# CIRCULAR MIGRATION AND MULTILOCATIONAL LIVELIHOOD STRATEGIES IN RURAL INDIA

# CIRCULAR MIGRATION AND MULTILOCATIONAL LIVELIHOOD STRATEGIES IN RURAL INDIA

*Edited by*
PRIYA DESHINGKAR AND JOHN FARRINGTON

# OXFORD

UNIVERSITY PRESS

YMCA Library Building, Jai Singh Road, New Delhi 110 001

Oxford University Press is a department of the University of Oxford. It furthers
the University's objective of excellence in research, scholarship, and education
by publishing worldwide in

Oxford New York

Auckland Cape Town Dar es Salaam Hong Kong Karachi
Kuala Lumpur Madrid Melbourne Mexico City Nairobi
New Delhi Shanghai Taipei Toronto

With offices in
Argentina Austria Brazil Chile Czech Republic France Greece
Guatemala Hungary Italy Japan Poland Portugal Singapore
South Korea Switzerland Thailand Turkey Ukraine Vietnam

Oxford is a registered trademark of Oxford University Press
in the UK and in certain other countries

Published in India
by Oxford University Press, New Delhi

© Oxford University Press 2009

ISBN 13: 978-0-19-5699-22-7
ISBN 10: 0-19-5699-22-X

Typeset in Kepler Std 10.5/12.5
by Sai Graphic Design, New Delhi 110 055
Printed in India at Rashtriya Printers, Delhi 110 032
Published by Oxford University Press
YMCA Library Building, Jai Singh Road, New Delhi 110 001

# Contents

# Tables, Figures, Maps, and Boxes

FIGURES

MAPS

BOXES

# Abbreviations

| | |
|---|---|
| BC | Backward Caste |
| BDO | Block Development Officer |
| CPR | Common Property Resources |
| CEO | Chief Executive Officer |
| EBC | Extremely Backward Caste |
| FC | Forward Caste |
| FGD | Focus Group Discussion |
| GSDP | Gross State Domestic Product |
| ILO | International Labor Organization |
| IFFCO | Indian Farmers Fertilizer Cooperative Limited |
| MDG | Millenium Development Goals |
| MO | Money Order |
| NELM | New Economics of Labor Migration |
| NREGA | National Rural Employment Guarantee Act |
| NREGS | National Rural Employment Guarantee Scheme |
| NTFP | Non-Timber Forest Product |
| OBC | Other Backward Caste |
| OC | Other Caste |
| ODI | Overseas Development Institute |
| RNFE | Rural Non-Farm Economy |
| SC | Scheduled Caste |
| SHARP | The Shastri Applied Research Project |
| ST | Scheduled Tribe |

# 1

# A Framework for Understanding
# Circular Migration

*Priya Deshingkar and John Farrington*

## Background and Rationale

Circular migration, much of it seasonal, is now an integral part of the livelihood strategies pursued by a large number of poor people living in agriculturally marginal areas. For individual households, it may be a precursor to more permanent out-migration, or an enduring phenomenon in its own right. While the drivers of migration are complex and diverse, important ones include the lack of sufficient local employment (both farm and non-farm), land fragmentation, and better opportunities in other high productivity and growth sectors. Common destinations include high growth areas such as irrigated agriculture, industrial parks, and urban areas. Earnings and savings from migration show tremendous variation by ethnic group, gender, occupation, wage rates, living costs, contracting arrangements, and debts. Some households barely manage to raise themselves above existing survival levels, while others accumulate wealth over time, but what is clear is that most would be worse off if they were depending solely on local employment.

This book is concerned with circular migration. This is defined as a temporary move from, followed by return to, the normal place of residence, for purposes of employment. The book pulls together case studies from some of the poorest and most deprived parts of India including southern Madhya Pradesh, the Telangana region of Andhra Pradesh, southern Rajasthan, and Bihar to show how important migration has become in sustaining and improving rural livelihoods. It also includes evidence from pockets of poverty in more prosperous areas where people belonging to socially disadvantaged groups depend on migration, for example, in irrigated tracts of Andhra Pradesh and parts of rural Bengal. The accounts presented in this book show that migration is complex, making it difficult to define watertight sub-categories, especially in relation to migration by the poor. As the examples in the book show, the migrant may have varying degrees of control over whether or not he or she moves and under what kinds of circumstances, blurring the distinction between voluntary and forced migration, the latter being tantamount to trafficking. Similarly, migration is often done through labour market intermediaries who give advances to the migrants or their families. Such an arrangement can be similar to debt-bondage but may also result in greater economic returns in the longer term, making it difficult once again, to distinguish migration from bonded labour. Finally, people may move to escape social discrimination or political persecution at home making it difficult to separate migrants from internally displaced people.

As we shall see in this chapter, the study of migration in India, indeed, throughout Asia, is complicated by the range of different conceptual frameworks that have been used. This makes it difficult to draw comparisons across studies. Below we present a conceptual framework intended to provide a measure of coherence across the studies contained in this volume. We approach the subject from a broad multidisciplinary perspective, examining the role of various economic and non-economic factors in shaping migration patterns and their impacts on the migrants themselves, their families, and society as a whole. We draw on concepts of vulnerability, social exclusion, social structure, political economy, and labour markets to understand the process of migration and how and why some sections of society have benefited more than others. The costs, risks, and benefits of migration are analysed not only in quantifiable terms but also on the basis of the personal accounts of migrants and their families.

Although the conceptual framework set out below draws on academic literature, ours is essentially a policy study: it reviews the empirical work available in order to draw out evidence-based policy conclusions. Our contentions are four-fold: first, that circular migration makes an important but underestimated contribution to the livelihoods of many rural people; second, and particularly through the construction industry, it contributes more strongly than policymakers and politicians recognize to economic 'transformation'[1]; third, that, under pressure from a strong middle-class urban electorate, governments take a generally negative, and often inaccurate, view of migration, labelling it a 'distress' phenomenon, doing little to ease the lives of migrants at destination, and providing support in rural 'source' areas, partly with a view to improving conditions there so that 'distress' migration will not take place; fourth, official statistics are neither collected nor presented in ways that would show the actual magnitude of circular migration, and governments have been tardy in making the necessary changes to regular surveys or to fund specific studies on circular migration.

To gather evidence which might support new policy departures against this fairly unsupportive policy background is not easy, and for this reason the evidence presented in this volume is uneven. Nevertheless, the sheer volume of circular migration, its importance to the livelihoods of the poor, and the scope for policy innovation are all such that a start has to be made somewhere, and this volume represents such a start.

MIGRATION THEORIES

Nearly all early economic theories of migration starting from Ravenstein's (1855) 'laws' of migration which linked distance to the volume of migration;[2] Lewis' (1954) dual economy model which saw a shift of people from the countryside to urban areas; Lee's (1966) 'push and pull' model[3] and Todaro's analysis of rural-urban migration (Todaro 1969; Harris & Todaro, 1970),[4] while being able to offer a partial explanation of why people move or want to move, have been more concerned with permanent migration and have paid little attention to circular migration.[5]

In the Todaro model, the migration decision depends on the migrant's expectations of earnings from formal sector urban employment, allowing for his or her assessment of the probability of an initial period of unemployment and/or of informal sector employment. Later work under the New Economics of Labour Migration (NELM) school of thought (Stark & Bloom 1985; Stark 1991) viewed migration as an outcome of different kinds of market failures including missing or incomplete capital and insurance markets. Migration is seen not as the decision of the individual alone but of the family that he or she belongs to, in order to minimize risks, diversify income sources, and ease financial constraints (Stark & Levhari 1982; Stark & Katz 1986; Taylor 1996) and the decision to migrate depends on the 'relative deprivation' of the household (Stark *et al.*, 1986; Stark & Taylor 1987, 1989). The entire family shares both the costs and rewards of migration (Stark 1991). Migration is thus a form of portfolio diversification by families. Remittances play an important role and represent an inter-temporal contractual arrangement between the migrant and the family. Families first invest in the migrants but do so in the expectation of returns in the form of remittances. Indeed, research by Rosenzweig (1988) shows that income transfers to rural households in India vary inversely with agricultural profits. Similarly, studies in the Matlab Thana of Bangladesh by Kuhn (2000) have found circular migration to work as a form of mutual cooperation and insurance between sending families and the migrants.

In contrast, Marxist analysis of migration views circular migration as an essential stage in capitalist production and development. It focuses on the class structure of the society to which migrants belong and examines the effects of national laws and regulation on migration. Marxist analysis thus tends to underplay the agency of the migrants in making decisions and influencing society. While the neo-classical position is that labour circulation between poor and more affluent areas benefits both labour-exporting and labour receiving areas, the Marxist school of thought emphasizes the negative and exploitative aspects of migration and views it as a process that suits capitalist production rather than the workers themselves. An important exponent of the Marxist school of thought is Jan Breman whose work on circular migration has been highly influential. We discuss it in more detail later in this chapter under theories of Indian circular migration.

Although the NELM model was an improvement over the Todaro model in explaining the decision to migrate by incorporating imperfect information and transaction costs into the analysis, it did not consider the political and social contexts in which migration decisions are shaped. While sociological research on circular migration has long noted the importance of kinship ties and social networks (see, for example, Mitchell 1959 on Africa), this kind of analysis remained on the margins of the mainstream migration discourse. But recent studies have once again emphasized that analysis need to understand both individual and family motives and the social structure within which migration occurs. Work by Arjan de Haan and Ben Rogaly (2002) for example, applies sociological theories such as Giddens' theory of structuration (1984), political economic analysis (Fine 2001), as well as gender analysis in order to understand the role of caste, ethnicity, gender, and power relations in shaping migration processes and also to understand how migration shapes society. Rogaly (1999) shows how temporary migrants in West Bengal are a source of social change in both destination and source areas among migrants, their employers, and also those who stay behind.

This body of research has also shown that migrant labour markets are highly segmented; that who goes where, for what, and on what terms is largely determined by social networks, skills associated with certain ethnic groups, historical precedents, and previous migration from the area. Rogaly (1999) argues that caste is one of the axes along which migration in West Bengal is segmented. The migration streams described in this book illustrate the complexity of migrant labour market segmentation along caste, age, and gender lines.

THE RELATIONSHIP BETWEEN CIRCULAR MIGRATION
AND DEVELOPMENT

The concept of mobility transition developed by the geographer Zelinsky (1971) offers an explanation of circulation, which he defines as 'a great variety of movements, usually short-term repetitive or cyclic in nature, but all having in common the lack of any declared intention of permanent or long-lasting change in residence.' Zelinsky combined demographic and modernization theories to argue that 'there are definite, patterned regularities in the growth of personal mobility through space-time during recent history, and these regularities comprise an essential component of the modernization process.' Based on his analysis of the Western experience he argues that a society will pass through four unilineal phases of mobility— pre-modern transitional, early transitional, late transitional, and advanced—during its transformation from a traditional subsistence to an urban–industrial state, in the course of which there is a 'vigourous acceleration of circulation'. The applicability of the theory to developing countries has been challenged by many (for example, Hugo 1982 in the case of Indonesia). Perhaps in response to such commentaries Zelinsky (1979) later noted that circulation is 'symptomatic of the problems of underdevelopment and will persist and increase in complexity as long as underdevelopment persists.'

Skeldon (1997) builds on Zelinsky's model and offers a different typology according to which there are five 'development tiers': the (1) old and (2) new core countries (e.g., Western Europe, North America, Japan) characterized by immigration and internal decentralization; (3) the 'expanding core' (e.g., eastern China, southern Africa, eastern Europe), where we find both immigration, and out-migration, and internal centralization (i.e., urbanization and rural-to-urban migration); (4) the 'labour frontier' (e.g., Morocco, Egypt, Turkey, Mexico, the Philippines and, until recently, Spain and Portugal), which are dominated by out-migration and internal centralization; and the so-called (5) 'resource niche' (e.g., many sub-Saharan countries, parts of central Asia and Latin America), with variable, often weaker forms of migration.

The migration situation found in India seems to lie somewhere between the expanding core and labour frontier countries defined by Skeldon (1997). But given the wide variation in migration patterns not just between different states but within states, districts, and even villages as we show in this book, generalizations and the development of typologies are difficult.

LOCATING MIGRATION WITHIN CONCEPTS OF LIVELIHOOD DIVERSIFICATION AND ECONOMIC TRANSFORMATION[6]

Migration is one means of diversifying out of low-income activities, mainly agriculture and also some non-farm traditional occupations. Other means of diversification include employment or own-enterprise in local higher-productivity farming or in the Rural Non-farm Economy (RNFE). Many view diversification as a first step at household level towards structural transformation at national level. Conventional theories of structural transformation (following Kuznets 1966, 1971) draw on the economic history of developed nations (Kuznets 1966, 1971). 'Transformation' is acknowledged to contain social elements, but conventionally is mainly defined in economic terms and includes:

- sectoral shifts away from low-productivity agriculture towards higher-productivity non-agricultural activity (but with employment shifting more slowly than production), and more recently away from industry to services;
- scalar shifts in size of productive unit, away from small family enterprises to national and multi-national corporations; and
- (of particular relevance for migration) spatial shifts, away from rural occupations and locations to urban.

Livelihood diversification is most clearly a potential step towards transformation where it is an attempt to seize improved opportunities within a growing and more flexible economy. But diversification can also be 'coping' in the sense of an enforced response to failing agriculture, recession, and retrenchment (e.g., Davies 1996; Scoones 1998; Francis 2000).

The livelihood prospects facing the poor as these three shifts take place are located not merely in economic, but also in political and social structures and processes, at both macro and micro levels. In rural areas where markets are acknowledged to be widely imperfect, these imperfections take the form of limitations imposed by social and political structures on the access to assets and opportunity by the poor, and thence on their capacity for free choice and rational economic decision-taking. One extreme conceptualization of transformation, that of neoclassical economists, maintains that choices are largely rational and unconstrained and that structural limitations are negligible. The opposing view is that structures are all-important and prevent markets from functioning almost entirely. It is important to position the present study in relation both to transformation and to conceptual tensions between neoliberalism and structuralism.

In relation to transformation, early policies in support of industrialization failed to generate the expected levels of urban employment creation and rural–urban population movement, and this spawned further thinking in several directions. One was to continue the pursuit of transformation via rapid industrialization and diversification of the national economy (e.g., Byres 1991, 1998, with some concessions to the 'appropriateness' of the technology). Another was to keep poor rural people in rural areas but improve their lot there, by improving farming (e.g., Lipton 1983, Lipton &

Longhurst 1989), or by promoting local diversification through intermediate technology and capitalization, fuelled by rising productivity in the small-scale farming sector (e.g., Mellor 1976). Yet another was to pursue regional[7] growth, but some advocating this (e.g., Haggblade *et al.*, 1989; Hazell & Ramasamy 1991), acknowledged that rural–urban markets are imperfect, and much sectoral output is at best only partly transferable: bulky staples, fresh perishables, and rural services in particular.

Critics of regional growth theory go beyond the analysis of market imperfections to concentrate on the power of ethnic and class ties (Harriss 1987), that is, what Hart (1994) refers to as the social logic of investment. These social structures and networks further modulate economic factors to create a highly diverse pattern of RNFE development that is temporally, spatially, and socially specific.

However, the prospects for improved livelihoods offered by the RNFE in the more agriculturally difficult parts of India are limited. The evidence suggests that it is not 'either agriculture or the RNFE' that is pre-eminent as a contributor to livelihoods, but, that in well-endowed locations 'both agriculture and the RNFE' are strong, whereas in remote areas characterized by combinations of poor communications, hilly topography, poor soils, and climatic uncertainty, neither one nor the other is strong.

Without a clearer understanding of the reasons for which people enter into new or diversified activities, and the social structures and processes that determine their opportunity sets—or lack of them— we are still far from understanding the mechanisms by which rural change, transformation, and diversification affect the poor. We are even further from understanding the ways in which they respond. In this context, Start and Johnson (2004) raise a number of questions in relation to livelihood diversification that can equally be applied to migration. Thus, do 'new' economic activities provide better or worse opportunities than those that existed before? Is diversification a strategic approach to an expanded opportunity, or a constrained response to a limited set of opportunities (that is, 'coping')? Has diversification offered the freedom and choice to move out of entrenched and dependent caste, class, or gender-based activities? These questions of balance between compulsion and choice, structure and agency are closely related to further questions on the social relations of production and exchange. What determines access to new and productive options and opportunities? Do markets work, or do social factors dominate access, production, and exchange? Have traditional rules of access and structures of inequality simply been reproduced and propagated in new areas of work? How can more equitable access be encouraged?

These issues remind us that the study of livelihood diversification is about more than multiple income sources; it relates to the current transformations of global, national, and local economies. The implications for rural societies, traditional ways of peasant life and well-being are paramount. Who will win and who will lose? Such questions will continue as key debates for social scientists in coming years.

There are two general ways in which we can address these questions. One draws upon a largely neo-liberal economic interpretation of the functioning of markets through individual preferences and rational choice. A second emphasizes the role that institutions and political economy play in constraining the access, opportunities, and choice that people face, and so the ways open to them for pursuing economic opportunities. Neither of these frameworks alone holds all the answers: each has a contribution to make to the understanding of migration in the context of rural livelihood diversification, but the respective contributions will vary according to the immense variations in rural context over time and space. From a policy perspective, the constraints of caste, class, and gender are important but not entirely insurmountable, and markets work to some degree within the constraints that they impose. On the other hand, to base policies on the assumption that rational choice alone governs the livelihood prospects of the poor is problematic since it is based on a fundamental misunderstanding of the ways in which people obtain (or are denied) access to new economic opportunities opened up through economic diversification.

DOMINANT THEORIES OF CIRCULAR MIGRATION IN INDIA

Migration, Social Structure, and Policy

An important voice in the debate on circular migration has been that of Jan Breman, a sociologist with years of research experience in India. Breman saw labour migration as the only survival option for people who were alienated from their land in the transition to capitalism. He argued that migrant labour benefits capitalist production, and migrants are exploited. Although he conceded that migration opened up an avenue for workers to move up the class ladder by changing from a 'semi-free' status in their villages to one of 'free' labourers in wage employment in neighbouring areas (Breman 1993), he also blames it for perpetuating exploitative relations and inequality.

Work migration is the mother and father of social inequality. By that statement we mean to say that migration starts from a differentiated situation. The social class of the migrant already predicts for what type of work the migrant has been qualified, equipped or not with education/skills and other forms of capital. The outcome of migration leads to further inequality in the sense that the most successful are able to further improve the economic and social status of the household to which they belong, while in the lower echelons of the work hierarchy migration does rarely result in structural improvement for the migrant and his/her family. (Breman 1997)

He continues:

Huge armies of labour continue to be on the move simply because in most cases employment is casual, conditioned by short term arrangements or even based on instant recruitment and dismissal. Not only men, but also women and children have been made mobile. Although in many cases footloose, these are not free labourers able to go wherever and whenever they want. Many have been contracted through advance payment which binds them to an employer or his agent, the jobber. Others remain attached by systems of delayed payment permitting them only to leave at the end of 'the job' or when the season is over. This footloose workforce can be found in the open air but is also 'domesticated' and kept indoors, away from the public eye, in the multitude of sweatshops that form the backbone of the informal sector economy. Although waged labour is far more important for migrants than self-employment, the first mode of payment is often hidden by practices of sub-contracting and piece work which prevail over time rates and regular hours of work.

Breman's work was instrumental in drawing out the differences in the migration experience of different castes. He found that lower castes and tribes are disproportionately represented in circular migration streams. His work has inspired an entire generation of researchers working on circular migration in India including David Mosse, Wendy Olsen and R.V. Ramanamurthy, and Ben Rogaly. This school of thought highlights the structural factors which lead to the exploitation of labour and often concludes that migrant labourers are no better off than bonded labourers (Mosse 2002, 2005; Olsen and Ramanamurthy 2002). We find the concepts very useful, especially the attention to the different migration experience of various social groups.

## Migration, Remittances, and Inequality

Another important school of thought stemmed from neo-classical economists' research on the drivers and impacts of migration. Lipton's (1980) widely quoted work argues that rural–urban migration does not equalize incomes, between or within regions for the following reasons:[8] First, the selective nature of migration, providing higher returns to the better-off and better-educated, prevents equalization *within* areas of origin. Second, there are costs and barriers associated with migration, including access to information about opportunities, which tends to steer the gains of migration to the rich. Third, absence of the most productive household members leads to a lowering of labour-intensity, which according to Lipton is 'socially maladaptive, especially in the medium run, while the rural work force is growing much faster than other, scarcer ... factors of production' (p.208).[9] Fourth, the volume of net remittances is usually low, and fifth, return migrants are likely to be the old, sick, and unsuccessful, and skills brought back are unlikely to be of much help.

However, the new evidence presented in this volume challenges many of these assertions: social networks have helped poor migrants to overcome some of the costs and barriers of entry into migrant labour markets. Circular migration rates among the poor are high and migration earnings may account for a significant proportion of household income, particularly among SCs and STs. Migration has helped many poor people to smooth consumption and a few to increase their asset base (see also Narain *et al.* 2005 study of 550 households in 60 villages in Madhya Pradesh and Dayal and Karan's 2003 study of 12 villages in Jharkhand). Only one of the studies (Bihar, chapter 6) in the volume documents severe labour shortages as a result of migration, in most cases 'surplus' labour migrates or farm management is not adversely affected if only one or two members from large families migrate.

In many cases even if migration does not reduce poverty, it can prevent further downward slide into poverty. Shah and Sah (2004) studied 212 households in a village in Madhya Pradesh and concluded that migration helped landless households to maintain their standard of living over a decade. Even when migration outcomes reduce poverty they may undermine social equity. Skeldon (2003) writes, 'Easy generalizations are impossible to make but it is likely that the relative impact of migration on poverty, and of poverty on migration, varies by level of development of the area under consideration.' Because migration can have differential impacts on different social groups, migration can offer those who possess more resources a route out of poverty while compounding the poverty of other groups. Numerous scholars have grappled with the question of whether or not migration increases inequality and several conclude that the answer is highly context dependent (Black *et al.* 2006; Skeldon 2003). Migration may also affect intra-household equity as women remain in the lower productivity agricultural sector while men transition into more productive jobs in urban areas (Dev and Evenson 2003). Nevertheless, although migration can increase income inequality, the relative impact of remittances on the poorest households should be large enough to significantly improve their quality of life even when wealthier households receive greater benefits from migration.

## Distress Migration and Urban Decay

While Breman and Lipton influenced academic research, the work of Shekhar Mukherji, of the Institute of Population Sciences at Bombay (now Mumbai) has been an important influence on the thinking of policy-makers in India since the 1970s. His concepts of distressed migration and urban decay were incorporated into various urban policies in India and have become firmly embedded in the discourse on urban poverty and development. He describes the process of distress migration and urban decay in five steps (Mukherji 2001):

First, masses of poor, landless, illiterate, and unskilled agricultural labourers and petty farmers from backward states make quantum leaps towards big metropolises like Calcutta, Bombay, Delhi, and Madras bypassing local small towns and small cities. This leads to acute urban involution, congestion, and decay. The proliferation of filthy urban slums, pavement dwellings, extreme squalor with very poor living standards characterize metros because they have failed to provide to the migrants minimum shelter and minimum subsistence employment. Ultimately this causes the growth of urban poverty, unemployment, extreme housing shortages, and frequent breakdowns of essential urban services (like water, electricity, sewerage, transport) are visible everywhere in such metropolises.

Second, metropolises have very limited employment-generating capacities under capital-intensive industrialization, and consequently, the incoming illiterate and unskilled migrants are absorbed only in very poorly paid urban informal sectors that are characterized by low productivity, cut-throat competition, insecurity, and exploitation. Although such migration helps to avoid starvation, it does not improve their economic condition adequately, or permit their social mobility. Rather, it leads to a colossal waste of human resources and of national potential. So migrants are in fact moving from rural poverty to urban poverty.

Third, as a result of such processes metropolises grow merely in population, not in prosperity. The mega cities of India are becoming merely over-blown villages, without urban culture and urban functional characteristics. Fourth, such mega cities deny the migrants even basic provisions of water, sanitation, and electricity. This leads to extreme squalor and filth and is very cruel towards poor children, women, the weak, the poor, the old, and the destitute. Fifth, such metropolises are very fast becoming the scenes of extreme social and economic inequalities creating a potentially dangerous situation which can lead to crime, violence, and class conflict.

Drawing together the strands of argument in the above literature in very basic terms, the overall conclusions are that circular migration is driven by poverty and leads to poverty. To put it simply, the policy conclusion following from this is that all efforts should be made to prevent migration through rural employment programmes and migrants should not be welcomed in towns and cities.[10]

The policy position remains largely unchanged despite a number of recent studies having shown that migration is increasing and can result in positive outcomes for the poor. Remittances are used for productive purposes ranging from farm inputs to non-farm enterprises to investment in education. Households also use remittances to fund social events like weddings or funerals, positively impacting the local economy and those community members who do not migrate. Other studies show that remittances are spent on healthcare or to repay debt. Ellis and Harris (2004) point out that remittances play an important role in the cumulative process of poverty reduction by diminishing the need for access to credit, which often serves as an obstacle to entrepreneurial endeavours. They also note that migration can lead to an accumulation of human capital and the transfer of ideas.

The Indian position is in sharp contrast to the position taken by China which, after years of obstructing the movement of people from rural areas to urban areas has now recognized the contribution that migration makes to urban development, and the importance of remittances for rural poverty reduction. Chinese scholars estimate that rural to urban migration accounted for 16 per cent of the country's total GDP growth over the past 18 years.[11] In 2004, remittances in China almost surpassed agricultural contributions to households, accounting for 40 per cent of rural household income.[12]

UNDOCUMENTED AND INVISIBLE

An important reason for the neglect and invisibility of circular migrants at the policy level is the lack of hard data. Official statistics tend to cover permanent migration and underestimate seasonal and circular migration. The two major sources of official statistics namely, the National Sample Survey and National Census of 2001 are discussed here in some detail. The 2001 Census provides detailed information on trends and patterns of migration at the district level but it does not tell us anything about circular migration. Although the 55th round of the NSS did collect data on temporary movements for work, it suggests that only 1 per cent of the population undertook such migration.

What Official Statistics Do and Do Not Tell Us About Migration

The two main sources of official statistics on migration are the National Census (2001 is the most recent) and the National Sample Survey (the 55th round of 1999–2000 is the most comprehensive). The National Census for 2001 shows the following trends:

During the reporting period, 30 per cent of the population or 307 million people were classified as migrants. Of these, nearly a third had migrated during the previous decade. Of the total of 98.3 million migrants, nearly 44 per cent had moved for marriage-related reasons (mainly women) and only 14.7 per cent had moved for employment. Other patterns revealed by the Census were:

- There were 32.2 million male migrants and 22.9 million female migrants.
- Among males the most important reason for migration was 'work/employment'.
- Rural to rural migration still dominated and accounted for 53.3 million; rural to urban migration was 20.5 million; urban to rural migration was 6.2 million, and urban to urban migration was 14.3 million.
- Inter-state migration has grown by 53.6 per cent. The total number of inter-state migrants was 42.3 million. Uttar Pradesh (-2.6 million) and Bihar (-1.7 million) were the two states with the largest net out-migration.

Table 1.1: Migration patterns based on National Census data for 2001

| Intra-state Migrants | Percentage | | |
|---|---|---|---|
| | Persons | Male | Female |
| Rural to rural | 60.5 | 41.6 | 68.6 |
| Rural to urban | 17.6 | 27.1 | 13.6 |
| Urban to rural | 6.5 | 8.6 | 5.6 |
| Urban to urban | 12.3 | 18.3 | 9.7 |
| Unclassified | 3.1 | 4.4 | 2.6 |
| *Inter-state Migration* | | | |
| Rural to rural | 26.6 | 20.7 | 32.7 |
| Rural to urban | 37.9 | 44.7 | 30.9 |
| Urban to rural | 6.3 | 6.1 | 6.4 |
| Urban to urban | 26.7 | 25.9 | 27.5 |
| Unclassified | 2.6 | 2.6 | 2.5 |

*Source:* International Organisation for Migration, India available at http://www. iomindia.migration_in_india.html

*The National Sample Survey*

The 55th round of NSS of 1999–2000 was the first to cover short-duration migration defined as: 'persons staying away from usual place of residence for 60 days or more for employment or better employment or in search of employment'. It estimates that roughly one per cent of the Indian population or 10 million people migrated temporarily (NSSO, 2001). But this is a gross underestimate. The true figure probably lies at around 100 million as adding up the numbers in major sectors and occupations employing migrant workers shows: the textile and garment industry employs 35 million of whom many are migrants; the construction sector employs 30 million workers; brick kilns employ around 10 million workers; there are 10 million street vendors; 8 million rickshaw pullers; 5 million truck drivers and helpers; 500,000 quarry and mine workers; 150,000 salt pan workers, and at least 100,000 workers in prawn processing.[13] In addition, at least half of the estimated 20 million domestic workers in India, waiters in small restaurants and room boys in small hotels are probably migrants.

The NSS data also fail to capture the important interstate migratory destinations. For example, the main destinations for migrants from Madhya Pradesh (MP) are Maharashtra and Uttar Pradesh (UP) (see Table 4.1 on page 47 of the NSSO report on migration [NSSO, 2001]). However, migration from MP to Gujarat does not appear to be significant. But field studies show high levels of migration to Gujarat from the south-western tribal districts of MP.

Both datasets seriously underestimate the mobility of rural people and the importance of migration in rural livelihoods. There are six major shortcomings of official data.

- They tend to underestimate short-term movements and thus underestimate or miss altogether, seasonal and circular migration which, according to recent village studies accounts for the bulk of migratory movements for work.
- Women's migration is not adequately captured because the surveys ask for only one reason for migration to be stated. This is usually stated as marriage and the secondary reason, that is, finding work at the destination may not be mentioned.
- They are particularly poor at capturing circular movements for

work and the contribution of remittances from such circular movements to household budgets. This is, in part, due to the failure to capture secondary occupations and under-reporting of short-term migration.

- They do not capture migration streams that are illegal or border on illegality, that is, various forms of child labour and trafficking for work.
- They do not capture adequately the movement of Scheduled Caste (SC) and Scheduled Tribe (ST) people mainly because these groups are engaged in short-term migration and this is not measured properly in the surveys for the reasons stated above. There are numerous case studies which show high mobility levels among these groups.
- They misrepresent the relationship between poverty and migration. While village studies show high levels of migration amongst the poor (not the poorest), official statistics show that migration is higher among better-off groups because they cover mainly permanent migration which has a higher representation of people from more affluent and better educated backgrounds.

Much of the quantitative evidence in the Indian literature on migration is drawn from these datasets and so inevitably exhibits a number of shortcomings. For example, Kundu's analyis of the 2001 Census showed a slowdown in permanent or long-term rural–urban migration rates despite increasing inter-regional inequalities, leading to the conclusion that migration is declining in India (Kundu 2003). Similarly, analysis based on NSS data can also be misleading; Dubey *et al.* (2006) argue on the basis of their analysis of the 1999–2000 round of the NSS that individuals from Scheduled Castes and Scheduled Tribes and those with little or no education are less likely to migrate to urban areas. Kundu and Sarangi (2007) compare migrant and non-migrant populations to argue that the probability of being poor among migrants (both urban–urban and rural–urban including seasonal migrants) is lower than among non-migrants.

In contrast to this body of literature, the main argument from data analysed in this book is that rural Indians are highly mobile (for example 40–82 per cent of the households in the Andhra Pradesh study, villages reported migration), especially among those who belong to the lower social strata, with low levels of education and few assets. The evidence presented also shows that circular migration is now an integral part of the livelihood strategies in agriculturally marginal areas. Scheduled Castes and Tribes[14] are especially mobile, travelling to a range of destinations including urban and rural locations. A framework for analysing circular migration is presented which draws on recent schools of thought dealing with the New Economics of Labour Migration (NELM) and the role of social networks. The analysis highlights the need for a different approach to circular migration as distinct from permanent migration to which most theories refer. Second, it recognizes the non-economic dimensions of the decision to migrate, and the impacts on the overall well-being of migrants on their families and ultimately on the society as a whole. The new analytical framework enables us to develop a more nuanced understanding of the migration process and better explains the wide diversity in circular migration patterns observed in India today.

## A FRAMEWORK FOR ANALYSING CONTEMPORARY FORMS OF CIRCULAR MIGRATION

The main challenge for migration researchers is to understand the diversity of circular migration, especially the diversity of segments in the migrant labour market, identify the institutional policy, social and economic dimensions of migration, identify which groups of migrants need what kinds of support and how this can be provided. Migration benefits some more than others and it is crucial for researchers and policy makers to understand who the winners and losers are, and how a more level playing field can be created.

We construct an analytical framework which is based on field evidence presented in this book, centred on the relationship between migration and agricultural development, geographical location (remoteness, overall development of the state), risk reduction, land ownership, education, skills, age, and how this intersects with ethnicity (caste, religion, and tribe), gender, and power relations.

### Coping and Accumulative Migration

We hypothesize that there are broadly two kinds of circular migration among the poor: circular migration by the poor[15] and the least educated which is mainly for survival and usually does not result in the accumulation of assets even if it allows the household to smooth consumption and manage risk. We call this kind of migration 'coping migration'. The other kind is circular migration undertaken by better-off households with some education, more assets, more skills and/or better social networks for portfolio diversification which often allows the accumulation of assets, savings, and investment. We call this kind of migration 'accumulative migration'. Such distinctions have been made by others but have often emphasized that most migrants are in the category of coping or survival migrants—Rogaly and Rafique (2003) note, for example, that 'seasonal migration is for most of those involved, a way of hanging on. For a small minority of migrants with land, supportive family structures, other social assets and/or other sources of income, remittances may remain available for investment in agriculture or to make an impression through conspicuous consumption'.

The research presented in this volume shows that knowledge and experience gained over time may allow a migrant to move up the ladder from survival to accumulative migration. Accumulation implies an increase in assets. These may generate further income streams—as, for instance, with investment in livestock—or may contribute to the well-being of the household with only indirect impacts on earning capacity, such as improvements to the family home. Accumulative migration tends also to be accompanied by higher levels or standards of consumption. Well-being is a subjective term and migrants' own assessments are relied on here. The second, 'better-off' category of migrants is very broad and includes those who are small and marginal farmers but also others who may have much larger holdings, and those employed outside agriculture.

Both categories are broad and diverse and include a wide variety of migration streams but the simple classification proposed here is intended to be 'manageable' for the purposes of facilitating policy discussion. Coping migration streams can become accumulative when work becomes available more regularly, when skills are acquired leading to better wages and improved security, and/or when workers deal with employers directly rather than through middlemen and agents. For example, unskilled construction work can start as coping but can become accumulative as work availability

improves. The reverse is also possible if work availability deterio-
rates as more workers come into the market and compete for the
same jobs.

It should be noted that the management of risk mentioned
above contains two broad elements. On the one hand are the risks
associated with migration—finding work, travel to and from places
of work, personal health and safety and security issues, the risks
of being underpaid, of loss of earnings during remittance, and so
on. On the other are the risks to livelihoods faced by the poor in
source areas, such as those associated with agriculture (low and
uneven rainfall, flooding, pests and diseases, problems of marketing
surpluses, and so on). Chapter 2 (by Badiani and Safir) in this
volume focuses on this latter category of risks, and, specifically,
attempts to test empirically whether migration, and the remittances
it generates, is used as a device for reducing the potential impacts of
climate-related risk.

Figure 1.1 contains a schematic representation of the types
of circular migration. The vertical axis represents earnings and
the horizontal axis represents skills and education. Migration
for survival usually involves those who belong to historically
disadvantaged groups such as the Scheduled Castes and Tribes as
well as some very poor categories of BCs known as the extremely

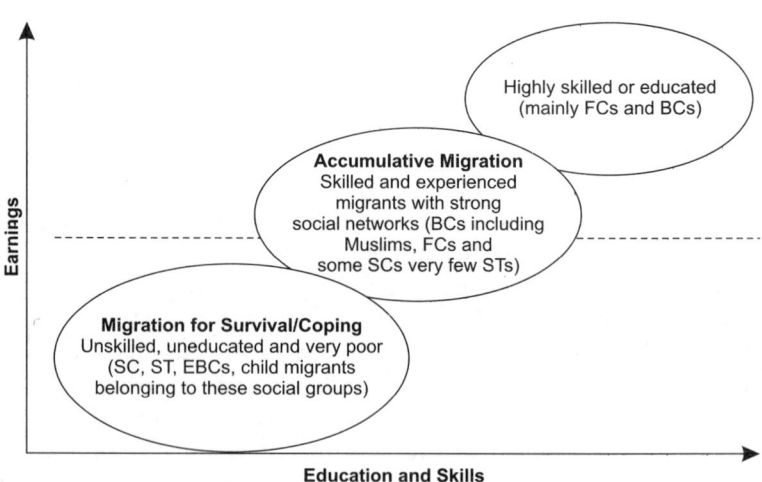

Figure 1.1: Types of Circular Migration

backward castes in states such as Bihar. These migrants travel short distances for the lowest paid manual work including harvesting or brick-kiln work. Examples include the migration of the Musahar in Bihar for brick-kiln work described in Chapter 6, the migration of STs in MP for crop harvesting in the Haveli area (Chapter 4), and the migration of the SCs in AP for construction work in the capital city of Hyderabad (Chapter 3). As in the case of the migrants studied by Jan Breman and David Mosse, recruitment is often done by labour market intermediaries and the terms of work are poor. Labour laws are rarely adhered to and late payment, underpayment, or even no payment are common especially in the case of brick-kiln workers where conditions are almost like bonded labour. Living and working conditions are unsafe, dirty, and difficult. These migrants often take an advance from the recruiting agent and the debt is repaid through their earnings. During the migration period, they are at the mercy of agents and contractors who control almost all aspects of their lives including their access to food, shelter, health care, etc. They often pay workers only pocket money for the whole working season and give them their wages only at the end, to ensure that they do not escape and that they work for as long as the agent or contractor wants.

Most of the money they earn is spent at the destination on food, healthcare and recreation and they hand-carry whatever little savings they have. This kind of migration often involves the entire family and children who accompany their parents, miss months of school and live in unhygienic and often dangerous conditions at the work site.[16] Adolescent girls are vulnerable to sexual abuse at the hands of the recruiting agents. Other types of migration that can be included under this broad category of migration are unskilled work in urban construction and work in mines and quarries.

Those who have more skills, education, and social networks are able to find better jobs in large cities such as Delhi and Mumbai in the rapidly expanding industrial, manufacturing, and service sector. This includes work in small units that make bags, footwear, embroidered fabrics, and clothes as well as plastic processing units and vehicle workshops. Work in restaurants and hotels as well as security firms is also a rapidly growing avenue for migrants who have completed secondary schooling and who have contacts in the city. This kind of migration is usually open to those who belong to the vast category of Backward Castes (BC) with some land. The migration is long distance and long term and migrants return for major festivals or family events. They send money through official (for example, postal money orders) and informal channels. The money is invested in the farm or in buying/upgrading other assets. Examples include the BCs in Bihar (Chapter 6), the Vaddis (also BCs) in Andhra Pradesh (Chapter 3) and skilled masons from MP (again mainly BCs) who work in urban centres in Gujarat (Chapter 4). In Bihar a type of relay migration has been observed where the father stays at home when the children grow up, and one or more grown up sons can migrate instead of him (Chapter 6). These circular migrants maintain strong links with source areas and jobs are often found by word of mouth.

In almost all cases (whether coping or accumulative), employment conditions frequently contravene labour regulations especially in relation to safety, exposure to toxic chemicals, and hygiene. The degree of illegality is more severe if the migrant is more socially and politically powerless. SC and ST migrants frequently occupy jobs at the lower end which are often in the category of dirty, dangerous, and degrading (the so-called 3-D jobs).

We further hypothesize that migrant labour markets are strongly segmented. In this regard we are in agreement with the findings of Rogaly (1999) who identified caste as a major axis of market segmentation. However, there are differences in form and degree of segmentation according to type of work. For instance, construction and harvesting work are open to all social groups. On the other hand, certain specialist tasks are not accessible for particular age, gender, religious or ethnic groups, and this classification embraces, but goes beyond, the caste-based distinctions made by Rogaly. People belonging to the stone cutter caste in Andhra Pradesh, for instance (Chapter 3) dig telecommunication trenches; Muslims from Bihar are often employed in the garment industry as tailors or for embroidering garments (Chapter 6); young boys from Scheduled Caste families in Bihar work in tea shops or in the carpet industry (Chapter 6); young tribal boys from south Rajasthan work in the textile markets of Gujarat (Chapter 5); young tribal girls from south Rajasthan work in cottonseed farms in Gujarat (Chapter 10), and teenaged tribal girls from southern Madhya Pradesh work as domestic maids in Maharashtra (Chapter 4). In fact, the autonomous migration of children is a growing phenomenon across India. All are highly specialized occupations with limited scope for moving across categories. Each has specific needs in terms of the kind of support needed. There is a high degree of movement between the less restricted occupations such as construction or work in restaurants and a migrant may change occupations more than once in a year depending on the season and job availability.

Several migration streams may exist in a single village. These are shaped by numerous factors including historical precedent, skills associated with certain ethnic groups and emerging employment opportunities in the region. Different household members may participate in different migration streams but they work towards a common goal which is portfolio diversification and risk spreading.

Although some migrants may progress from coping to accumulative migration over time, the majority remain in the same position. We argue that this is not because of migration *per se* but because of a combination of factors including poor education levels, discrimination against certain castes, tribes and religions, and a hostile policy and institutional environment, all of which intersect with each other to perpetuate the exclusion of certain kinds of migrants from mainstream employment and citizenship and thus keep them from breaking out of poverty. The poorest survival migrants work on terms that have many elements of coercion and bondage and face the greatest denial of rights. The overall policy environment in India is far from migration-friendly. This is manifested in numerous rural development programmes which try to offer *in-situ* alternatives to migration. Urban authorities regard migrants as a menace and the police routinely harass them as they are not perceived as citizens and are treated as illegal residents. Some examples of major policies that have impacted on migration are listed in Table 1.2.

Regardless of whether migrants are working for survival or on more accumulative trajectories, they live and work in poor conditions and have no access to pro-poor schemes, such as the PDS and health care. This is an enormous gap in service provision because poor circular migrants are among the poorest and most vulnerable groups in the country. If the government fails to reach them, it will affect India's prospects of reaching the MDGs.

Table 1.2 Policies impacting on migrants in India

| | |
|---|---|
| Urban development projects | The Master Plans of major metropolises such as New Delhi openly aim to keep migrants out. |
| Rural employment projects | The National Rural Employment Guarantee Act (NREGA) aims to reduce rural–urban migration by creating jobs in rural areas. |
| Natural resource management projects | Watershed development projects aim to improve the natural resource base and its capacity to sustain rural livelihoods and thus reduce outmigration. |

*Source*: Authors.

The pyramid below represents the policy and institutional environment for circular migrants. Only those few on the top with access to formal jobs are in a position to enforce laws in their own favour through the judiciary but, for the vast majority the policy environment and the institutions that shape the labour market actually work against their interests.

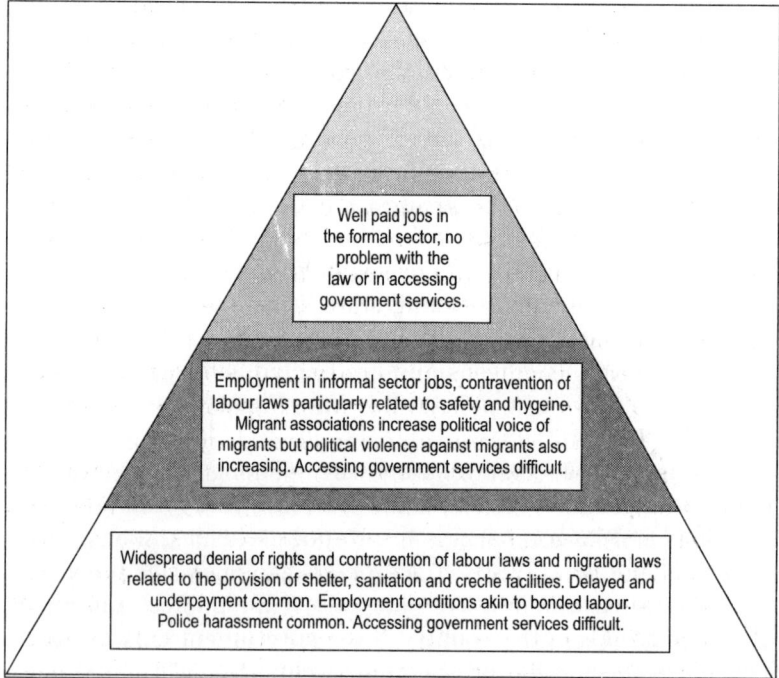

Well paid jobs in the formal sector, no problem with the law or in accessing government services.

Employment in informal sector jobs, contravention of labour laws particularly related to safety and hygeine. Migrant associations increase political voice of migrants but political violence against migrants also increasing. Accessing government services difficult.

Widespread denial of rights and contravention of labour laws and migration laws related to the provision of shelter, sanitation and creche facilities. Delayed and underpayment common. Employment conditions akin to bonded labour. Police harassment common. Accessing government services difficult.

Figure 1.2: Policy and Institutional Environment for Circular Migrants

## Creating a Migrant-Friendly Policy Environment

Recall the three factors that we blamed for perpetuating poverty among migrants: poor education, discrimination, and a hostile policy environment. While improving education levels among migrants and removing discrimination require a sustained campaign at several levels and are already part of the national development strategy, policy reform aimed at improving the lives of migrants has received inadequate attention and has hitherto been limited to framing labour laws. But as we saw, these have proved to be largely ineffectual, and laws that recognise the *multi-locational* nature of rural livelihood systems are needed. At present all laws related to subsidized food and other pro-poor schemes are based on the assumption that populations are more or less static. There is a need to recognize that people move around and need to be able to access services wherever they are.

We argue that if the obstacles to migration are removed and if the policy environment is made more migrant-friendly, the returns to migration will improve and the hardships faced by migrants will be reduced. Two kinds of changes will be needed. One is to provide support to accumulative migrants so that they can remit their money safely and efficiently, and invest it in more productive uses if they want to do so. The second kind of support involves the provision of improved social protection to the poorest and most vulnerable 'survival' migrants and is more challenging from a policy viewpoint.

Conceptually, social protection encompasses a set of publicly-mandated actions—carried out by the state or privately—that address risk, vulnerability, and chronic poverty. Traditional social protection mechanisms have existed for a long time, such as, informal loans among friends, but our focus here is on more formal actions undertaken by the state, by NGOs, or by others (even the private commercial sector) with state support. Social protection can seek to prevent the occurrence of an adverse event, to mitigate its effects, or to enhance the capacity of poor people to cope with its effects. Vulnerabilities can also be addressed in a transformative vein by, for example, the promotion of collective action for workers' rights, or support to farmers' organizations. Social protection can take numerous forms (Box 1.1).

---

Box 1.1: Forms of social protection

*Social assistance*, including social transfers such as pensions for the elderly, and allowances for the widowed, disabled, orphans, and vulnerable children. Some take specific forms such as stipends or vouchers for attendance at school, or the provision of school meals or uniforms.

*Public works*, to provide cash or food for the able-bodied when they can find no other work, but also to create communal assets.

*Transfer or subsidized purchase of assets*, either in cash or in kind, and strengthened access to shared assets by the poor.

*Actions to improve labour standards*, including minimum wage enforcement and health and safety provisions.

*Subsidized access to services*, such as health and education, or to make good market failures, such as weakly-functioning markets for personal insurance, especially among the poor dispersed across remote rural areas, whether for health, accident, life, or property.

*Risk-reducing interventions* in productive sectors, including insurance of crops and other productive assets.

---

Certain forms of social protection have a long history in India. For instance, from the examples in Box 1.1, the provision of health and basic education, and of subsidized basic goods (staple foods, kerosene) under the Public Distribution System (PDS) are important to rural households, but the provision of these is premised on a more-or-less static population. A head of household entitled to these benefits finds it difficult to acquire them when she/he moves to a different location within the same state, and impossible when moving to another state. To make such benefits 'portable' is a high priority for policy. To do so within the same state should not present major difficulties, but to make them accessible by migrants working temporarily in other states will require high level agreements between states on budgetary provisions, registration procedures, etc. Though it may take some time to reach agreement on these, the very process of discussions may generate benefits by giving circular migration a higher policy profile. It may also help to generate further necessary services and forms of protection such as housing for migrants at destinations, and improved health and safety in the workplace. Throughout the following chapters, the ways in which migration itself can be socially protecting are discussed. In those chapters, specifically on migrant support (Chapters 5, 10, and 11) social protection is discussed not only in relation to migrant workers themselves, but also in relation to those left behind.

In sum, our understanding of migration indicates that:

- Long distance circular migration is higher from less developed and more remote locations.
- Short distance migration and commuting[17] are higher from less developed locations that are near developed locations.
- Migration is least amongst the poorest but highest among the poor (including landless and marginal farmers).
- The poorest migrants (mainly SCs and STs) are disproportionately represented in short-distance circular migration streams.
- Migrants from better-off households with more education and skills (mainly BCs) are disproportionately represented in long distance circular migration.
- Earnings rise sharply with the acquisition of skills.
- Different household members may participate in different migration streams but they work towards a common goal which is portfolio diversification and risk spreading.

CHAPTERS IN THIS BOOK

The above account is a highly generalized conceptualization to illustrate the diversity of circular migration within the broad category of poor migrants and to draw policy attention to the different needs for support of different groups of migrants at different points in the life cycle of the household. The case studies presented in the book provide a more detailed picture by location and specific cultural and historical context. Examples of migrant support that show potential for scaling up are also presented towards the end of the book.

Although, all of the chapters are on the common theme of migration, they approach the subject from different disciplinary perspectives and analyse the issue from a different disciplinary lens. But rather than resulting in a diverse hotchpotch that has little cohesion we feel that this diversity allows us to view the problem in its entirety and rich complexity. Thus, while earlier chapters in the volume emphasize the economic reasons and impacts of migration, later chapters emphasize the non-economic aspects of migration using a range of different methods and approaches and the final chapters take a completely pragmatic and policy focused approach.

The chapter by Badiani and Safir (Chapter 2) is based on an econometric analysis of a panel dataset constructed from the Village Level Studies (VLS) data collected by the International Crop Research Institute in the Semi-Arid Tropics (ICRISAT) in Mahabubnagar district in Andhra Pradesh and in two districts in Maharashtra. They find that an increase in aggregate rainfall decreases the probability of migration and the number of days of migration, while it has the opposite effect on off-farm agricultural wage labour. Positive idiosyncratic shocks increase the probability of migration while they decrease the number of days of work in the village. The two chapters by the ODI team on MP and AP (Chapters 3 and 4), also based on panel datasets collected from six villages in each state in 2001, 2003, and 2006, document high levels of circular migration and commuting and a highly diverse and segmented migrant labour market with variable returns. In AP, the incidence of commuting showed a marked increase, migration was associated with acquiring skills and being upwardly mobile and was relatively more important for poorer social groups. In MP, circular migrants and commuters far outweigh permanent migrants. Earnings were spent mainly on consumption and paying off debts.

In contrast, the next four chapters highlight other dimensions of the migration process. The chapter by Khandelwal and Joshi (Chapter 5) provides valuable insights into the nature of migrant labour contracts, the role of social networks and power relations in shaping the outcomes of migration through case studies of ice cream vendors, textile workers, brick-kiln workers, and loaders in Rajasthan. The case studies provide evidence of the many market imperfections that permeate rural labour markets and render simplistic demand and supply analyses meaningless. The authors provide a number of suggestions for specific migrant support programmes for these sectors. The study in Bihar by Deshingkar *et al.* (Chapter 6) shows that even within the broad category of poor migrants working in the informal sector, there are important differences: those belonging to the broad category of Other Backward Caste (OBC) with dynamic social networks and skills are able to save and invest money in improving their asset base, compared to tribals and the lowest caste groups who are barely able to smooth and raise their consumption levels. Child migration is on the rise and this is the most vulnerable group of migrants. The authors conclude that the poorest need migrant support programmes built on social protection principles, whereas upwardly mobile migrants need support for safe and efficient remittance mechanisms as well as institutional and technical support for investing their earnings. The Bihar study also highlights inter-generational dimensions of migration, that is, sons follow in the footsteps of their parents and become the main migrant as the parents 'retire', a phenomenon that has been variously termed as 'relay' or 'serial' migration in studies from other parts of the world.

The study by Shah in Jharkhand (Chapter 7) shows that economic reasons alone cannot explain migration which may, in fact, be driven in some cases by the desire to break free of restrictive social norms in the village and engage in relationships, including amorous relationships, away from home. Shah also argues that Jharkhand activists and policy-makers' construction of migration as a problem is as much about their vision of how the new tribal state *ought* to be as about exploitation. Migration to the kilns is seen by them as a threat to the purity and regulation of the tribal citizen. This moralizing perspective creates a climate that, paradoxically, encourages many young people to flee to the brick kilns where they can live freely. She argues that the new puritanism at home helps to reproduce the conditions for capitalist exploitation and the extraction of surplus value. The study of migration in tribal areas of Madhya Pradesh by Llewellyn (Chapter 8) draws from in-depth interviews with men and women migrants to explore the ways in which landless and land-poor tribal workers negotiate credit and labour arrangements. The chapter engages with feminist and structuralist discourses and shows how workers' decisions to migrate, their material experiences of migration, and the meanings, they construct from them are informed by their social identities.

The next chapter by Rao (Chapter 9) focuses on the policy dimensions of migration and examines the impact of the NREGA on migration based on fieldwork conducted in eight villages in Andhra Pradesh and Madhya Pradesh in February 2007.

On a positive and practical note, the chapter by Aajeevika Bureau, one of the largest and most successful migrant support programmes in India (Chapter 10), offers options for civil society organizations, the private sector, donors, and the government to work together on enhancing skills, providing educational support, issuing ID cards, and creating awareness on migrant rights. The chapter in this section by Deeptima Massey (Chapter 11) describes informal social protection mechanisms used by family members left behind in West Bengal based on fieldwork done in 2006.

The book ends by spelling out the policy options available to promote the positive dimensions of migration and to counteract both the negatives and the constraints (Chapter 12). It does so in the knowledge that policy is mediated through the pressures exercised by political constituencies, and that the actions of those responsible for making and implementing policy will be constrained by these. Two broad kinds of support are recommended:

NOTES

1. Economic transformation, among other things, is shorthand for a process of modernization of the economy in which urban-based activity outstrips rural, with a shift of population from rural- to urban-based employment. Transformation is discussed in more detail below.

2. The laws are as follows: 1. The greatest body of migrants travel short distances. 2. This produces currents directed towards great commercial centres. 3. Each current has a compensating counter-current in the opposite direction. 4. Both currents display similiar characteristics 5. Long distance movements are directed towards great commercial centres. 6. People in urban areas migrate less than people in rural areas. 7. Males migrate more over long distances and females migrate more over short distances.

    Additions to these laws: 8. Most migrants are between 20–34 years of age. 9. People mainly move for economic reasons. 10. Urban housing development is inadequate for the influx of migrants so ghettoes/shanties are formed.

3. 'Pushes' are the negative features of the source area such as lack of employment and deteriorating agriculture and 'pulls' are the attractions of the destination such as better paid jobs. Whilst these concepts have intuitive appeal, they are of little analytical use. The worse are source area conditions, the more appealing appear potential destination area conditions. The reality is that, like a pair of scissors, both blades do the cutting, and, as in basic demand and supply models, the interaction between the two determines to some extent the equilibrium quantity and price, recognizing always the influence of structural rigidities, as we explore below.

4. According to this model, the migration decision is based on expected income differentials between rural and urban areas, not wage differentials. This implies that rural–urban migration in a context of high urban unemployment can be economically rational if expected urban income exceeds expected rural income. The model further asserts that an equilibrium will be reached when the expected wage in urban areas, adjusted for the unemployment rate, is equal to the marginal product of an agricultural worker.

5. Circulation has meant different things to different analysts. Anthropologists and sociologists studying the movement of workers in Northern Rhodesia were among the first to coin the term labour circulation (Wilson 1941; Mitchell 1961, 1969).

6. This section draws on Start & Johnson 2004.

7. i.e., regions within countries, not internationally.

8. Cited in de Haan 1999.

9. de Haan (1999), p. 208.

10. This negative view of migration in not unique to India. On the whole governments and donors tend to view migration as a negative phenomenon and seek to inhibit rather than facilitate labour flows. For example, a survey of 41 Poverty Reduction Strategy Papers (PRSPs), carried out by the Centre for Migration Research at Sussex University, illustrates the negative light in which governments view labour mobility. Twentyone PRSPs did not mention migration at all while the remaining papers referred to migration in negative terms, often suggesting that rural to urban migration be controlled or eliminated (Ellis and Harris 2004, p. 9).

11. Deshingkar (2006), p. 9.

12. Ellis and Harris (2004), p. 6.

13. Estimates of textile workers from Ministry of Textiles http://texmin.nic.in/msy_20010621.htm; construction workers from Chen (2007); brick kiln workers from ILO (2005); numbers of street vendors from GOI (2004); estimates of rickshaw pullers from the Centre for Rural Development which runs rickshaw banks in several states; truck drivers from an HIV/AIDS control programme reported in *Business World* (2008); mine and quarry workers from Ghosh and Roy (2007); estimates of salt pan workers from BOBP–IGO (2006).

14. These groups accounted for more than 250 million people in 2001 (167 millions SCs, 86 millions STs and other minorities). Official statistics show that SCs and STs are more deprived than other social groups. At the all-India level, poverty among STs was about two times higher than non-SC/STs, the poverty gap ratio being 2.10 and 1.7 times higher among SCs compared to non-SC/ST groups. But there were variations across states. The disparity between SCs and non-SC/ST groups was particularly high in Punjab, Haryana, and Rajasthan with poverty disparity ratios of 5.31, 3.98, and 3.72 respectively. Thus, poverty among the SCs was about five times

higher in Punjab, about four times higher in Haryana, and about two and half times higher in Rajasthan than the rest of the non-SC/ST population (Thorat and Mahamallik 2005).

15. As distinct from the poorest (very close to categories such the very poorest, the extreme poor, the ultra poor as defined by various researchers and aid agencies ) who would be unable to work being too young or old, sick, or disabled.

16. The America India Foundation (AIF 2006) estimates that at least 6 million children in India miss school because they migrate seasonally with their parents.

17. Daily commuting.

## REFERENCES

AIF, *Locked Homes, Empty Schools: The Impact of Distress Seasonal Migration on the Rural Poor*, New Delhi: America India Foundation/Zubaan, 2006.

Black, R., C. Natali, and J. Skinner, 'Migration and Inequality', Background paper for the World Development Report, Development Research Centre on Migration, Globalisation, and Poverty, UK: University of Sussex, 2006.

Breman, J., *Beyond Patronage and Exploitation: Changing Agrarian Relations in South Gujarat*, Delhi: Oxford University Press, 1993.

———, *Footloose Labour: Working in India's Informal Economy*, Cambridge: Cambridge University Press, 1996.

Breman, Jan, Otto van den Muijzenberg, and Ben White, 'Labour Migration In Asia', Clara Working Papers on Asian Labour, IIAS/IISG, Amsterdam, 1997.

*Business World*, 'CSR Special Apollo Tyres HIV initiative', 18 May 2008. http://wvw.businessworld.in/content/view/4655/4763

Byres, Terence J., 'The Agrarian Question and Differing Forms of Capitalist Agrarian Transition: An Essay with Reference to Asia', in Jan Breman and Sudipto Mundle (eds), *Rural Transformation in Asia*, Oxford: Oxford University Press, 1991.

———, 'Introduction: Development Planning and the Interventionist State Versus Liberalisation and the Neo-liberal Ideal State: India, 1989–96', in T. Byres (ed.), *The State, Development Planning and Liberalisation in India*, Delhi: Oxford University Press, 1998.

Centre for Rural Development http://www.crdev.org/rb.asp. Guwahati, Assam.

Chen, M., *Skills, Employability and Social Inclusion: Women In The Construction Industry*, Harvard University: WIEGO Network, 2007.

Connell, J., B. Dasgupta, R. Laishley, and M. Lipton, *Migration from Rural Areas: The Evidence from Village Studies*, Delhi: Oxford University Press, 1976.

Davies, S., *Adaptable Livelihoods: Coping with Food Insecurity in the Malian Sahel*, London: Macmillan, 1996.

Dayal H., and A. K. Karan, *Labour Migration from Jharkhand*, New Delhi: Institute for Human Development, 2003.

de Haan, A., 'Livelihoods and Poverty: The Role of Migration — A Critical Review of the Migration Literature', *Journal of Development Studies* 36 (2), 1999, pp. 1–47.

de Haan, A. and B. Rogaly (eds), *Labour Mobility And Rural Society*, London: Frank Cass, 2002.

Dev, S. M., and R. E. Evenson, 'Rural Development in India: Rural, non-farm, and Migration', Working Paper # 187, Stanford Center for International Development, Stanford, California, Oct. 2003.

Deshingkar, P., 'Internal Migration, Poverty and Development in Asia', *IDS Bulletin* 37 (3), 2006, pp. 88–100.

Deshingkar, P. and D. Start, 'Seasonal Migration For Livelihoods, Coping, Accumulation And Exclusion', Working Paper no 220, London: Overseas Development Institute, 2003.

Dubey, A., R. Palmer-Jones, and K. Sen, 'Surplus Labour, Social Structure and Rural to Urban Migration: Evidence from Indian Data', *The European Journal of Development Research*, 18 (1), March 2006, pp. 86–104.

Ellis, F. and N. Harris, 'New Thinking About Urban and Rural Development', Keynote Paper for DFID Sustainable Development Retreat, University of Surrey, Guilford, 13 July 2004.

Fine, B., *Social Capital versus Social Theory: Political Economy and Social Science at the Turn of the Millenium*. London: Routledge, 2001.

Francis, E., 'Rural Livelihoods, Institutions and Vulnerability in South Africa', Paper presented at the DESTIN Conference on 'New Institutional Theory, Institutional Reform and Poverty Reduction', London School of Economics, 7–8 September 2000.

Giddens, Anthony, *The Constitution of Society: Outline of the Theory of Structuration*, Berkeley: University of California Press, 1984.

Government of India, National Census of 2001, Ministry of Home Affairs, Government of India.

Haberfeld *et al.* 'Seasonal Migration of Rural Labour in India', *Population Research and Policy Review* 18 (4), 1999, pp. 73–89.

Harriss, B., 'Regional Growth Linkages from Agriculture', *Journal of Development Studies*, 23 (2), 1987, pp. 275–89.

Harris, J., and M.P. Todaro, 1970, 'Migration, Unemployment and Development: A Two Sector Analysis', *American Economic Review*, 60, 1970, pp. 126–42.

Haggblade, S., P. Hazell, and J. Brown, 'Farm-non-farm Linkages in Sub-Saharan Africa', *World Development* 17 (8), 1989, pp. 1173–1201.

Hart, G., 'The Dynamics of Diversification in an Asian Rice Region', in B. Koppel, et al (eds.) *Development or Deterioration: Theories, Experiences and Policies*, Oxford and New York: Oxford University Press, 1994.

Hazell, P. and C. Ramasamy, *The Green Revolution Reconsidered: The Impact of High Yielding Varieties in South India*, Baltimore, MD: Johns Hopkins University Press, 1991.

Hugo, G.J., 'Circular Migration in Indonesia', *Population and Development Review*, 8 (1), 1982, pp. 59–84.

Kuhn R.S., 'The Logic of Letting Go:Family and Individual Migration from Rural Bangladesh', *Working Paper Series* 2000–09, Labor and Population Program, Santa Monica, California: The RAND Institute, August 2000.

Kundu, A, 'Migration and Urbanisation in India in the Context of Poverty Alleviation', presentation at the International Conference and Workshop on 'Policy Perspectives on Growth, Economic Structures and Poverty Reduction', Beijing, China, 3–9 June, 2007. http://www.networkideas. org/ideasact/Jun07/Beijing_Conference_07/Amitabh_Kundu.ppt#261,3, Slide 3.

———, 'Changing Agrarian System and Rural Urban Linkages in India in the Context of Social Viability', http:/fao.org/es/ESA/Roa/pdf/6_Social / Social Viability_India.pdf

Kundu, A., and N. Sarangi, 'Migration, Employment Status and Poverty: An Analysis across Urban Centres', *Economic and Political Weekly*, 27 January 2007, pp. 299–306.

Kuznets, S., *Economic Growth of Nations. Total Output and Production Structure, Cambridge*, MA: Harvard University Press, 1971.

———, *Modern Economic Growth*, New Haven, CT: Yale University Press, 1966.

Lee, E.S., 'A Theory of Migration', *Demography*, 3(1), 1966, pp. 47–57.

Lewis, V.A., 'Economic Development with Unlimited Supplies of Labour', *Manchester School*, 22, May 1954, pp. 139–91.

Lipton, M., 'Migration from Rural Areas of Poor Countries: The Impact on Rural Productivity and Income Distribution', *World Development* 8 (227), 1980, pp. 1–24.

———, 'Labour and Poverty', World Bank Staff Working Paper 616, Washington DC: World Bank, 1983.

———, and R. Longhurst, *New Seeds and Poor People*, London: Unwin Hyman, 1989.

Ministry of Urban Development, 'Economic Growth of Nations. Total Output and Production Structure'. New Delhi, 1988.

Mitchell, J.C., 'Labour Migration in Africa South of the Sahara: The Cause of Labour Migration', *Bulletin of the Inter-African Labour Institute* 6, 1959, pp. 12–47.

———, 'Wage Labour and African Population Movements in Central Africa', in K.M. Barbour, and R.M. Prothero (eds), *Essays on African Population*, London: Routledge and Kegan Paul, 1961.

——— (ed.), *Social Networks in Urban Situations: Analysis of Personal Relationships in Central African Towns*, Manchester: Manchester University Press, 1969.

Mellor, J., *The New Economics of Growth: A Strategy for India and the Developing World*, Ithaca: Cornell University Press, 1976.

Mosse, D., S. Gupta, M. Mehta, V. Shah, and J. Reas, 'Seasonal Labour Migration in Tribal (Bhil) Western India', Report to DFID India, New Delhi, KRIBP Working Paper, Centre for Development Studies, University of Wales, Swansea, 1997.

Mosse, D., S. Gupta and V. Shah, 'On the Margins in the City: Adivasi Seasonal Labour Migration in Western India, *Economic and Political Weekly*, 9 July 2005, pp. 3025–38.

Mosse, D., 'Brokered Livelihoods: Debt, Labour Migration and Development in Tribal Western India', *Journal of Development Studies* 38(5), June 2002, pp. 59–87.

Mukherji S., 'Low Quality Migration in India: the Phenomenon of Distress Migration and Acute Urban Decay, paper presented at the 24th IUSSP (International Union for Scientific Study of Population) Conference, Salvador, Brazil, August, 2001.

Narain, U., S. Gupta, and K van 't Veld, 'Poverty and the Environment: Exploring the Relationship between Household Incomes, Private Assets, and Natural Assets', Working Paper no. 134, Centre for Development Economics, Department of Economics, Delhi School of Economics, 2005.

NSSO, *Migration in India 1999-2000*, NSS 55th Round, Report no. 470, National Sample Survey Organisation, Ministry of Statistics and Programme Implementation, Government of India, September 2001.

NIUA, *State of India's Urbanization*, National Institute of Urban Affairs, New Delhi, 1988.

Olsen, W., and R. V. Ramanamurthy, 'Contract Labour and Bondage in Andhra Pradesh (India)', *Journal of Social and Political Thought*, 1(2), June 2000. http://www.yorku.ca/jspot

Rogaly, B, 'Dangerous Liaisons? Seasonal Migration and Agrarian Change in West Bengal, in B. Rogaly', B. Harriss-White, and S. Bose (eds), *Sonar Bangla? Agricultural Growth and Agrarian Change In West Bengal and Bangladesh*, New Delhi/London/Thousand Oaks: Sage, 1999, pp. 357–80.

Rogaly, B., and A. Rafique, 'Struggling to Save Cash: Seasonal Migration and Vulnerability in West Bengal, India', *Development and Change*, 34 (4), 2003, pp. 659–81.

Ravenstein, E., 'The Laws of Migration', *Journal of the Statistical Society*, 48, 1885, pp. 167–235.

Rosenzweig, M., 'Labor Markets in Low Income Countries', in H. Chenery and T.N. Srinivasan, (eds), *Handbook of Development Economics*, Vol. 1. North Holland, Amsterdam: Elsevier, 1988.

Scoones, I., 'Sustainable Rural Livelihoods: A Framework for Analysis', IDS Working Paper 72, Brighton: Institute of Development Studies at the University of Sussex, 1998.

Shah A., and D.C. Sah, 'Poverty among Tribals in South West Madhya Pradesh: Has Anything Changed Over Time?', *Journal of Human Development*, 5(2), July 2004, pp. 249–63.

Skeldon, R., *Migration and Development: A Global Perspective*, Essex: Longman, 1997.

——, 'Migration and Poverty', Paper presented at the Conference on 'African Migration and Urbanization in Comparative Perspective', Johannesburg, South Africa, June 4–7, 2003.

Stark, Oded, and David E. Bloom, 'The New Economics of Labor Migration', *American Economic Review* 75(2), 1985, pp. 173–8.

Stark., O., and E. Katz., 'Labour Migration and Risk Aversion in Less Developed Countries', *Journal of Labor Economics*, 4(1), 1986, pp. 134–49.

Stark, O. and J. Edward Taylor, 'Testing for Relative Deprivation: Mexican Labor Migration, Harward University Migration and Development Program Discussion Paper (U.S.): No 26: 1–37 December, 1986.

——, 'Relative Deprivation and International Migration', *Demography*, 26(1), 1989, pp. 1–14.

Stark, O., J.E. Taylor, and S. Yittzhaki, 'Labour Migration, Income Inequality and Remittances: A 16 Case Study of Mexico', Development Research Department, World Bank, Washington, 1987.

——, 'Remittances and inequality', *Economic Journal*, 96(383), 1986, pp. 722–40.

Stark, O. (1991), The Migration of Labour, Cambridge: Basil Blackwell, 1991.

——, and D. Levhari, 'On Migration and Risk in LDCs', *Economic Development and Cultural Change*, 31, 1982, pp. 191–6.

Start, D. and C. Johnson, 'Livelihood Options? The Political Economy of Access, Opportunity and Diversification', Working Paper no 233, London: ODI, 2001.

Thorat, S., and M. Mahamallik, 'Persistent Poverty—Why Do Scheduled Castes And Scheduled Tribes Stay Chronically Poor', Paper presented at CPRC-IIPA Seminar on 'Chronic Poverty: Emerging Policy Options and Issues', September 29 and 30, Indian Institute of Public Administration, New Delhi, 2005.

Todaro, M.P., 'A Model of Labor Migration and Urban Unemployment in Less Developed Countries', *The American Economic Review*, Vol. 59, 1969, pp. 138–49.

Todaro, M., 'Internal Migration in Developing Countries: A Survey', in R. A. Easterlin (ed.), *Population and Economic Change in Developing Countries*, Chicago: University of Chicago Press, 1980, pp. 361–402.

Wilson, G., 'An Essay on the Economics of Detribalisation in Northern Rhodesia', Rhodes Livingston Paper no. 5, Rhodes-Livingston Institute, 1941.

Zelinsky, Z., 'The Hypothesis of the Mobility Transition', *Geographical Review*, 61(2), 1971, pp. 219–49.

Zelinsky, W., 'The Demographic Transition, Changing Patterns of Migration', in *Population Science in the Service of Mankind*, P. Morrison (ed.), International Union for the Scientific Study of Population: Liege, 1979, pp. 165–88.

# 2

# Circular Migration and Labour Supply
## Responses to Climatic Shocks

*Reena Badiani and Abla Safir*

## INTRODUCTION

The income and well-being of rural households in developing countries continues to be affected by climatic shocks and in particular by rainfall patterns. Insurance markets are incomplete, in the sense that they do not allow households to hedge themselves against all of the risks that they are exposed to. In the face of liquidity constraints and a lack of savings or borrowing opportunities, household investments in human capital, health, nutrition and consumption may fluctuate substantially due to shocks. The consequences for households who are unable to absorb shocks can be bleak, including an increased risk of malnutrition, the withdrawal of children from school and the loss of productive assets Rose (1999), Jacoby and Skoufias (1997), Rosenzweig and Wolpin (1993), Dercon and Krishnan (2000) and Hoddinott (2006)). The consequences of drought can be even worse. In Andhra Pradesh and Maharashtra, the states in which our study villages are located, newspapers have documented an increase in the suicide rates of farmers during severe droughts (Sainath, 2006).

This paper hopes to add another dimension to the literature on how households manage risk. We examine whether households respond to climatic shocks through their labour supply, in particular through circular migration. Much attention has been paid to long-term and permanent migration as a means of managing risk or as a means of investing in higher return activities. Studies of remittances as a risk diminishing mechanism focus on the correlation of income and shocks between the location of migration and that of the sending region. Stark and Rosenzweig (1989) use the earlier wave of the ICRISAT dataset that we use to examine how marriage location patterns of women can be a means of reducing the variability of incomes. De la Briere et al. (2000) study the motivation behind sending remittances in the Dominican Republic; they find that whether remittances play an insurance role or can be seen as a strategic bequest depends on a number of individual and household characteristics. However, only a few works tackle the decision of migration *per se* as a means of managing risk. Whilst the study of permanent migration has been quite extensive (Lucas (1997) provides a good overview), work on circular or temporary migration has been more limited. To our knowledge, no other empirical work has studied whether circular migration occurs in response to shocks, *ex-post*. That this is the case is surprising given the high levels of short-term mobility in many countries across the world. For example, Yang (1992) reports that the population of temporary migrants in China was estimated to be between 10 million and 50 million in a sample of large urban areas.

Understanding why people leave their place of residence in search of short-term employment elsewhere is a challenging task since it requires knowledge of how labour markets on the local, district, and state-wide levels function. Several theoretical explanations for the phenomenon of temporary migration can been given, including its role as a means to earn money for a particular project ('target saving', Lucas (1997)), as a 'mistaken' permanent migration (Lucas (1997)), as a coping mechanism, as an *ex-ante* risk management strategy or as a response to differentials in earnings between rural and urban areas. Each of these explanations, however, also implies a mirrored statement about the functioning of local markets. For example, if circular migration acts as a coping mechanism, this implies that either wages, demand or both in local labour markets are insufficient to allow households to smooth shocks. This also signals failures in local insurance and credit markets. Similarly, if migration is used as an *ex-ante* risk management strategy this implies that the *ex-post* risk management strategies available in the village are inadequate to deal with shocks. Furthermore, it implies that the risks faced in the destination labour market are not strongly covariant with those of the initial residence.

Given the strong need to examine local labour markets to fully understand why households migrate, we combine our study of circular migration with a study of village labour market responses to shocks. Our study focuses on households' labour market responses to idiosyncratic and aggregate rainfall shocks. We examine whether the days of agricultural wage work, circular migration and non-agricultural work are responsive to idiosyncratic and aggregate shocks. Unfortunately we do not have access to data on own-farm labour so we are unable to examine whether households increase the work conducted on their own farms in response to income shocks. The setting for our study is 6 villages surveyed intermittently since 1975 by the International Crops Research Institute in the Semi-Arid Tropics (ICRISAT), India.

The chapter is structured as follows. In Section 2 we describe the dataset employed and discuss the incidence of both permanent and circular migration in the villages since data collection commenced. Section 3 introduces the empirical strategy we use to estimate the impact of climatic shocks, namely rainfall, on household labour supply and section 4 presents our results. Section 5 concludes.

DATA AND HISTORY OF MIGRATION

Data

The Village Level Surveys (VLS) were initiated between 1975 and 1984 in six villages in Andhra Pradesh (Aurepalle and Dokur in Mahabubnagar district) and Maharashtra (Shirapur and Kalman in Sholapur district, and Kanzara and Kinkheda in Akola district). The intensive and meticulous surveying procedures followed by ICRISAT led to the generation of one of the most influential and illuminating data sets in development economics. Information from 40 households was collected in each village using 12 questionnaires designed to cover the key aspects of income generation and consumption. The sample in each village was stratified by land holding size rather than providing a representative sample of the village; a given year of data therefore covers small, medium, and large landholders, as well as landless labourers in equal proportion.

We refer the interested reader to the ICRISAT Manual (1985) and Walker and Ryan (1992) for more detailed information regarding the panel between 1975 and 1985.

Four of the six original ICRISAT villages were revisited in 1992; one village in each of the original Maharashtra districts was dropped due to an increased survey burden as a result of picking up household split-offs.[1,2] Attempts were made to resurvey as many of the original VLS households and their split-offs as possible. A total of 199 split-off and continuation households corresponding to 132 original households were picked up in a three-round panel during the 1992-93 agricultural year. Interested readers should refer to Chung (1998).

ICRISAT resumed data collection in the VLS villages in 2002, covering the agricultural year from June 2001 to May 2002. At that time, the aim was to obtain a representative sample of the village including many of the original households and supplemented by additional households. When data collection recommenced in 2002, the panel was expanded to 446 households, of which 264 contained individuals present in the earlier period; we call this subset of households the continuation sample. The household surveys used in 2002 were designed to be compatible with the intensive surveys conducted between 1975 and 1984. However, the data emanating from the earlier period were collected using an intensive three-weekly survey methodology, whereas the data emerging from the later rounds were collected using a yearly recall at the termination of the agricultural year. The comparability of the two periods is discussed in greater detail in Badiani et al (2006). We will only present here the essential aspects necessary for the understanding of this paper.

In 2005, information was collected on all individuals related to the earlier and later VLS—4796 individuals living in 1398 households, of which 619 households were still residing in the villages and 734 households were households linked to permanent migrants. From the 240 original households in 1975, the VLS traced 1964 individuals living in 939 different households, of which 546 were households residing elsewhere and 393 were households in the villages. From 2005, all households in the villages linked to the earlier and later VLS were surveyed using a monthly survey, which was designed to ensure full comparability with the earlier VLS.

## Permanent and Circular Migration in the VLS

Since the VLS started in 1975, the study has registered a substantial movement of individuals and households into and out of the six villages. In the earlier VLS period, migration flows were limited in size and consisted predominantly of permanent migratory movements. The surveys conducted in 1992 indicate that circular migration had become an occupational choice for some households in the villages. These trends are supported by the data collected since 2002, in which circular migration has become an important employment source for some households.

The changes in the nature and magnitude of circular and permanent migration flows witnessed during this period in the VLS villages appears to be reflective of overall migration trends in India. Using data from the National Census, Roy (1991) reports that internal migration, as measured by individuals no longer residing at their place of birth, increased from 166.7 million to 207.6 million migrants between the 1971 and 1981 rounds. Estimates of the number of short-term or circular migrants in India are based upon informal estimates due to a lack of nationally representative data [Deshingkar (2005)]. Available evidence suggests that the number of circular migrants has increased during the 1980s and 1990s in eastern (Ghosh and Sharma (2005)) and in western India (Breman (1996)).

### Migration between 1975 and 1984

Both permanent and circular migration have been prevalent in the VLS since the earlier rounds, albeit at a smaller magnitude. Of the 40 households in each of the six villages in 1975, approximately 10 per cent had permanently migrated by 1984. Whilst data on circular migration was not systematically picked up in the earlier VLS, Walker and Ryan (1990) provide qualitative evidence indicating that circular migration was present in the earlier period, and indeed increased in Aurepalle and Dokur post 1983 as a 'response to off-farm opportunities, mainly rickshaw pulling and construction work in Hyderabad'. Approximately 40 per cent of households in the Andhra villages contained an individual who had left the village for employment purposes in the agricultural year 1985–86 (Walker and Ryan, p. 27).[3] They document the early presence of formal arrangements facilitating migration, with the presence of subcontractors in Dokur allowing villagers to migrate for periods of five to eight months. Whilst there is no substantive evidence on the magnitude of the flows of migrants, movements were viewed as small enough to be considered of no significance to previous studies of the ICRISAT villages.

## Circular Migration in 1992

In the survey conducted in 1992, data on circular migration is available for a subset of four of the six villages (with the number of original and split-off households linked to the old-VLS surveyed in brackets): Aurepalle (64), Dokur (39), Shipapur (49) and Kalman (45). In each of the 3 rounds of data collection, questions were asked on all individuals who were classified as permanently residing in the village but who had left for at least a week during the last four months. The purpose of migration was recorded, along with the number of weeks the individual was absent for and whether any monetary transfers had been made between the migrant and the members of the household still residing in the village. The occurrence of circular migration for work is spread across households in the sample: 26 (45 per cent) in Aurepalle, 15 (39 per cent) in Dokur, 14 (29 per cent) in Shirapur, and 10 (22 per cent) in Kalman. The higher rates of migration seen in the villages in Andhra Pradesh in 1985/6 were still witnessed in 1992. At an individual level, of the 1025 working age individuals surveyed in 1992, 123 individuals declared having worked outside of the village at some point during the year.

Circular migrants appear to have a higher level of education than the sample average at all ages. By 2005 the individuals who engaged in circular migration in 1992 also have much higher rates of permanent migration for work purposes and circular migration than those who did not. This would suggest that circular migration, which we study in this paper as a short-term income generating activity or a way to cope with shortfalls of other income sources, may be part of a longer-term individual or household strategy. At a household level, 37 per cent of households with a circular migrant in 1992 had at least one circular migrant between 2001/2 and 2004/5, compared to 29 per cent for non-migrant households in 1992/3. On an individual level, 45 per cent of migrants in 1992/3 were still conducting circular migration post-2001 compared to 17 per cent of non-migrants.

*Migration post-2001*

Data on circular migration using yearly recalls was collected in the new VLS surveys from 2002 onwards; this is the data which we employ in this study. Table 2.1 summarizes the incidence of temporary migration at a household level by village. Whilst the number of households reporting a circular migrant is clearly greatest in Andhra Pradesh, a sizeable fraction of households in Maharashtra report engaging in circular migration. What is interesting for our purposes is that the number of households engaging in circular migration fluctuates year-on-year: whilst nearly half of the households surveyed in Aurepalle conducted circular migration at some point between 2001–2 and 2004–5, in a given year, only a quarter of households reported engaging in it. Figure 2.1 shows the yearly movements which motivate our basic story: as can be seen, the raw data indicate a negative correlation between circular migration and monsoon rainfall. In years during which rainfall has been plentiful, the sampled households' average number of days of circular migration falls. For one village, this pattern may not be pertinent: Kinkheda in Akola district. This village, along with Kanzara, was characterized by Walker and Ryan (1992) as being one of the most amenable to agricultural production, with fertile soil and reliable rainfall patterns. The higher levels of income per capita and asset holdings seen in these two villages may partially explain their lower levels of circular (and indeed permanent) migration. Other explanations at a village level, such as village level infrastructure, are also likely to contribute to the explanation. Since we only have data on 6 villages, however, these village level factors cannot be examined.

Of the 1814 individuals present between 2001–2 and 2004–5, 197 had engaged in circular migration at some point during the period. The characteristics of temporary migrants in this period are similar to those seen in 1992–3—migrants are predominantly young males with higher levels of education at all ages than the rest of the sample. At the household level, the differences between the income and asset levels of the two groups seem insubstantial. Interestingly there are statistically significant differences in the demographic profiles of the two groups: households with circular migrants comprise, on average, an extra individual in the household and an extra half male.

Table 2.1: Households with Migrants

| | Andhra Pradesh | | Maharashtra | | | |
|---|---|---|---|---|---|---|
| Village | Aurepalle | Dokur | Shirapur | Kalman | Kanzara | Kinkheda |
| Number of Households | 100 | 81 | 88 | 94 | 95 | 31 |
| 2001–2 | 14 (14%) | 31 (39%) | 12 (14%) | 5 (5%) | 7 (14%) | 2 (6%) |
| 2002–3 | 25 (25%) | 33 (41%) | 11 (13%) | 4 (4%) | 1 (2%) | 6 (19%) |
| 2003–4 | 23 (23%) | 30 (38%) | 10 (11%) | 11 (12%) | 9 (21%) | 7 (22%) |
| 2004–5 | 27 (27%) | 35 (40%) | 7 (8%) | 12 (13%) | 9 (21%) | 5 (16%) |
| At least once 2001/2–2004/5 | 43 (43%) | 45 (40%) | 19 (8%) | 18 (13%) | 14 (21%) | 6 (16%) |

Note: Number of households reporting at least one temporary migrant for work purposes. The figures in brackets are the percentage of households in the village sample who have a temporary migrant.
Source: VLS Survey, 1992.

In addition to having experienced an increase in the number of circular migrants since the earlier VLS, the villages have seen a gradual increase in the number of individuals permanently leaving the villages. Permanent migration for work purposes increased throughout the period, particularly towards the end of the 1990's. Between 1975 and 1985 on average 2.7 people migrated permanently for work purposes per year and village, from 1985 to 1992 this figure rose to 3.8 and in the subsequent period, 1992 to 2005, on an average 10 individuals migrated for work purposes per year. These figures are small in absolute terms as well as relative to those of other low-income countries.[4] The low levels of permanent migration highlight the importance of considering circular migration in the Indian context, since it is likely to be an important route for households to generate income outside of their agrarian villages.

## Labour Participation in the ICRISAT Villages

Other substantial changes in the occupational structure of the villages appear to have been occurring, alongside an increase in circular migration over time. Table 2.2 summarizes the number of days of labour conducted by households by occupational type in the

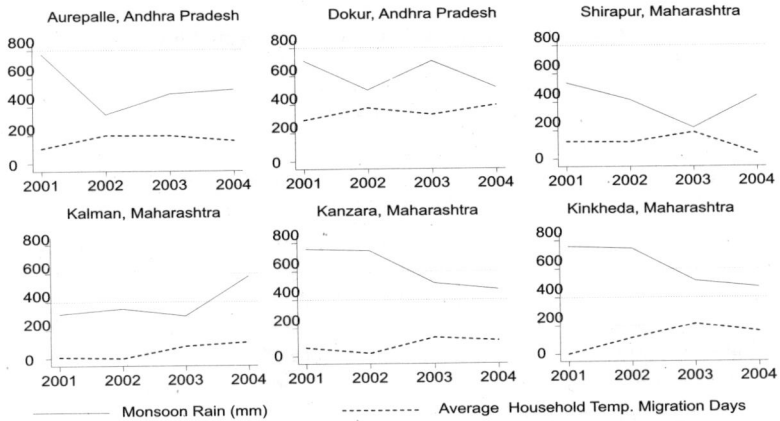

Temporary migration has been scaled; a different scale is used in each State

Figure 2.1 Temporary Migration and Monsoon Rainfall

earlier and later samples. Off-farm work is split into different types (circular migration, agricultural wage work and non-agricultural work). We define an individual, and thus the household he belongs to, as working for an agricultural wage if he reports working in the agrarian sector within the village for a wage or salary. Non-agricultural work is defined as non-agrarian occupations, such as business and trading or caste related occupations conducted within the village.

The patterns seen in the continuation sample (i.e. the sample of 264 households containing at least an individual present both in the old VLS and in the new survey) and whole sample (i.e. the 240 households interviewed between 1979 and 1984 and the 446 households interviewed from 2002) are broadly similar; therefore we focus on the continuation sample. The figures reported represent the labour market activity of households engaged in a given occupational type. The number of days devoted to labour market activities has increased substantially over the period, from 77 days per adult to 156. Part of this increase is attributable to agricultural wage work, which has more than doubled over the period from 49 days to 88. Non-agricultural work has also expanded substantially from 44 days per adult to 121. In addition, households have seen a large decrease in the percentage of income emanating from farming. For those households participating in the labour market, the mean

Table 2.2: Changes in Occupational Structure between
1975–84 and 2001–04

| | Continuation Sample | | Whole Sample for each period | |
| --- | --- | --- | --- | --- |
| | 1979–84 | 2001–04 | 1979–84 | 2001–04 |
| *Farming* | | | | |
| Total income per capita (1983 Rs) | 842.6 | ·1796.9 | 812.8 | 1636.9 |
| | (627.30) | (1760.60) | (606.02) | (1544.60) |
| % of Total income | 44.3 | 29.3 | 37.3 | 18 |
| Farm days per hectare | 140 | 77.1 | 138.7 | 71.1 |
| (hired and own) | (98.09) | (66.07) | (97.20) | (72.50) |
| % Household participating | 81 | 70 | 78.5 | 56 |
| *Total off-farm employment days* | | | | |
| % Income from labour market | 43.6 | 44 | 45.6 | 45.3 |
| Days per adult | 76.6 | 156 | 76.8 | 145.8 |
| | (57.67) | (109.73) | (57.50) | (95.96) |
| % Household participating | 84.5 | 85.8 | 78.1 | 86.3 |
| *Circular Migration* | | | | |
| Days per adult | – | 81.6 | – | 93.3 |
| | (43.90) | | (60.80) | |
| % Household participating | – | 13.1 | – | 16.7 |
| *Agricultural wage labour* | | | | |
| Days per adult | 51.8 | 89.8 | 43.3 | 82.9 |
| | (51.90) | (64.00) | (50.00) | (63.80) |
| % Household participating | 69.9 | 62.6 | 65.6 | 61.4 |
| *Non-agricultural work* | | | | |
| Days per adult | 44.2 | 120.6 | 44.7 | 105.5 |
| | (43.00) | (114.40) | (44.20) | (97.80) |
| % Household participating | 55 | 53.1 | 54 | 52.2 |
| *Involuntary Unemployment* | | | | |
| Days per adult male | 14.2 | 14.8 | 14 | 15.3 |
| | (24.80) | (36.90) | (22.90) | (38.10) |
| Number of households | 458 | 574 | 721 | 1806 |
| No household members | 6.1 | 4.9 | 6 | 5.1 |

*Notes:* Statistics for the whole sample 2001–04 are for the six villages and cover all time periods. Those for the whole sample 1979–85 cover households in three villages—Aurepalle, Shirapur, and Kanzara. The continuation sample comprises of 149 households linked to 91 original households in three villages who were present and cultivating throughout the period: both between 1979 and 1984 and between 2001 and 2004. Data are only presented for those households engaging in the activity—therefore the number of days of circular migration is given for those 16 per cent of households reporting positive days of circular migration. Farming income as a percentage of total income is given for households cultivating on owned or rented land. The statistics presented are unweighted. Comparisons between the original and full sample may therefore partially reflect changes in the sampling design across periods. Standard errors are given in parentheses.

proportion of household income generated in the wage labour market has stayed stable in relative terms, at approximately 45 per cent of household income, although it has increased substantially in absolute size. While we cannot compare across the two periods, we can see how important circular migration is now. Amongst households conducting circular migration, income from this source accounts for 32 per cent of total income.

Since the number of non-agricultural opportunities within the villages seems to have increased substantially throughout the period, an interesting question which we hope to address is whether households are able to shield themselves from climatic variation through increasing the number of labour days devoted to non agricultural work. Since non-agricultural work is generally based within the village, and may therefore be subjected to demand shocks related to climatic variation, it provides an interesting contrast to circular migration responses to climatic variation.

ECONOMETRIC SPECIFICATION AND IDENTIFICATION

We want to estimate the impact of aggregate and idiosyncratic rainfall shocks on the number of days of labour supply and circular migration. Since some households do not carry out any labour market activities, we estimate the days of agricultural wage labour, non-agricultural labour and temporary migration allowing for the censoring of labour supply.[5] We estimate the following model:

$$l^k_{ht} = \beta_1 rain_{vt} + \beta_2 rain_{vt}{}^*C_{h2001/2} + \beta_3 rain_{vt}{}^*AW_{h2001/2} + \beta_4 rain_{vt}{}^*NA_{h2001/2} + \beta_5 X_{ht} + u_h + u_t + \varepsilon_{ht}$$

where $l^k_{ht}$ refers to either migration, agricultural wage work or non-agricultural work by household h in year t; $rain_{vt}$ is a measure of rainfall during monsoon in village v in year t; $C_{h2001/2}$ refers to the income emanating from agricultural and allied activities by household h in 2001–2; $AW_{h2001}$ refers to earnings from agricultural wage work in 2001–2; $NA_{h2001}$ refers to non-agricultural earnings; $X_{ht}$ controls for household demographic characteristics; $u_t$ controls for time trends common to the six villages, for example structural changes in the labour market or inflation; and $u_h$ includes fixed unobserved household characteristics that may be correlated with the household shock and influence labour decisions. Lastly,

$\varepsilon_{ht}$ includes time-varying shocks other than rainfall as well as measurement error in data collection.

Our measure of the aggregate village level shock, rain$_{vt}$, is the difference between total rainfall during the monsoon season in a given year and the long term average measured between 1990-1 and 2000-1.[6] Average levels of rainfall may be correlated with levels of migration in the village. For example, crop profits may be higher in those villages with high rainfall, and average levels of temporary migration are lower since there is more work or higher wages available in the village. Our interest lies in *changes* in rainfall over time within a village and their correlation with changes in migration patterns of households in a given village.[7]

We measure the idiosyncratic shock by using the interaction of monsoon rainfall with a measure of a household's exposure to the shock. The general idea is that a household which contains individuals who are engaged in off-farm activities or had a lower proportion of income emanating from agriculture may be less reliant on agricultural income and less exposed to rainfall variation than a household whose income from cropping is high and who has no other income generating activities. We define two dummy variables indicating whether a household earns income from cropping and non-agricultural activities in 2001-2 as a proxy for a household's exposure to shocks and capacity to diversify, respectively. In addition, we measure a household's exposure to agricultural wage work by separating agricultural wage participation into 3 groups: those households whose agricultural wage income is strictly positive and who fall into the bottom half of the agricultural wage income distribution in 2001-2 (the median income from agricultural wages is 3600 Rs.); those whose income falls between the 2nd and 3rd quartiles (75 per cent of the sample earn less than 12000 Rs. from agricultural wage labour); and those who fall in the last quartile (those earning greater than 12000 Rs). We interact these variables with monsoon rainfall to estimate the shock faced by a specific household in a given agricultural year. Our estimations are therefore carried out on the sample between the 2002-3 and 2004-5.[8]

The aggregate shock differs from the idiosyncratic shock in that it affects the average level of income in the village through directly altering the marginal product of productive assets and labour inputs. Signing the impact of the aggregate shock on agricultural wage labour is not obvious and depends on the distribution of land within each village and possible differing elasticities in the demand and supply of labour between small, medium and large farms. Typically, if the elasticity of the demand for wage labour to the aggregate shock in medium and large farms is larger (in absolute value) than the elasticity of the supply of own-farm labour by small farmers who are likely to be the most active landowners taking part in the agricultural wage labour market, then the total effect of the aggregate shock is going to be positive: i.e. agricultural wage labour is going to increase in good years and decrease in bad years.

A household's crop income is a measure of the household's reliance on agriculture—a household that conducts farming is likely to face a larger absolute negative shock when rainfall is poor than a household that does not. Non-agricultural income is viewed as a measure of a household's potential to diversify outside of the agrarian sector: if a household generated income from non-agricultural activities in 2001–2, it should be less affected by the impact of rainfall on agrarian activities. A similar effect may be considered for agricultural wage labour. Labour demand is likely to vary with rainfall since the marginal product of labour in agrarian activities is a function of climatic conditions. Village level wages will therefore vary with climatic conditions since they are likely to adjust to equilibrate labour demand and supply. If they do not adjust completely because of wage rigidities then the demand for labour is likely to decrease. Households which have large levels of agricultural wage income may be affected by rainfall variation through changes in labour market conditions and, while we expect them to be affected more strongly than non-agricultural households, it is unclear whether they suffer from shortfalls in rain more than independent farmers.

Since measures of the household's exposure to the shock are likely to be correlated with unobserved household characteristics, we include household fixed effects to control for unobserved time invariant heterogeneity between households. The fixed effect $u_h$ allows us to control for household fixed characteristics that may be correlated both with the shock and labour supply. For example, risk aversion may be important in this framework: we expect a more risk-averse household both to select into less risky occupations (therefore being less prone to shocks) and at the same time migrate less because migration also has uncertain returns. A more risk averse household may also have a higher supply of agricultural wage labour as an ex-ante insurance mechanism. Therefore, such a household would have lower shocks on average than other households; he would also migrate less than other households, this last phenomenon not due to the lower shock on average but actually to the household risk aversion. Without the fixed-effect estimation, we would not be identifying the impacts of the shocks but we would be comparing different households whose fixed unobserved characteristics would determine both the magnitude of shocks and the off-farm labour supply.

We use Honore's 1992 fixed-effects estimator, which is suitable for short panels.[9] In the case of temporary migration however, understanding the decision to migrate *per se* is of additional interest to us. Moreover, since the proportion of households migrating is at most 20 per cent in a given year, the censored regression model may be ill-suited because it constrains regressors to have the same effect when going from 0 to 1 day of migration as when going from 100 to 101 days, while we may expect the two decisions to be quite different. We therefore additionally estimate Logit regressions to estimate correctly the impact of the shocks on the decision to migrate.

RESULTS

The results are presented in Table 2.3. The results for the Logit specification, which examines migration decisions on the extensive margin, are presented in column (a) and the results for the censored model are presented in columns (b) thru (d).

The estimated coefficients indicate that circular migration may be a coping mechanism for some rural households in the sampled villages: the number of days of circular migration increase when rainfall decreases. In the estimation of the decision to migrate, the impact of rainfall is negative although not significantly different from zero, indicating that aggregate rainfall may be less important on the extensive margin than on the intensive margin. For households who were engaged in farming during the 2001–02 agricultural year, the negative effect is reinforced, as is indicated by the negative coefficient on the interaction between rainfall and the crop income dummy, i.e. households engaged in farming during 2001–02 are less likely to migrate in *good years* and, symmetrically, are more likely to do so in

Table 2.3: Fixed Effects Estimates of Labour Supply Responses to
Aggregate and Idiosyncratic Shocks

| | Decision to Migrate (Logit specification) | Total household days devoted to different labor market activities (Honore's fixed-effect estimator) | | |
| --- | --- | --- | --- | --- |
| | Circular Migration | Circular Migration | Agricultural Wage Work | Non-Agricultural Work |
| | (a) | (b) | (c) | (d) |
| Monsoon rainfall | -0.00501 | -1.398*** | 0.3050** | 0.1374 |
| | (0.00349) | (0.4253) | (0.1442) | (0.2519) |
| Monsoon rainfall* Farming in 2001/2 | -0.00495* | -0.7549** | -0.1369 | -0.00128 |
| | (0.0029) | (0.3889) | (0.1155) | (0.1803) |
| Monsoon rainfall* Non-agricultural work in 2001/2 | -0.00312 | 0.2766 | 0.06605 | -0.0402 |
| | (0.00319) | (0.5592) | (0.1157) | (0.1609) |
| Monsoon rainfall* Levels of agricultural wage work in 2001/2 | | | | |
| —Low | 0.00263 | 0.8842*** | -0.4355** | 0.3232 |
| | (0.00430) | (0.6953) | (0.1791) | (0.2997) |
| —Intermediate | -0.00061 | 0.6651 | 0.002755 | -0.3929* |
| | (0.00375) | (0.5851) | (0.1402) | (0.2267) |
| —High | 0.00922** | 1.5780*** | 0.01946 | -0.05488 |
| | (0.00365) | (0.5823) | (0.1441) | (0.2248) |
| Number of male adults in household | 0.72191* | 238.80*** | 42.82** | 30.15 |
| | (0.42829) | (67.90) | (19.03) | (29.99) |
| Average migration wage (village–year) | -.03015* | -3.9240 | -1.115 | 2.201* |
| | (0.01799) | (3.1570) | (0.7651) | (1.251) |
| Average agricultural wage (village–year) | -0.13211* | -21.41 | 4.175 | -2.676 |
| | (0.07461) | (17.45) | (2.913) | (4.309) |
| Chi–square test (p–value (%)) | 27.57 | 39 | 59.8 | 24.5 |
| | (0.38) | (0) | (0) | (1) |
| Number of observations | 285 | 1339 | 1339 | 1339 |

Source: Authors.
Notes:* significant at 10%; ** significant at 5%; *** significant at 1%
Each specification includes controls for time dummies. Standard errors are given in parentheses.
Agricultural wage income in 2001-2 is split into 4 categories, depending on whether households generated no income from this activity the 'zero' category, which is the reference category; the first half of the distribution ('low'), the third quartile ('intermediate') and the fourth quartile ('high').

*bad years*.[10] In contrast, the impact of rainfall is attenuated or even completely compensated for households who conducted agricultural wage work. Households which conducted some agricultural wage work allocate fewer days to migration in *good years* but less so than households which conducted farming or no agricultural wage work at all.[11] The positive coefficient on the interaction between rainfall and the high agricultural wage income group reverses the effect of rainfall. For this group, the total impact of rainfall is positive: they are more likely to migrate when rainfall increases and they also migrate for longer periods. One possible interpretation comes from migration costs. As circular migration may be costly, households that want to diversify their income through wage work may use an increase in their income (due to better rainfall) to finance the cost of migration. We are unable to validate this explanation since we do not have appropriate data on the cost of migration.

Aggregate rainfall has a positive effect on days of agricultural wage work, except among those households whose earned income from agricultural wage work lies in the *low* category. For this group, agricultural wage labour decreases as rainfall increases. The average positive impact of rainfall on agricultural wage work is an interesting corollary to the migration estimates which showed that the number of days of circular migration increased in bad rainfall years. Demand for circular migrant labour, in contrast to village level agricultural labour demand, is unlikely to be correlated with local climatic conditions. The results indicate that households may use circular migration opportunities as a means of responding to localized shocks. Households whose income is very sensitive to rainfall, such as households who crop, are the most likely to use circular migration in *bad years* while households that take part actively in the agricultural wage labour market may use temporary migration both as a coping mechanism as well as a more general income generating scheme. Unfortunately, our data do not contain information on own-farm work for all years of the panel making us unable to test whether the overall number of days worked by the household increased overall in response to rainfall variation or were just reallocated amongst activities.

The impact of the number of adult males is interesting. An additional male adult in the household increases the length of circular migration by eight months and also strongly increases the probability that a household sends a migrant away. As mentioned previously, households with circular migrants comprise, on average, 0.5 male adult more than other households. The addition of a household male also has a strong positive effect on agricultural wage work, increasing total wage work by 43 days.

The coefficients on average village-level wages for circular migration and agricultural wage work are mostly not significant and difficult to interpret when they are. Circular migration is negatively correlated with agricultural wages, a result we would expect; more puzzlingly, migration is negatively correlated with circular migration wages as well. Similarly, non-agricultural work is positively correlated with circular migration wages. The wage measures used in this chapter are the average of observed male wages amongst those conducting circular migration or agricultural wage work. As such they measure at best equilibrium wages and are likely to be an imperfect proxy for the actual wage offers received by workers, particularly in the case of the wage rate earned during circular migration. As a robustness check on the impact of idiosyncratic shocks, we estimate the specifications including village-year dummies[12]; the main results of this chapter remain robust to this change in specification.

Non-agricultural work is not significantly impacted by any of our measures of shock, aggregate or idiosyncratic. What's more, the interaction of the indicator of non-agricultural income in 2001-02 with rainfall does not have any impact on temporary migration. Although non agricultural income could be a means of diversification, which could shelter households from rainfall variations and therefore induce them to migrate less, it may also be more of a medium to long-run income generation scheme and therefore exhibit less variation in employment in the short-run.

CONCLUSION

In this chapter we have used panel data on six villages in rural India to examine household labour supply responses to climatic shocks. We separate the labour supplied by a household into three categories: labour conducted whilst having temporarily migrated away from the village; agricultural wage work and non-agricultural work conducted in the vicinities of the village. We find that the number of days of circular migration conducted by a household is responsive to climatic variation: circular migration increases when rainfall is low. Agricultural wage labour is also found to be responsive to rainfall variation, whilst non agricultural work within the village is non-responsive.

The results presented in this chapter imply that circular migration is responsive to climatic variation at a village level. However this explanation is likely to be only a part of the determinants of circular migration: the households which are most responsive to climatic variation are those households with a large reliance on agriculture. As such, the choice of income generation strategy for a household is likely to have implications on its propensity to migrate. Enhancing our understanding of the choices that households make between alternative occupations within the village is likely to be crucial for understanding which households are the most likely to engage in circular migration as a coping mechanism.

NOTES

We thank Esther Duflo for suggesting the estimation we conduct and helpful comments on earlier work. We thank Sylvie Lambert for many helpful comments on this chapter.

1. Split-off households are those which occur from the division of former VLS households - for example children of former VLS households creating their own new household after marriage. A continuation household is one which had the same household head in 1984 and 1992.

2. Kalman in Sholapur and Kinkheda in Akola were dropped since inter-district variability was considered to be greater than intra-district variability.

3. This figure is not verifiable using the VLS surveys since data collection had already terminated at that time.

4. The migration figures may under-report income related migration since familial co-movements, which are often part of the same flow, are reported as 'migration for familial reasons'. In addition, since the sample under consideration covers only the old-VLS households the demographic profile of this sample may be weighted against younger migrants as we reach the end of the period.

5. Labour supply is characterized as 'censored' since for those households who choose not to work, labor supply is set to zero. Ordinary Least Squared gives inconsistent parameter estimates since desired labor supply may in fact be negative for these households but is scaled up to zero. With a cross-section, we could estimate labor supply using a tobit specification, which is a particular form of censored regressions that assumes the error term to be normally distributed and homoscedastic. Because we conduct

estimates using a panel dataset and want to allow for household level fixed-effects, we use Honore's (1992) semi-parametric estimator which does not constrain the error term to be normal and gives consistent estimates even in short panels.

6. The rainfall data used in this study come from the Indian Meteorological Department. Villages were matched to the nearest rainfall station. The monsoon season covers the period between June and September.

7. Migration wages may however react to village rainfall since migration contractors may have to increase offered wages in years when village level rainfall is high while they may decrease them in years when rainfall is low. In addition, if rainfall is spatially covariant, wages from migration may covary with rainfall. Since we have observed that migrants often travel long distances to their destinations, it is unlikely that rainfall co-movements will affect the entire wage schedule they face. However, if rainfall co-movements are actually important then the relative returns of migrating to different locations will vary according to the size and covariance of rainfall shocks observed in each region. The only solution for this would be to control for wages in the most frequented migrant destinations. However this is quite difficult because we only observe wages *ex-post* to migration occurring, we do not observe wages as offered by contractors.

8. We exclude the year in which we calculate the household's exposure since a failure to do so would expose our estimates to reverse causality: in a given year, a household could decide to migrate temporarily and, as a consequence of the migration decision, this household could decrease its cropped area or crop income. This may occur if, for example, hired and family labour are imperfect substitutes and the optimal level of family labor required to cultivate the household's land is greater than that available after the migration decision has been made.

9. Honore's (1992) semi-parametric trimmed least absolute deviations estimator is employed since, as noted by Heckman and MaCurdy (1980), the inclusion of household specific fixed effects into a Tobit regression may yield biased estimates in short panel data. This estimator assumes that errors are independently and identically distributed across time.

10. The total impact of rainfall for these households is obtained by adding the coefficient on rainfall (−1.398) to the coefficient on the interaction of rainfall with the dummy indicating cropping activity in 2001–02 (−0.7549), the total impact then is −2.152, which is stronger than the −1.398 impact of monsoon rainfall alone.

11. The coefficient on the interaction of rainfall with the level of agricultural wage work in 2001–02 must be understood as the impact relative to the reference category which is 'Zero', i.e. households who did not participate in the agricultural wage labor market. In this case, for the 'zero' category, the coefficient on rainfall is −1.398 while for the 'low' category, the impact of rainfall is −1.398+0.8842.

12. Since rainfall varies by village and by year, we cannot conduct estimates with both village-year dummies and measures of rainfall. Including village-year dummies allows us to control for rainfall but also for other factors such as labor market conditions, such as wages, specific to each village.

REFERENCES

Badiani R., S. Dercon and P. Krishnan, 'Income, Consumption, Nutrition and Assets in Villages in India 1975–2004: Revisiting the ICRISAT village level studies', Working Paper, 2006.

Bantilan M.C.S. and K.V. Anupama 'Vulnerability and Adaptation in Dryland Agriculture in India's SAT: Experiences from ICRISAT's Village-Level Studies' Working Paper Series Socioeconomics and Policy ICRISAT, No 13.

Breman, J., *Footloose Labour: Working in the Indian Informal Economy*, Cambridge: Cambridge University Press, 1996.

Chung, K., 'The Contribution of ICRISAT Mandate Crops to Household Food Security: A Case Study of Four Rural Villages in the Indian-Semi Arid Tropics' Information Bulletin no. 52. Hyderabad, India: The International Crops Research Institute for the Semi-Arid Tropics, 1998.

De la Brière, B., E. Sadoulet, A. de Janvry and S. Lambert, 'The Role of Gender, Age, and Family Composition in Explaining Remittances', *Journal of Development Economics*, 68 (2) 2002, pp. 309–28.

Dercon, S. and P. Krishnan, 'In Sickness and in Health: Risk Sharing within Households in Rural Ethiopia', Journal of Political Economy, 108 (4) 2000, pp. 688–727.

Deshingkar, P., 'Maximising the Benefits of Internal Migration For Development', IOM Background Paper, 2005.

Deshingkar, P. and S. Grimm, 'Voluntary Internal Migration', ODI Working Paper, 2005.

Ghosh, P. P. and A. N. Sharma, 'Seasonal migration of rural labour in Bihar', *Labour* and *Development*, Vol. 1 No 1 July–December, 1995.

Hoddinott, John, 'Shocks and their Consequences across and within households in Rural Zimbabwe', *Journal of Development Economics*, February 2006.

Honore, Bo, 'Trimmed Lad and Least Squares Estimation of Truncated and Censored Regression Models with Fixed Effects'. *Econometrica*, 60 May 1992, pp. 533–65

Jacoby, H.G. and E. Skoufias, 'Risk, Financial Markets and Human Capital in a Developing Country', *The Review of Economic Studies*, 64 (3) July 1997, pp. 311–35.

Kundu, A., 'Urbanisation and Urban Governance, Search for a Perspective Beyond Neo-liberalism', *Economic and Political Weekly*, No. 29, July 19, pp. 3079–87, 2003.

Lucas, R. E.B. and O. Stark, 'Motivations to Remit: Evidence from Botswana', *Journal of Political Economy*, 93 (5) October 1985, pp. 901–18.

Rose, E., 'Consumption Smoothing and Excess Female Mortality in Rural India', *Review of Economics and Statistics*, 81:1 pp. 41–9, 1999.

Rosenzweig, M. and O. Stark, 'Consumption Smoothing, Migration, and Marriage: Evidence from India', *Journal of Political Economy*, 97(4), 1989, pp. 905–26.

Rosenzweig, M., 'Payoffs from Panels in Low-Income Countries: Economic Development and Economic Mobility', *American Economic Review*, papers and proceedings, (May 2003), pp. 112–16.

Rosenzweig, M. and K. Wolpin, 'Credit Market Constraints, Consumption Smoothing, and the Accumulation of Durable Production Assets in Low-Income Countries: Investments in Bullocks in India' *The Journal of Political Economy*, 101(2), 1983, pp. 223–44.

Sainath, P., 'Distress Up, Suicides Appalling' *The Hindu*, November 22, 2006.

Townsend, R., 'Risk and Insurance in Village India', Econometrica 62, (May 1994), pp. 539–92.

Walker, T. S. and J.G. Ryan (1990), Village and Household Economies in India's Semi-Arid Tropics, Baltimore: Johns Hopkins.

Yang, X., 'Temporary Migration and Its Frequency from Urban Households in China', *Asia-Pacific Population Journal*, 7(1), 1992, pp. 27–50.

# 3

# The Evolving Pattern of Circular Migration
## Household Surveys in Andhra Pradesh

*Priya Deshingkar, Laxman Rao, Shaheen Akter, and John Farrington*

## INTRODUCTION

The poorest southern state, Andhra Pradesh has made rapid advances in the IT and retail industry and has some of the most rapidly urbanizing centres in India. Yet, the differential pattern of growth has meant that high growth pockets co-exist with some of the poorest and underdeveloped rural areas in India. For many of the poor living in these underdeveloped areas, migration and commuting are the only ways of accessing the benefits of growth in other locations. Migration has helped them in managing risk, smoothing consumption, and earning enough to invest in a better future.

This chapter examines the changing patterns of migration and commuting in the southern Indian state of Andhra Pradesh. The evidence presented is based on the analysis of three surveys conducted in 2001–2, 2003–4, and 2006–7 in six villages in Andhra Pradesh. Three districts were covered representing the three regions of the state: Medak district in Telangana, Chittoor in Rayalseema, and Krishna in Coastal AP. Two villages were selected from each district with one being relatively remote and the other well connected. Descriptive statistics and multivariate analysis are used to gain an understanding of the importance of migration earnings for the poor, differences in migration patterns by location, caste and other factors that influence income. Qualitative data are used to shed light on segmentation in the migrant labour market by caste, gender, and age and identifying vulnerable groups of migrants. The chapter with an overview of the context within which migration occurs followed by a description of migration and commuting patterns, incomes generated and how these have changed since 2001. The chapter concludes with a discussion on the policy implications of the findings.

THE CONTEXT

Andhra Pradesh is the poorest southern state but has a dynamic and growing IT sector and receives a large flow of remittances from abroad which fuel the economy. It is the fifth largest state in India both in terms of geographical area (276,814 sq. kms) and population (76 million) comprising 23 districts, 1105 revenue *mandals*,[1] 29,994 villages, and 65,505 habitations. There is a great deal of diversity and disparity in terms of agro-ecology, irrigation, infrastructure, and public and private investment. There are three broad regions which are culturally and historically distinct: Coastal Andhra, Telangana, and Rayalaseema.[2]

Although Andhra Pradesh ranks low among south Indian states on human development indicators, it has succeeded in reducing income poverty substantially over the last 60 years.[3] Official statistics

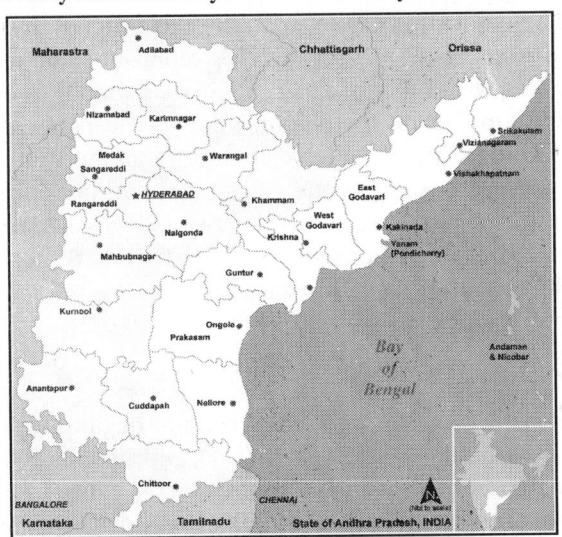

Map 3.1: Map of Andhra Pradesh
*Source*: http://en.wikipedia.org/wiki/Image:Kosta,png

show that agriculture continues to sustain nearly 65 per cent of the workforce. Agriculture is characterized by a large proportion of landless people as well as marginal and small farmers who together account for 80 per cent of operational holdings covering 43 per cent of the cultivable land. Almost 60 per cent of the holdings are below one hectare. Rural labour productivity is low and earlier increases in real wages have slowed down. As in the rest of India, Scheduled Castes and Tribes are disproportionately represented among the poor. The origins of rural labour migration for manual work in Andhra Pradesh can be traced back to the pre-independence era. Rural labourers were mobilized for executing major public works in both rural and urban areas. For instance, migrant labourers from Mahabubnagar district migrated to irrigation project sites such as the Nizamsagar project.

Migration has been an important way of coping with environmental shocks and stresses. Drought studies show the pervasiveness of migration, particularly in drought prone areas. For example, a study in a village in Kosgi Mandal in Mahbubnagar district shows that 60 per cent of the farmers owning between 10 to 20 acres of land were migrating (Reddy 2002). Another survey conducted in 1989–90 in three villages of the same district shows that circular migration occurs in all cultivating classes with the exception of those holding more than 20 acres of land (Reddy 2003). Small and medium farmers from this area were more likely to migrate seasonally to other rural locations to supplement their income during the lean season.

Recent studies in AP indicate that the incidence of migration has increased. For example, the village level studies conducted by ICRISAT over the last three decades in two villages of Mahbubnagar district covering, 1164 households show that both seasonal and permanent migration have increased during the reference period (see Chapter 2 and also Deb et al. 2002).

METHODOLOGY

Data were collected through three rounds beginning in 2001–2, repeated in early 2005 for the year 2003–4, and again in 2006–7. Data were collected from 6 villages in 3 districts (see Table 3.1 below).

The first survey had three rounds: a census of all the households in the study villages covering 4,647 households, and two seasonal surveys covering a smaller stratified sample of 40–80 households

## Table 3.1: Study Regions and Villages

| Andhra Pradesh | | |
|---|---|---|
| Krishna (Coastal Andhra) | Chittoor (Rayalseema) | Medak (Telangana) |
| KO (well connected)    KA (remote) | OP (well connected)    VP (remote) | GU (well connected)    MD (remote) |
| Agricultural prosperous, canal irrigated, Paddy, Pulses, Sugarcane· <br> • Mixed caste but FC dominated <br> • Polarized land distribution.· | Semi arid, tank, and tube well irrigated, well connected with large cities, Groundnut, Paddy, Mulberry, Tomato <br> • BCs emerged as powerful in remote village recently <br> • More equitable land holdings | Semi arid, socially backward, mainly tank irrigated or rain-fed agriculture, Sorghum, Paddy, Cotton, Maize <br> • Traditional caste hierarchy <br> • Land distribution still along feudal lines in remote village |

*Source*: Authors.

(depending on the size of the village). Stratification was done by land-holding and caste. This survey showed that migration was occurring in all villages to varying degrees. However, analysis was hampered by the limited data on migration because the main focus of the survey was livelihood diversification, debt, and village governance. Although some idea of the diversity and complexity of migration was gained from focus group discussions and key informant interviews, detailed quantitative analysis could not be undertaken.

The second and third rounds of data collection were designed with the purpose of understanding migration in greater detail. The 2003–4 round completed in early 2005 covered the same households as the 2001–2 seasonal surveys. But there was roughly a 5 per cent decrease as some of the households in the previous survey had split up or moved out of the village. Data were collected on the year of first migration, type of work, skill levels, number of days worked, earnings, expenditure, sources of information, and remittance spending patterns.

The most recent survey (in two rounds) completed in April 2007 focuses on migrating households alone and further refines questions on migration. It captures income from migration in detail, that is, cash, in-kind, and advances as well as expenditure by end use. It includes questions on occupational mobility with a view to understanding the links between spatial mobility and occupational mobility. Migration information was collected from all six villages in the 2001–2 and 2003–4 panels; however the village KA was dropped from the 2006–7 panel due to very low levels of migration. The sample size was thus 360 households for the first two rounds and 300 for the last round.

## HOW IT ALL BEGAN

An important common trigger for migration from the semi-arid villages of Medak and Chitttoor was drought. Other factors that have shaped migration in recent years include emerging opportunities in irrigated agriculture, industry and urban areas. The specific history of migration varies a great deal by village and social group. For example, group discussions in MD indicated that the Lambada started to migrate to sugar mills around 37 years ago when farmers from irrigated areas came to the village looking for hard-working labourers to cut their cane. Lambadas were given preference over others because of their reputation for being hard working and also because they owned bulls and carts which are essential for transporting the harvested cane to the sugar factory. In the case of the Mudiraj (BCs) from the same village, migration began after a major drought in the late 1960s known as 'Makkala Karuvu' or the corn drought because people were reduced to eating maize which was the cheapest grain available. Other migration streams have evolved due to specific skills of workers as in the case of the earth workers from VP who belong to the caste of Vaddi. The Vaddi were traditionally well and grave diggers. They began migrating around forty years ago as the demand for their traditional occupation waned. Early migrations were through contractors and agents from government departments who were looking for workers to help them with building roads and in other public works. They later moved on to working for private sector cable network companies as trench diggers and for construction companies in levelling land for new developments.

## GROWING NUMBERS

Discussions in all the villages indicate that on the whole, the incidence of migration has increased over the years especially after economic liberalization in the early 1990s. Although there were fluctuations in the numbers migrating from year to year depending on the duration and severity of drought, the availability of work through public works programmes, and watershed development programmes, the general trend is increasing mobility. Data on the year of first migration and commuting (not shown in Table 3.2) shows that for 55.4 per cent, the year of first commuting/migration falls between 2000 and 2006 and for 40.3 per cent the first year of commuting/migration fell between 2003 and 2006.

There has also been a shift in destinations towards metropolises. This corroborates the trend noted by other studies conducted in the last five years (for example, Deshingkar et al. on Bihar in this volume, studies by Action Aid in Andhra Pradesh). More than half of all circular migrants went to destinations outside the state, 34 per cent travelled within the state, and 15 per cent within the district. Migrants from Medak and Krishna districts migrate to Hyderabad and their counterparts in Chittoor district migrate to Bangalore. International migration occurs mainly from the coastal villages; the highest numbers were from the prosperous village KO.

The first survey conducted in 2001–2 found migrants in all the villages studied but the magnitude of migration varied a great deal: while the well connected villages of GU and OP had only 4 per cent and 9 per cent of their households migrating (but a larger number of commuters as we discuss later), remote villages had a much larger proportion of households with at least one migrant (Table 3.2). In VP, the remote village in Chittoor, this proportion was 33 per cent and in MD, the remote village in Medak district, it was 78 per cent.

A comparison of the last two rounds shows that the number of households with at least one person working outside the village had increased from 41 per cent in 2003–4 to 54 per cent in 2006–7; average annual increase is more than 3.3 per cent.

MIGRATION AS A RISK SPREADING AND ACCUMULATIVE STRATEGY

A majority of circular migrants are poor. Nearly 60 per cent of the households with circular migrants in the 2006–7 sample were marginal farming households and a quarter were landless households. For these households many of whom are SCs, STs, and BCs, migration is a household strategy for managing risk where one or more members go away from the village to find work. In the case of the poorest households, entire families migrate as we see in the case of SCs in Medak. Commuting is equally important for the

Table 3.2: Incidence of Migration in AP Villages, 2001–2

| AP villages | Census | | Sample | |
|---|---|---|---|---|
| | Total number of households | % of households with at least one member migrating | Total number of households | % of households with at least one member migrating |
| OP | 214 | 9 | 40 | 10 |
| VP* | 553 | 33 | 60 | 29 |
| KO | 1429 | 10 | 80 | 6 |
| KA* | 464 | 15 | 60 | 17 |
| GU | 1560 | 4 | 80 | 4 |
| MD* | 427 | 78 | 40 | 75 |
| Total | 4647 | 17 | 360 | 19 |
| | Chi$^2$ 5df =1433*** | | Chi$^2$ 5df =107*** | |

Source: Household Census, AP 2001–2.
Note: * remote villages, other villages are well connected.

Table 3.3: Frequency and Percentage Distribution of Households with at least One Person Working Outside the Village (Migrants and Commuters)

| | Village | Numbers | | | % | | |
|---|---|---|---|---|---|---|---|
| | | Yes | No | Total | Yes | No | Total |
| 2006/7 | OP | 25 | 15 | 40 | 62.5 | 37.5 | 100.0 |
| | VP | 33 | 27 | 60 | 55.0 | 45.0 | 100.0 |
| | KO | 38 | 42 | 80 | 47.5 | 52.5 | 100.0 |
| | GU | 38 | 42 | 80 | 47.5 | 52.5 | 100.0 |
| | MD | 29 | 11 | 40 | 72.5 | 27.5 | 100.0 |
| | Total AP | 163 | 137 | 300 | 54.3 | 45.7 | 100.0 |
| 2003/4 | OP | 15 | 25 | 40 | 37.5 | 62.5 | 100.0 |
| | VP | 21 | 39 | 60 | 35.0 | 65.0 | 100.0 |
| | KO | 26 | 54 | 80 | 32.5 | 67.5 | 100.0 |
| | GU | 28 | 52 | 80 | 35.0 | 65.0 | 100.0 |
| | MD | 33 | 7 | 40 | 82.5 | 17.5 | 100.0 |
| | Total | 123 | 177 | 300 | 41.0 | 59.0 | 100.0 |

Source: Panel datasets 2003–4 and 2006–7.

poor—just over half the commuters were marginal farmers and more than 40 per cent belonged to the category of landless indicating that this type of mobility is also central to the livelihoods of the poor. As we describe in the remainder of the chapter, whether or not migration remains at the level of coping or becomes more accumulative, depends on a number of factors including improved work availability, rising wages, cutting out intermediaries, and improving skills.

## CHANGES IN MIGRATION STREAMS

Different migration streams in the study villages were first charted in 2003 (published in Deshingkar and Start 2003). We identified two accumulative migration streams and two coping migration streams.[4] The accumulators were sugarcane cutters from Medak who have earned well on account of their long-standing relationship with sugarcane farmers and, earth workers from Chittoor whose skills are in great demand for digging trenches for cable networks and building roads. These were unskilled construction workers from Medak, who on account of the unreliability of work and high expenses in the city, were able to earn just enough to survive and, agricultural labourers from the villages in Krishna district who migrated for low-paid harvesting work. This chart was updated for the present chapter based on the last two rounds of data collection (see Chart 3.1).

The situation has changed now with new opportunities emerging, changing wage rates, and work availability. While some new migration streams have emerged with fresh contacts in new destinations, others have ceased to exist because of the availability of better opportunities in urban locations as the case studies and qualitative accounts below show. Some streams that were earlier in the category of coping such as migration from MD to Hyderabad for construction work, are now more accumulative.

### Sugarcane Migration on the Decline

In 2003, rural–rural migration for sugarcane harvesting to nearby sugar factories within the district and in the neighbouring districts (Medak, Nizamabad, Karimnagar) was one of the most important migration streams in Medak. Since then many have given up sugarcane cutting because they cannot afford the bulls and cart. Some stopped migrating after they had saved enough to sink a tubewell (Box 3.1). Younger people are exploring opportunities in Hyderabad and do not want to do sugarcane work. Construction work which was risky in 2003 has become more remunerative and predictable because of the booming construction sector. It is emerging as the dominant migration stream following the decline of cane cutting.

Chart 3.1: Coping and Accumulative Migration Streams in AP Villages in 2006–7

| AP Village name and characteristics | Caste, skill and asset base of migrants | Type of work and when | Who migrates | Source, amount and purpose of credit/advance | Coping or accumulative and wage rate | Impact on migrant household and source location |
|---|---|---|---|---|---|---|
| VP, Narsapur hamlet: far from urban centres, unirrigated agriculture, sericuture was important until 2002. | Vaddi (BC) skilled earthworkers, small and marginal farmers, good contacts with government officials who award contracts. | Non Farm: Digging trenches for cable networks, preparing new plots for development. Migrate in all seasons, more in rabi. | Able bodied men and sometimes their wives. New/young families all members migrate. In older/larger families couples take turns so that others can care for livestock, farm and children. | Contractor pays for food, transport, and shelter, until they get paid for the work at the end of the contract. | Accumulative and always has been. Average in 2003 was Rs 110 and now Rs 150 per day. | Increase in wealth, much construction work and drilling of tubewells in village, buying more land from neighbouring villages. They are educating their children in good schools. |
| VP – SC hamlet | Mala (SC) marginal farmers | Used to migrate with Vaddis on 'lighter' jobs in plantations and for the Forest Department. Now migrating with them for higher return digging work. | Able bodied men. Women used to migrate when household economic situation was very bad but now mainly men. | Vaddi contractor/leader takes care of food and shelter and deducts the amount from wages. | Was coping because low paid and erratic work. Becoming accumulative Rs 100/day work availability good. | Used to help survival during lean season and drought. Now contributing to improved standard of living. Reduced dependency on moneylenders. |

| | | | | | | |
|---|---|---|---|---|---|---|
| OP – dry, partly tank irrigated. Near district capital. | Mixed | Migrate for 15-30 days at a time to nearby urban centres and irrigated farms. | Single person from household, men, and women. | None | Accumulative. Average earning is Rs 70 per day and work is available all year round. | Better paid than local casual labouring. |
| MD – remote, unirrigated Very large number of marginal and submarginal holdings. | Mudiraj (BC), and Lambada (ST). Small and marginal farmers. | In 2003 rural–rural migration for sugarcane harvesting within the district and to neighbouring districts (Nizamabad, Karimnagar) was the most important kind of migration. Now migration for construction work in Hyderabad is on the rise. It is emerging as the dominant migration stream following the decline of cane cutting. | Two-three adults from a household together with their children. Pair of bulls and cart essential | Employer (cane farmer) at destination (sends word in advance of the migration season). No middleman or contractor. | Accumulative in 2003, started as coping migration in the 1970s. In 2003 migrants could save up to Rs 3000 per month after meeting expenses and paying off debt. Most families returned with a saving of at least Rs 20,000 in a season. But construction work is seen as even better paid than that with recent increases in wage rates to Rs 100–150 a day for unskilled workers. | More wealth but children's education suffered during sugarcane harvesting, working conditions difficult. Construction work is in locations that are better connected to the village and frequent trips home are possible. |

Contd...

Chart 3.1 (contd...)

| | | | | | | |
|---|---|---|---|---|---|---|
| MD — remote unirrigated. Very large number of marginal and submarginal holdings. Much of the land is unproductive. | Madiga, Mala (SC), poor Mudiraj (BC), marginal farmers. | Construction labour in Hyderabad. Although risky in 2003 this work has become more remunerative and predictable because of the booming construction sector. | Young men, families with young children. | They continue to borrow from moneylenders but are no longer dependent on them for meeting basic needs. | Becoming accumulative. Rs 100-150 per day. Work is available almost all year round. | Earnings are used to clear debts, buy land, pay for marriage expenses, educate children and to pay for medical care. Although it still involves many personal risks and dangers, it is resulting in savings and spending on improving the standard of living. |
| KO, KA — canal irrigated, prosperous. In KO very large proportion of landless households, KA has more smaller holdings but land is highly productive | Mala, Madiga (SC), Gowda (BC). Some of them are tenant farmers. | In 2003, short duration migration (only 15-20 days a year) for agricultural work to other coastal districts was widespread. Now only commuting for agricultural work is seen. But permanent migration to urban locations by the educated/skilled poor from upper castes is on the rise. | Able-bodied men and women, no children. | None | Coping. Rs 50 per day and ½ kg of rice. | Without this work they would have to borrow money. |

*Source:* Authors.

---

BOX 3.1: SUGARCANE MIGRATION WANING

Case 1: Rajaiah (SC), a 60 year old man used to migrate seasonally to villages around the Ganesh Sugar Factory in Sangareddy. He did this for 15 years and the work involved cutting and transporting sugarcane. He would migrate in a group with his two daughters and son-in-law. He dug a tubewell four years ago with the money he saved from seasonal migration. He now grows two crops in a year. Two years ago Rajaiah also arranged the marriage of his younger daughter. This reduced labour availability in the household so they gave up sugarcane harvesting. His son-in-law started commuting to Narayankhed town (the Mandal headquarters) to work as construction worker.

Case 2: Suresh (20) is among several youth in MD who have been migrating to Hyderabad for the last 3 years to work at construction sites. He dropped out of high school to help his family with farming. He learnt about opportunities in construction work from friends and relatives already working in Hyderabad and migrated to Hyderabad in 2005 carrying two pairs of clothes and 25 kg of rice. He stayed with his friends in a rented room in the city. He worked as a casual worker and also under contractors. He used to get a daily wage of Rs 100 three years ago but now he gets Rs 150. He visits his village for festivals and he gives his parents some money each time he visits. He is clearing debts and saving money for his sister's marriage.

---

## More Castes Migrating For Digging Work From Chittoor

The recent trend in VP of Chittoor district is a rise in the number of migrants from diverse caste backgrounds to Bangalore. Until a few years ago, temporary migration to Bangalore had mostly been confined to the Vaddis (BCs). Now Other Castes (OC) such as the SCs and OBCs have joined this migration stream. They work under the Vaddis. The work in and around Bangalore involves clearing and levelling new plots for construction, building roads and drains, and erecting electricity poles. There is plenty of work available and earnings are in the region of Rs 100 per day. Although this kind of migration is not resulting in any immediate accumulation of assets, it is helping to improve the standard of living (Box 3.2).

BOX 3.2: DIGGING WORK IN BANGALORE

Veeraswamy is a 45 year old SC labourer with half an acre of rainfed land. He lives with his wife and two children in the SC hamlet of VP village. His family has been poor for many generations and traditionally worked as farm workers. Both he and his wife are illiterate. The son studied up to class X and the daughter dropped out of school at the age of 10. They grow paddy on their land and it provides some grain for their own consumption. Until recently Veeraswamy and his wife worked as casual agricultural labourers on farms in the village. He was paid around Rs 60 and she was paid Rs 50 for a day's work. But they were able to get work for only 40 days in a year so they had to supplement local work with commuting to the town of Punganur 25 km away. Only Veeraswamy would commute to work as a construction labourer. He would get paid around Rs 80 a day and the work was erratic. The family was always in debt and there was never enough to eat. Then in 2003, Veeraswamy started migrating to Bangalore with groups of SCs from his village under a Vaddi *mestri* from the other hamlet in VP. He migrated for 2–3 months at a time and went up to three times a year. He started on a daily wage of Rs 100 and this went up to Rs 120 in 2006–7. The Vaddi *mestri* takes a Rs 25 cut from the daily wage for providing the workers with food. The construction company provides temporary accommodation.

The money from migration has helped the family to eat regularly and eat better food. They have also started to repay old debts and Veeraswamy is looking forward to a good wedding for his daughter. His wife continues to work in local fields. Although they are still among the poor in the village, they feel that their life is better than it was before.

COMMUTING ON THE RISE

There has been a more than doubling in the proportion of commuters in Andhra Pradesh between the last two surveys. This dramatic change can be explained by the growing road network, improved communications, and the growth of small towns.

Although commuting has increased mainly as a result of urbanization there is also some commuting for agricultural work

Table 3.4: Frequency and Percentage of Different Types of Mobility in
Andhra Pradesh , India, 2003–4 and 2006–7

| Mobility type | 2003–4 | | 2006–7 | |
|---|---|---|---|---|
| | N | % | N | % |
| Commuters | 47 | 22.8 | 119 | 44.4 |
| Circular migrants | 100 | 48.5 | 83 | 31.0 |
| Permanent migrants | 59 | 28.6 | 66 | 24.6 |
| Total | 206 | 100.0 | 268 | 100.0 |

Source: Authors.

to nearby villages. In GU village, close to the industrial belt on the outskirts of Hyderabad, a majority of commuters are industrial workers and the sharp rise in the number of commuters is attributable to the reopening of two major industries around the village (which had been closed down in the early 2000 due to labour disputes). The other major stream of commuters in Medak consists of the self-employed youth plying auto rickshaws between villages and urban centres. In the well-connected village of OP in Chittoor on the other hand, commuters travel to the district headquarters 15 kms away, to work at construction sites, in hotels/restaurants, and shops. Commuters from the more remote village VP work in both farm and non-farm work in nearby villages since there are no major towns nearby. Short duration migration which was widespread in Krishna district in 2003 has almost disappeared now. Now there is only commuting for agricultural work, mainly by SC women. A small number of people also commute to work as drivers and cleaners. Survey results are consistent with the FGDs and key informant interviews; rural–rural migration has indeed reduced dramatically with the increase in commuting.

HAS MIGRATION REDUCED POVERTY?

The literature on migration and poverty suggests that although migration can reduce poverty, the outcome depends very much on the kind of migration. Research by Rogaly and Rafique (2003) in West Bengal and research by Reddy in Andhra Pradesh (2003), for example, shows that for a majority of migrants it is no more than a way of surviving and coping (see also Chapter 1 for a more detailed discussion on this issue). Indeed our sample also shows that migration money is most often used for 'consumption' (60 per cent of the respondents said this). This is usually interpreted with slightly negative undertones as if spending on consumption is somehow not productive. However, improved consumption can have far-reaching positive effects on household well-being by improving nutrition, labour productivity, and reducing sickness and debt. Paying off debt was next in importance followed by purchase of agricultural inputs. Paying for medical treatment was listed as the second most important use by 35 per cent of the respondents followed by paying off debt and consumption.

However, there are clear differences in spending patterns and needs by caste (Table 3.10). Nearly 86 per cent of STs for example, mentioned consumption as the most important use of migration and commuting earnings. Although this could mean that they are so poor that they have to spend most of their earnings on basics such as food, case studies and interviews show that the STs in our sample are not the poorest. Most of them are Lambadas who have some assets and migration has helped them to improve their consumption level. None of them mentioned paying off debt as an important use of their money. Although they do still borrow money, they are less dependent on money lenders than they used to be.

On the other hand, it was mentioned by a fifth of the SC households as the most important use. This is because many SCs work in occupations where recruiting is done by an agent against advances. The migrant then has to repay the advance or debt through the work that they do. This system of recruitment is common in occupations such as brick-kiln work, certain kinds of construction work, and road digging and even in sugarcane harvesting. Proportionately more BCs (18 per cent) said that they would use earnings from migration and commuting to save and invest compared to only 8 per cent of SCs. Interestingly health and education were not mentioned by the

Table 3.5: Percentage Distribution of Households Ranking the Top Use (or Plan to Use) of Mobility Earnings by Purpose and Caste Category, 2006–7

|  |  | Caste category | | | | Total |
|---|---|---|---|---|---|---|
|  |  | ST | SC | BC | OC |  |
| Use | Consumption | 85.7 | 58.3 | 56.6 | 70.4 | 61.2 |
| group | Education and health |  | 12.5 | 6.6 | 7.4 | 7.5 |
| rank 1 | Investment and savings | 14.3 | 8.3 | 18.4 | 11.1 | 14.9 |
|  | Paying off debt |  | 20.8 | 18.4 | 11.1 | 16.4 |
| Total |  | 100.0 | 100.0 | 100.0 | 100.0 | 100.0 |

*Source*: Authors.

STs but were mentioned by 13 per cent of SCs as an important use of their earnings. This suggests that even though the STs are better off than many of the SCs in the sample, they place less importance on the education of their children. However case studies show otherwise.

It is therefore difficult to establish on the basis of quantitative data alone how and why migration earnings are used in a particular way and what their impacts are. Case studies provide important insights into how migration fits into the household's strategy for improving its standard of living and improving prospects for future generations.

---

BOX 3.3: DRILLING TUBEWELLS AND SPENDING ON EDUCATION—
SCs AND STs IN MEDAK, ANDHRA PRADESH

Lingaiah (SC) is 50 year old illiterate labourer who lives in MD, the remote village in Medak district. He and his wife live with their two sons and the sons' families in the same house. Lingaiah's family was landless in the past but he was given an acre of dryland by the government during a land reform programme some years ago. The land yielded very little and both he and his wife continued their traditional occupation of working as agricultural labourers in the local landlord's field. Then about ten years ago, his elder son began to migrate to Hyderabad for construction work. The village is only four hours away from Hyderabad by bus and many other people migrate to the city. The son got married and took his wife with him a couple of years later. But when they had children they left them with Lingaiah and his wife in the village. The son and his wife come back to the village every two months and bring money, clothes, and gifts for the parents and children. They take rice back with them. The rice is obtained by the parents as wages for their labouring work in the fields. Even when they need to buy rice it is cheaper in the village to buy from farmers rather than paying town prices in Hyderabad. The second son started migrating eight years ago. The family in the village was able to eat better and send the children to school because of the money brought back by the sons. This was a major step for a family where several generations have been illiterate. They have also managed to borrow Rs 30,000 to dig a tube well. They were able to borrow

Contd...

Box 3.3 Contd...

because their creditworthiness has improved in the eyes of the moneylenders who know that they have two migrant sons who can repay the debt. The tube well has raised their status in the village and they are now able to take two crops on their land. Both sons and their wives live in rented rooms in Hyderabad for around Rs 500 a month.

Lingaiah says that all families like his are doing the same in the village. If the parents are relatively young and healthy, the sons leave their children in the village and they use migration money to eat better, educate their children, invest in tube wells, or improve their houses.

Case 2. Kishan Nayak is a 50 year old Lambada (ST) living in the same village. He lives with his wife and five children. He owns 1.5 acres of dry and rocky land and has encroached on an acre of forest department land. He grows rainfed sorghum and paddy on his farm. Kishan has been migrating for sugarcane harvesting within the state for the last 20 years. At first it was just him and his wife who were migrating but later both of his sons started to accompany them and he now has four earning members in the house. He started migrating when recruiting agents from the sugarcane mills came to his village to find workers to harvest the cane. He bought a couple of bulls and a cart with borrowed money and started migrating. The recruiting agents gave workers an advance which they would use to buy essentials and repay the debt. The advance would be paid off through their earnings. In 2006 a team of three workers and a bullock cart could save Rs 30,000 in a season of cane cutting. Now the first son migrates with Kishan and his wife. The second son goes to work with another person from the village who also owns a bullock cart. He earns Rs 5000.

The family is no longer in debt and over the years they have improved their living standard considerably. Kishan spent on his eldest daughter's wedding and did not have to borrow. He has built a larger house with a separate kitchen/storage room and a separate shed for the cattle. He now plans to dig a tube well.

As a community Lambadas have done well through migration. They are now migrating on their own without recruiting agents because they know the market well. They are also investing in the education of their children and the younger generation is going into white collar jobs. There are now 2 police constables, 2 school teachers, 1 assistant engineer, and 1 construction supervisor in the Lambada hamlet.

There are less clear cut cases than these where the costs and risks of migration may outweigh the benefits. An example is the migration or trafficking of children for work where the extra income may help to feed the family but at the cost of the child's education. Andhra Pradesh has the largest number of child workers in the country. The most notorious sector for employing child labour is cottonseed production which employs around 200,000 children but other rural occupations and small town enterprises are also child labour intensive such as domestic work, tea shops, eateries, and textile shops.

Although it was difficult to collect hard data on the number of child workers in the study villages, it was often mentioned in Medak and Chittoor that boys from poor dalit families would be sent to work as attached labourers or live in servants (see Box 3.4).

COSTS, RISKS, DISCRIMINATION, DANGER

The surveys and interviews revealed that unskilled migrants usually work in occupations that are classified as the 3 D occupations

---

BOX 3.4: CHILD LABOUR IN CHITTOOR

Ramaswamy is a 40 year old SC labourer in the VP with half an acre of rainfed land on which he grows rice. Both he and his wife are illiterate and work as casual labourers on local farms. They have two children, a son aged 15, and a daughter aged 12. The son is working in a small eatery in the nearby town of Punganur. He stays on the premises and comes back during festivals. The daughter is going to school. The son is paid Rs 1000 a month with food and accommodation. In exchange for their son's labour, the parents were paid half of his annual salary in advance. This money has made a huge difference to the family. They can eat regularly and can buy some clothes. Although the parents realize that the work is gruelling — from 7 in the morning to 10 at right in unhygienic and uncomfortable conditions, they feel that this is a better option than local work.

(dirty, degrading, and dangerous) and the work is far from 'decent' because there are usually no contracts or social security. Those belonging to lower castes and tribes are often discriminated against in several ways (underpaid, treated with contempt, not provided basic amenities). Migrants travel, live, and work in highly insecure conditions and women and girls are more burdened by extra work and are also more vulnerable to sexual exploitation. Creches are hardly ever provided by contractors even though they are meant to do so by law and the migrants' children miss months of school or drop out altogether. Men and women do not receive equal pay and working hours are long. Olsen and Ramanamurthy (2000) show the variety of insidious ways in which migrant construction workers are exploited by *mestries* or recruiting agents ranging from trapping them in bonded labour by paying less than subsistence level, extracting overtime and child labour, and using caste-based and patriarchal modes of oppression to maintain exploitative labour relations. The system survived because mestries are seen as those who save the labourers in distress by offering work when otherwise they might starve. However, the system of *mestris* is now on the wane. Although it survives in some of the most poorly connected pockets of AP, we heard several accounts of workers migrating on their own. Similar observations were made by a Council of Social Development resurvey of 1000 households in Mahbubnagar (Rao 2004), where it was noted that the system of *mestris* is on the decline.

Our discussions with migrants also show that they have very little understanding of health hazards and risks in construction, mining, and industry. They are also not aware of their risk of catching killer diseases such as HIV/AIDS and tuberculosis.

THOSE STAYING BEHIND

The research team found a few instances of families left behind facing difficulties due to the absence of migrating members from their household. The difficulties faced by those left behind is a common theme in the migration literature (see Kothari 2002 and Seeley 2008; see also Chapter 10 in this volume). In our study villages it was mainly widows whose sons had migrated and women in nuclear families whose husbands had migrated that faced the greatest problems in the village. But such cases were relatively uncommon. The majority of migrants belonged to large households where there was sufficient surplus labour within the household to manage the family farm or business effectively in the absence of the migrant. It was also common for male relatives to help women whose husbands or sons had migrated. While the relatives of the poorest migrants found it difficult to have their concerns heard at village council meetings, families of more powerful migrants such as the Vaddi were able to retain a presence in village institutions.

QUANTITATIVE ESTIMATES OF INCOME FROM MIGRATION AND COMMUTING

A significant finding is that commuting has now become a more important source of income for households with at least one person working outside the village. In 2006–7 it accounted for more than a quarter of net annual income in such households. Cultivation came second and accounted for 24 per cent followed by circular migration accounting for 20 per cent (Table 3.6). The results for AP are thus very different than MP (Chaper 4) where circular migration was the most important source of income for households with mobile earners. Agricultural labouring occupied fourth rank in AP while salaried occupations and local non-farm work were more important in MP. Table 3.6 shows the importance of commuting and migration (including remittances) to the households with mobile workers.

Table 3.6: Proportionate Share of Household Net Income (Gross income— Enterprise Cost) from Migration and Other Sources by Village for Households with One Member Working Outside the Village, 2006–7

| Activity | OP | VP | KO | GU | MD | Total |
|---|---|---|---|---|---|---|
| Commuting | 30.5 | 13.9 | 16.9 | 49.9 | 4.4 | 26.1 |
| Cultivation | 11.2 | 30.9 | 14.9 | 24.3 | 30.3 | 23.5 |
| Circular migration | 20.1 | 34.6 | 8.0 | 2.4 | 41.5 | 19.9 |
| Agricultural labour | 5.1 | 4.6 | 24.7 | 6.7 | 3.2 | 8.2 |
| Remittance | 16.0 | 5.8 | 17.1 | 0.1 | 7.0 | 7.6 |
| Service, craft & trade related | 11.5 | 0.8 | 6.3 | 9.6 | 9.1 | 6.8 |
| Livestock | 5.0 | 6.7 | 0.0 | 0.2 | 1.2 | 2.9 |
| Salary | 0.6 | 0.0 | 9.3 | 3.7 | 2.0 | 2.8 |
| Sharecropping/leasing | 0.0 | 2.8 | 2.4 | 1.6 | 1.4 | 1.8 |
| Non-farm wage labour | 0.0 | 0.0 | 0.0 | 1.5 | 0.0 | 0.4 |
| Other elementary | 0.0 | 0.0 | 0.4 | 0.0 | 0.0 | 0.1 |
| Total | 100 | 100 | 100 | 100 | 100 | 100 |

Source: Authors.
Note: The share was calculated for households having migrants/commuters as income data were not collected for other households.

Overall such households derive more than a half (54 per cent) of their total household income from commuting and migration. Unfortunately the absence of data from a control population (that is, where there are no migrants or commuters) makes it difficult to establish the relative importance of mobility as an income source for the entire village. But given that the proportion of mobile households varies between 47 per cent and 72 per cent (average over 54 per cent), it is evident that income from outside the village is important.

### Migration Earnings Important for STs and Commuting Important for SCs

Further disaggregation of the data by caste and tribe reveal interesting differences (Table 3.7). While circular migration accounts for 74 per cent of the net annual income for STs, it accounts for only 13 per cent of the income of SCs, 28 per cent of the income of BCs, and 3 per cent of the income of OCs.* On the other hand, commuting accounts for 38 per cent of the income of SCs, 26 per cent of the income of OCs, and 22 per cent of the income of BCs, but only 11 per cent of the income of STs. The SC commuters are predominantly farm workers and the wage income from this activity makes the largest contribution to the household income; it is higher than the income

Table 3.7: Proportionate Share of Household Net Income
(Gross Income—Enterprise Cost) from Migration and
Other Sources by Caste Category, 2006–7

| Activity | % share of net annual income | | | |
| --- | --- | --- | --- | --- |
| | ST | SC | BC | OC |
| Commuting | 11.0 | 37.7 | 22.8 | 26.7 |
| Circular migration | 74.1 | 13.4 | 28.5 | 3.4 |
| Remittance | 0.0 | 8.5 | 3.0 | 14.7 |
| Salary | 0.0 | 2.7 | 2.9 | 3.1 |
| Service, craft & trade related | 0.0 | 2.7 | 8.6 | 7.2 |
| Cultivation | 7.4 | 11.9 | 18.1 | 39.8 |
| Agricultural labour | 6.0 | 20.1 | 8.8 | 1.2 |
| Livestock | 0.0 | 3.1 | 4.0 | 1.6 |
| Sharecropping/leasing | 0.0 | 0.0 | 2.4 | 2.2 |
| Non-farm wage labour & other elementary | 1.5 | 0.0 | 0.9 | 0.0 |
| Total | 100 | 100 | 100 | 100 |

Source: Authors.
Note: * OC is other castes and icludes upper castes that are included in the category of FC in other states.

they derive from the local farm work. The upper castes also obtain a large proportion of their income from commuting but in contrast to the SCs they are mostly in better paying non-farm activities such as the self-employed and white collar jobs. This suggests that STs are not able to find employment in nearby towns and villages, whereas other castes are. Consequently STs are more dependent on migration. If policy recognizes this fact and interventions can improve the returns to circular migration, STs will be important beneficiaries.

## Permanent Migration Earnings Important for Upper Castes

Remittances from permanent migration accounted for 15 per cent of the income of OCs and 9 per cent in the case of SCs but much less for other groups (Table 3.7). Key informant interviews showed that many OC families in Coastal Andhra have migrants in big cities in the state and elsewhere in India and even other countries such as the US. The OCs drew as much as 40 per cent of their income from cultivation, much higher than any other group. For the STs, it accounted for only 7 per cent of the net annual income and for the SCs and BCs 12 per cent and 18 per cent respectively.

The STs appear least diversified and heavily dependent on migration whereas other groups are more diversified and earn from a variety of sources. The OCs however appear to have a strong agricultural base and diversify through commuting for maximizing their gains from options nearby. The OCs receive remittances mostly from skilled and/or white collar and the self-employed migrants. By contrast, the SC and the BC families receive remittances mostly from unskilled or semi-skilled migrants.

## Determinants of Income

The relationship between the daily wage rate and human capital factors including age, experience, education, and skill and social factors such as gender, status of the worker, location of the job, type of job, and caste were examined for circular migrants and commuters through multivariate analysis using 2003–4 and 2006–7 data (Tables 3.11 and 3.12). Permanent migrants were not included in this analysis. The variations in daily earnings were associated with socio-economic factors more than human capital variables; the exception was skill, which was significantly positively associated with daily wages. According to the analysis of 2003–4 data, a skilled person's earnings predicted by the regression model are 54 per cent higher than an unskilled person. The predicted earnings are higher for skilled persons belonging to both poorer and less poor quintiles but the skill variable was statistically significant only for less poor quintiles. In the absence of education data specifically for migrants, household level aggregate of schooling years collected during the 2001–2 census survey was used as a proxy. Experience was measured as the length in years from first migration to the survey year. Experience and education were expected to be associated with higher earnings. While this was true in most quintiles, the result appeared to be inconclusive for quintiles 4–5, and the reason for this is not clear. Females earned less than males due to discrimination in pay rates. Commuters earned significantly less than circular migrants. Not only are there fewer women migrants and commuters, but they also earn less than their male counterparts. Regression results reveal that women migrants belonging to the three poorer quintiles were earning about 16 per cent less each day than men in 2003–4 which further widened to 25 per cent less in 2006–7.

Those who were paid partly in kind received less cash than those who were paid only in cash. Dummy variables representing destination, land ownership, caste, and occupation type did not perform consistently probably due to diversity/complexity in the migration market. Overall, migrants belonging to the schedule tribes, schedule castes and backward castes earned less than those belonging to higher castes, but the result is significant at less than 5 per cent. The result was positive for the less poor STs possibly because they are not disadvantaged in the job market. Wage rates differ significantly between seasons but only for the less poor quintile groups where migrants in the summer season earned more than those who migrated in the *rabi* season who in turn earned more than *kharif* season migrants.

Multivariate analysis shows that caste differences are decreasing in importance but women are still disadvantaged and in the poorer groups women are even more disadvantaged. Overall, village specific differences are not significant except that wage rates in GU are significantly higher. This is probably due to the fact that GU is a well-connected industrialized village near Hyderabad. Quintile based analysis produced more significant village differences. The poor earned high rates in all well-connected villages but the less poor earned higher rates in all villages compared to OP. In Bangalore, where most of the migrants from Chittoor work, wage rates are relatively higher. Mobile workers from Krishna district have the lowest incomes because unlike Medak, a large proportion of them are commuters working in agriculture with lower wages.

The results for the most recent year confirm that skills are being rewarded and the gap between men's and women's earnings grew because women remained in lower skilled and poorly paid jobs. The differences in the wages of skilled and unskilled as well as gender differences in wages were more marked among poorer groups showing that the poor are less upwardly mobile and especially poor women. Statistical performance of education and experience variables appeared better. Caste differences appear to have decreased which reflects the overall situation of Indian society today. Village specific differences were mostly insignificant at 5 per cent level. One striking result is that most non-farm occupations do not have higher wage rates; the exception are professionals who do earn more.

Commuters worked for lower rates than circular migrants, even though our earlier tabular analysis showed that commuting provided the largest share of household annual income in mobile households in 2006–7.[5]

PROSPECTS FOR UPWARD MOBILITY

The question that often bothered the research team was whether migration was a dead-end prospect or whether it offered the poor chances of upward mobility. The last survey included questions on skills and changes in skills.

Skill Profile and Occupation of Migrants in 2003–4 and 2006–7

In 2003–4 the construction sector was the largest employer of both migrants and commuters, followed by agriculture and then salaried jobs. The construction sector continued to be the largest employer in 2006–7 but the relative proportion of migrants and commuters employed in it declined considerably (Table 3.9). On the other hand, the relative importance of industry and service sectors grew. Based on workers' assessment of their own skills we conclude that the overall skill level in both construction and agriculture improved between 2003–4 and 2006–7. While about two-thirds assessed

## Table 3.8: Determinants of Income among Migrants and Commuters 2003–4

| | All sample | | Quintiles 1–3 | | Quintiles 4–5 | |
|---|---|---|---|---|---|---|
| | Coefficient | p–values | Coefficient | p–values | Coefficient | p–values |
| (Constant) | 4.213 | .000 | 3.975 | .000 | 1.526 | .252 |
| Age (years) | .002 | .539 | .006 | .041 | .013 | .131 |
| Migration experience | .004 | .585 | .012 | .156 | −.042 | .042 |
| Years of schooling in household[a] | .001 | .625 | .002 | .558 | .031 | .027 |
| Gender ( female = 1) | −.187 | .006 | −.157 | .023 | −.204 | .189 |
| Skilled worker = 1 | .539 | .000 | .487 | .000 | .215 | .363 |
| Commuters = 1 | −.370 | .000 | −.782 | .000 | .132 | .642 |
| Migration to large town = 1 | .068 | .602 | −.289 | .063 | −.183 | .631 |
| Kind wage, yes = 1 | −.728 | .002 | −.462 | .021 | | |
| Migration at kharif season = 1 | −.035 | .727 | .095 | .402 | −.706 | .015 |
| Migration at summer season = 1 | .044 | .617 | .028 | .766 | 1.036 | .007 |
| Landless = 1[b] | −.094 | .237 | −.028 | .744 | .588 | .220 |
| Medium, small and large farm = 1 | .006 | .941 | −.145 | .076 | 1.378 | .135 |
| Service, craft & trade jobs = 1[c] | .065 | .582 | .334 | .050 | −.326 | .375 |
| Construction job = 1 | −.146 | .176 | .049 | .674 | −.176 | .496 |
| Industry/machine operator = 1 | −.008 | .950 | .226 | .139 | .481 | .172 |
| Elementary job = 1 | −.094 | .450 | −.154 | .268 | 1.001 | .034 |
| Schedule tribe=1 | −.720 | .000 | −1.027 | .000 | .283 | .739 |
| Schedule caste = 1 | −.063 | .583 | −.153 | .278 | .399 | .169 |
| Backward caste = 1 | −.190 | .079 | −.151 | .267 | −.924 | .013 |
| VP = 1 | −.073 | .648 | −.013 | .946 | 2.494 | .010 |
| KO = 1 | .130 | .333 | .678 | .003 | 1.177 | .061 |
| KA = 1 | −.049 | .736 | −.832 | .007 | 1.196 | .040 |
| GU = 1 | .260 | .000 | .506 | .001 | 1.142 | .061 |
| MD = 1 | .035 | .539 | .254 | .145 | | |
| N | 160 | | 114 | | 40 | |
| F value | 8.92 | 0.00 | 10.83 | 0.00 | 3.76 | 0.00 |
| R–square | 0.61 | | 0.75 | | 0.83 | |
| Adj R–square | 0.55 | | 0.68 | | 0.61 | |

*Source*: Livelihood options study: Census survey 2001–2, Panel survey 2005.
*Note*: Dependent Variable: Natural log of daily migration earnings.
a) These household level data are taken from the 2001–2 Census survey; b) Base is marginal farm; c) Base occupation is agriculture (includes forestry and fishery).

Table 3.9: Determinants of Income among Migrants and Commuters
2006–7

|  | All sample | | Quintiles 1–3 | | Quintiles 4–5 | |
|---|---|---|---|---|---|---|
|  | Coefficient | p–values | Coefficient | p–values | Coefficient | p–values |
| (Constant) | 4.001 | .000 | 3.983 | .000 | 3.968 | .000 |
| Age (years) | .007 | .020 | .006 | .021 | .013 | .036 |
| Migration experience | .002 | .001 | .000 | .562 | .001 | .129 |
| Years of schooling in household[a] | .005 | .065 | .009 | .001 | .000 | .944 |
| Gender (female = 1) | –.183 | .016 | –.247 | .000 | –.138 | .409 |
| Skilled worker = 1 | .243 | .001 | .146 | .035 | .268 | .095 |
| Commuters = 1 | –.362 | .000 | –.456 | .000 | –.229 | .216 |
| Migration to large town = 1 | –.118 | .285 | –.081 | .454 | .071 | .791 |
| Migration at kharif season = 1 | –.109 | .282 | –.107 | .325 | –.105 | .625 |
| Migration at summer season = 1 | –.272 | .003 | –.174 | .027 | –.331 | .135 |
| Landless = 1[b] | .012 | .871 | .023 | .756 | –.020 | .903 |
| Medium, small and large farm = 1 | –.032 | .760 | –.061 | .545 | .222 | .388 |
| Professional job = 1[c] | .606 | .000 | .008 | .977 | .625 | .025 |
| Service, craft & trade jobs = 1 | .005 | .965 | –.044 | .699 | .103 | .672 |
| Construction job = 1 | –.070 | .529 | .089 | .373 | –.130 | .640 |
| Industry/machine operator = 1 | –.040 | .712 | –.065 | .539 | .005 | .981 |
| Elementary job = 1 | –.145 | .238 | .038 | .695 |  |  |
| Schedule tribe=1 | .212 | .166 | .061 | .665 | .714 | .104 |
| Schedule caste = 1 | .027 | .806 | .114 | .266 | .034 | .896 |
| Backward caste = 1 | .066 | .513 | .139 | .133 | .041 | .860 |
| VP = 1 | .220 | .047 | .167 | .118 | .173 | .462 |
| KO = 1 | .238 | .052 | .315 | .006 | .142 | .617 |
| GU = 1 | .193 | .085 | .202 | .075 | .136 | .571 |
| MD = 1 | .347 | .020 | .202 | .188 | –.011 | .976 |
| N | 201 | | 114 | | 87 | |
| F value | 6.67 | 0.00 | 4.35 | 0.00 | 2.60 | 0.00 |
| R–square | 0.46 | | 0.53 | | 0.47 | |
| Adj R–square | 0.39 | | 0.41 | | 0.29 | |

*Source*: Livelihood options study: Census survey 2001–2, Panel survey 2006–7.
*Note*: Dependent Variable: Natural log of daily migration earnings.
a) These household level data are taken from the 2001–2 Census survey; b) Base is marginal farm; c) Base occupation is agriculture (includes forestry and fishery).

themselves as unskilled in 2003–4, the skill status improved noticeably in 2006–7. The progress is impressive in all villages, and was especially high in the villages VP and MD, probably because the base was exceptionally low in 2003–4. Both villages are relatively remote and underdeveloped. The kinds of skills acquired by these workers can be learned relatively quickly. For example, migrants from MD working in Hyderabad as unskilled loaders had graduated to semi-skilled work such as mixing concrete within a few months.

In the peri-urban village of GU most commuters work in the nearby pharmaceutical industries as unskilled workers. They learn/upgrade their skills in a couple years to mixing formulas and operating machinery. On the other hand, learning skills is relatively low in the prosperous Green Revolution village of KO because there is not much scope for improvement in tasks like harvesting, transplanting, and weeding. It would appear therefore, that upward mobility is greater in non-farm occupations.

Table 3.10: Frequency Distribution of Migrants by Skill Status

| Village | Skill status 2003–4 | | | Skill status 2006–7 | | | |
|---|---|---|---|---|---|---|---|
| | Skilled | Unskilled | Total | Skilled | Semi Skilled | Unskilled | Total |
| OP | 19 | 6 | 25 | 22 | 13 | 6 | 41 |
| VP | 9 | 25 | 34 | 34 | 23 | 9 | 66 |
| KO | 23 | 16 | 39 | 24 | 17 | 14 | 55 |
| GU | 17 | 17 | 34 | 30 | 12 | 11 | 53 |
| MD | 9 | 65 | 74 | 14 | 18 | 21 | 53 |
| Total | 77 | 129 | 206 | 124 | 83 | 61 | 268 |

*Source*: Authors.

## Circular Migrants Acquire More Skills but SCs, STs, and Women Fare Poorly

Respondents were asked to mention the number of new skills they had learned since they began working outside the village. The analysis reveals they learned up to three skills since migration and the number of skills learned varies between type of mobility, caste status, and gender. More than 20 per cent of the circular and permanent migrants were able to learn more than two skills. Scheduled tribes learned only one skill and very few SCs learned more than one skill. Only 6 per cent of the women acquired two skills against 21 per cent men. So in terms of skill progression, permanent migrants, upper castes, and men were better off. There is a need to understand the kinds of barriers faced by SCs and STs in acquiring skills. While it can be surmised that these will be related to their social status and exclusion from training programmes and information sharing, it would help to gain a more nuanced understanding of the level at which this occurs and what needs to be done to overcome it.

CONCLUSION

The findings of the three sample surveys show a broad trend: mobility from rural Andhra Pradesh has increased since 2000. The proportion of households with at least one commuting or migrating member has steadily increased from 19 per cent in 2000-1 to 41 per cent and 54 per cent in 2003-4 and 2006-7 respectively. But the results of more detailed and comparable surveys of 2003-4 and 2006-7 show a clearer trend characterized by a sharp increase in the number of commuters across the study villages from 47 to 119 and a marginal increase in the number of permanent migrants from 59 to 66. The rise in commuting mostly to urban locations is, among other things, driven by growing opportunities in construction and services because of the rapid growth of small towns across rural AP. However, access to these opportunities is not equal: for STs, jobs in nearby towns appear to be less accessible than they are to other caste groups because of their skills that are mainly suited to agricultural work, their lower levels of education and because of discrimination against them. STs are therefore more dependent on circular migration.

Migration has helped many poor households eat more regularly, pay off debts and invest in health, education, and agriculture all of which contribute to raising the standard of living of the household. Migration has also helped in gaining skills and higher incomes. However, SCs, STs, and women acquire fewer skills because of their disadvantaged position in society. Overall, migrants belonging to schedule tribes, schedule castes, and backward castes earned less than those belonging to higher castes.

The process of migration is risky, difficult, and expensive and migrants need urgent support in a number of key areas such as education, housing, access to pro-poor programmes including the PDS and health care. In sum, there is an urgent need for recognition at the policy level of the importance of migration and the rapidly growing importance of commuting for rural livelihoods. This will have implications for planning in a number of sectors including urban development, rural development, urban infrastructure, housing, transport, and the flexibility of pro-poor services and programmes. These questions are revisited in the final chapters of the book which examine existing support measures and future needs.

NOTES

1. *Mandal* is an administrative tier between district and gram panchayat.
2. The districts within each are: *Coastal Andhra:* Prakasam, Srikakulam, Vizianagaram, Krishna, West Godavari, East Godavari, Guntur, Vishakhapatnam, and Nellore; *Telangana:* Mahabubnagar, Nalgonda, Karimnagar, Medak, Warangal, Nizamabad, Adilabad, Rangareddy, Khammam, and Hyderabad; *Rayalaseema:* Anantapur, Kurnool, Chittoor, and Cuddapah.
3. Planning Commission estimates show that rural poverty in Andhra Pradesh has declined from 15.92 per cent in 1993–4 (NSS 50th Round) to 11.05 per cent in 1999–2000 (NSS 55th Round). However Deaton and Dreze (2002) estimate the incidence of rural poverty in Andhra Pradesh at 29.20 per cent in 1993–4 and 26.20 per cent in 1999–2000.
4. For a definition see Chapter 1.
5. The share of commuting income was less than half the share of circular migration income in 2003–4.

REFERENCES

Deaton, A. and J. Drèze, 'Poverty and Inequality in India, A Re-examination', *Economic and Political Weekly*, 7 Sept. 2002, pp. 3729–48.

Deb, U. K., G.D. N. Rao, Y. M. Rao, and R. Slater, 'Diversification and Livelihood Options: A Study of Two Villages in Andhra Pradesh, India 1975–2001', Working Paper 178, Overseas Development Institute, 111 Westminster Bridge Road, London SE1 7JD UK, 2002.

Dev, M. S., and S. Subrahmaniyam, 'Regional Disparities in Andhra Pradesh at the Millennium', in Y.V. Krishna Rao and S. Subrahmanyam (eds), *Development of Andhra Pradesh, 1956-2001: A Study of Regional Disparities*, Hyderabad: NRR Research Centre, 2002.

———, and Padmanabha Rao, *Poverty Alleviation Programmes in Andhra Pradesh: An Assessment* (commissioned by Planning Commission of India), Hyderabad: Centre for Economic and Social Studies, 2002.

Deshingkar, P. and D. Start, 'Seasonal Migration for Livelihoods in India: Coping, Accumulation and Exclusion', ODI Working Paper 220, London: Overaseas Development Institute, 2003. http://www.odi.org.uk/publications/working_papers/wp220.pdf

Government of Andhra Pradesh (Planning Department), *Economic Survey 2003-4*.

Kothari, U., 'Migration And Chronic Poverty', Institute for Development Policy and Management, University of Manchester, Chronic Poverty Research Centre.

Olsen, W. and R. Murthy, 'Contract Labour and Bondage in Andhra Pradesh, India', *Journal of Social and Political Thought*, 1(2), June 2000, http://www.yorku.ca/jspot/2wkolse nrvramana.htm.

Prasad, P., *Famines and Droughts: Survival Strategies*, Jiapur/Delhi: Rawat Publications, 1998.

Rogaly, B and A. Rafique, 'Struggling to Save Cash: Seasonal and Vulnerability in West Bengal, India', *Development and Change*, 2003, pp. 659–81.

Rao, V. D., 'Study of Migration Trends among Palamur Labour in Mahbubnagar District of Andhra Pradesh: A Revisit after a Decade', Hyderabad: Council for Social Development, 2004.

Reddy, B., Drought-Proneness and Labour Migration: Socio-Economic Impact in a Telangana Village, unpublished M.Phil. dissertation, Department of Anthropology, University of Hyderabad, 2002.

Reddy, D.N., 'Economic Reforms and Travails of Circulating Labour of Dry Regions: A Case Study of Palamur Labour in Andhra Pradesh', *Labour & Development*, 9 (2), December 2003, pp. 2341–52.

Seeley, J., 'Social Protection by and for Temporary Work Migrants and their Households in Northwest Bangladesh', *Research Report*, Development Research Centre on Migration, Globalization and Poverty, University of Sussex, 2008.

Subrahmanyam, S., 'Regional Disparities in Andhra Pradesh at the Millennium', in Krishna Rao Y.V. and S. Subrahmanyam (eds), *Development of Andhra Pradesh, 1956–2001: A Study of Regional Disparities*, Hyderabad: NRR Research Centre, 2002.

# 4

# The Evolving Pattern of Circular Migration

## Household Surveys in Madhya Pradesh

*Pramod Sharma, Sushil Kumar, Priya Deshingkar,*
*John Farrington, and Shaheen Akter*

## INTRODUCTION

After being classified as a lagging or 'BIMARU'[1] state for a number
of years, rapid improvements have been noted recently especially
in Madhya Pradesh in relation to agriculture and infrastructure.[2]
But growth has been uneven and drought-prone and forested
tribal districts in the south of the country have continued to rank
among the worst poverty traps in the country (Shah 2007). People
from these districts are heavily dependent on circular migration for
meeting their every day needs. Without migration, a majority of the
poor would not be able to spend on health, festivals, and ceremonies
and would face the risk of sliding deeper into poverty.

This chapter examines the changing patterns of migration in the
poor and tribal dominated state of Madhya Pradesh. It is based on
the analysis of three surveys conducted in 2001–2, 2003–4, and 2006–
7 in six villages in Madhya Pradesh. Three districts were covered
representing the three regions of the state: Tikamgarh district in
Bundelkhand, Ujjain in Malwa, and Mandla in Mahakoshal. Two
villages were selected from each district with one being relatively
remote and the other well connected. Descriptive statistics and
multivariate analysis were used to gain an understanding of the
importance of migration earnings for the poor, differences in
migration patterns by location, caste, and the factors that influence
the likelihood of migration. Qualitative data were used to shed light

on segmentation in the migrant labour market by caste, gender, and age and identifying vulnerable groups of migrants. The chapter begins with a description of the context in which migration occurs followed by basic statistics on the incidence of migration and how this has changed over the three rounds. Following that details of earnings by caste and landholding are presented, followed by regression analysis on the determinants of income. Changes in specific migration streams are discussed using the results of focus group discussions and key informant interviews. Finally, recommendations for policy reform and interventions are made.

## THE CONTEXT

Madhya Pradesh has the largest population of scheduled tribes among all states and a high proportion of scheduled castes. Of the total of 45 districts, 23 are predominantly tribal. The major tribes of Madhya Pradesh are Gonds, Baigas, Bhils, Oraons, Korkus, Sahariyas, and Kols. Landlessness, nominal and unproductive landholdings, and the inability to invest in farming continue to characterize the tribal population of the state. The share of marginal and small farmers in the total landholding area and the number of holdings in the state increased from 9.6 per cent in 1970–1 to 21.5 per cent in 1995–6, an increase of 75 per cent in terms of land under small and marginal farmers.

The central part of Madhya Pradesh is relatively more developed in terms of farming, mines, industries, business centres and urbanization. This is where the non-tribal population is concentrated.

## The Employment Situation in MP

Official statistics suggest that employment in Madhya Pradesh is largely, rural and non-industrial in nature. According to the National Sample Survey, nearly 75 per cent of rural workers depended on agriculture in 1999–2000, but agriculture accounts for only 35 per cent of the GDP. However, as we shall see there is much hidden diversification because many people work outside agriculture for part of the year.

Casual labour forms a substantial part of the total labour force and has been growing: the proportion of workers who were casual increased from 32 per cent for males and 38 per cent for females in 1993–4 to 37 per cent for males and 44 per cent for females in 1999–2000. There has been an increase in the share of marginal and small farmers in area and number of holdings. Around 61 per cent of the landholdings belonged to marginal and small farmers in 1995-6 (Commissioner of Land Records and Settlement, Gwalior, MP cited in the 2002 *Human Development Report*) who are under-employed and work as labourers to supplement their incomes from farming. According to the 2001 Census, 28.7 per cent of the workers in the state are agricultural labourers and most of them are concentrated in the southern tribal and forested districts. The Bundelkhand region in the north-east which straddles the Uttar Pradesh-Madhya Pradesh border has fewer agricultural workers. The vast majority of the workforce (around 94 per cent) including agricultural labour, construction labour, and labour in traditional leather tanning, forestry, fishing, bidi rolling, household industry, village artisans, and urban informal workers are poor and in the unorganized sector.

Rural non-farm employment (RNFE) in Madhya Pradesh stagnated after 1987–8 for both males and females and by 2002 Madhya Pradesh had the lowest share of rural non-farm employment to total rural employment in the country (*Human Development Report* 2002). RNFE was limited to certain areas such as the Sagar, Damoh, Katni, Jabalpur, Narsimhpur in central Madhya Pradesh, Gwalior, Bhind, Morena in the north, Ratlam, Ujjain, Indore in the western Malwa plateau, and the Hoshangabad, Bhopal belt in the centre of the state.

They all share certain features namely zones of agricultural prosperity, proximity to a large urban conglomeration and some industrial or industrial service based activity. They are also associated with specific crops or types of produce, such as mustard associated with Bhind and Morena, and soybean associated with Ujjain and Ratlam. Many of these are important destinations for migrants.

Of the 45 districts in the state, 16 have less than 20 per cent of the workforce in non-farm employment. According to studies conducted by (NRI) on rural non-farm employment in Madhya Pradesh,[3] the main barriers to entry into RNEF include the following: inadequate credit facilities especially for small entrepreneurs the size of landholdings is one of the underlying factors for the poor extent of RNFE. A smaller number of landowners means a higher concentration of livelihood resources through agriculture, which

Map 4.1: Map of Madhya Pradesh
*Source*: Maps of India

in turn leads to more exploitative tendencies and the attempt to subjugate people through the unending cycle of indebtedness.

In circumstances where both farm and non-farm options for employment are highly limited, circular migration has emerged as an important livelihood strategy. Much of the migration is seasonal, and is undertaken by people who are classified as labourers — both agricultural labourers and non-farm labourers. The poor southern districts are labour exporting areas. The labour surplus situation in the southern districts co-exists with a shortage of labour in the diversifying centres mentioned above and drives much of the intrastate migration.

HISTORICAL PRECEDENTS

Past studies have shown that migration patterns vary a great deal in terms of who goes, for how long, where, for what, and on what terms. Studies by David Mosse and colleagues undertaken under the DFID-funded Western India Rainfed Farming Project, provide insights into The migration patterns in the last decade Mosse et al 1997, 2002, 2005. Rapid surveys undertaken between December 1996 and April 1997 of 2,588 households in 42 villages covered found that 65 per cent of households and 48 per cent of the adult population were involved in seasonal migration in 1995–6 (Mosse et al., 1997, Mosse *et al.* 2002). The area covered Bhil tribal villages in the contiguous districts of Jhabua (western Madhya Pradesh), Banswara (southern Rajasthan), and Panchmahals (eastern Gujarat). On an average two to three household members migrated for five to five-and-a-half months each in a year. Roughly 42 per cent of the migrants were women and this proportion did not show much variation across locations. A few years later Virgo et al. (2003) studied the same area and found that in many villages up to three-quarters of the population was absent between November and June.

METHODOLOGY

Data were collected through three rounds beginning in 2001–2, repeated in 2003–4, and again in 2006–7. Three contrasting districts were chosen for study in the regions of Malwa, Bundelkhand, and Mahakoshal. Malwa in the west is a semi-arid, tubewell irrigated region with highly fertile black cotton soil, high soyabean production, and relatively high urban and industrial development. The region was originally a combination of two princely kingdoms and has a common local language (Malwi). The proportion of tribals is low, but that of scheduled castes is high. Bundelkhand is in the north-east, near the border with Uttar Pradesh. It is highly feudal and caste ridden. Land distribution is highly uneven. The region is semi-arid with low fertility red-black soil but high irrigation coverage and good tank distribution. Mahakoshal lies in the east and is a predominantly Gond tribal area with forests and black soil. Rice and traditional minor millets are grown, mainly for subsistence. There is little industrial development but the rate of urbanization has picked up in the last five years.

Two villages were selected in each district, one well-connected in terms of road connectivity and proximity to market and urban centres, and the other relatively remote. It was hoped that the study of such contrasting villages would provide insights on the importance of connectivity, rural-urban links, and market links in livelihood diversification.

Each round involved more than one survey. The 2001–2 round began with a census covering 1,297 households in all six villages. The census collected data on basic household characteristics such as household structure, education, age, gender, occupations, asset

Table 4.1: The Study Regions and Villages

| Madhya Pradesh | | | | | |
| --- | --- | --- | --- | --- | --- |
| Ujjain (Malwa) | | Tikamgarh (Bundelkhand) | | Mandla (Mahakoshal) | |
| PR[4] (near) | LJ ( far) | SM (near) | MB ( far) | GG (near) | PT ( far) |
| Agricultural prosperous. Deep black cotton soils, semi-arid, tube-well irrigated, Soybean and Wheat. • Mixed caste • Polarized land distribution | | Average agricultural development. Medium to shallow black soils, well and tank irrigation, Soybean, Pulses, Rice, and Wheat. • Caste hierarchies from feudal legacy • Polarized land distribution | | Hilly, forested, often infertile shallow black soils, limited irrigation and limited spread of intensive agriculture. Minor millets, Rice, Wheat, and Pulses. • Large number of tribals • More equitable land holdings | |

*Source*: Authors.

ownership, and whether or not the household had a migrant. This was followed by two seasonal surveys covering a smaller stratified sample of 302 households (40–80 households per village depending on the size of the village). Stratification was done by landholding and caste. The primary purpose of the 2001–2 round was to collect data on livelihood diversification. The data on migration were minimal.

The next round in 2003–4 was undertaken with the specific purpose of collecting more detailed data on patterns of migration, livestock keeping, and landownership and leasing using three different questionnaires. Another resurvey on the patterns of migration was done in 2006–7. While the 2003 resurvey covered all 6 villages as before, the last round covered only 5 because the richest village, namely PR, had such low migration rates that it did not seem to make sense to survey it. The total sample size was 264 households. Of these, 136 had migrants and these households were surveyed twice: once after the *kharif* season in October to cover the preceding summer season (March–May) and the *kharif* season (June to September), and again after the *rabi* season in March to cover the preceding months of the *rabi* season (October to February).

During each round, key informant interviews and focus group discussions were conducted at the same time as the questionnaire survey. Key informants included migrant labourers, their family members, *gram pradhans* (head of local government), members of the *gram panchayat* (local government), village and block level government officials (gram sachiv/village secretary, BDOs), labour recruiting agents (*mukkaddams*), CEO–zila panchayat (district administration), donor funded livelihood projects, the police, and NGOs. Focus Group Discussions (FGDs) were held with women and men in each *tola* (locality of a village delineated on the basis of caste/tribe/religion).

## WHO MIGRATES

In all three rounds, migrants from the study villages were mainly young men in the age group of 25–35. The proportion of women among migrants appears to change with the change in economic status of the household. In the poorer households, entire families migrate whereas in the slightly better off households only the men migrate. When couples migrate they take young children with them leaving only old people and older children in the village. In 2006–7 only 23 per cent of the circular migrants were women as compared to 28.1 per cent in the previous round. This may indicate a general improvement in the status of some of the migrating households. Although skill levels have improved slightly over the years (discussed later), migrants among the poorer categories were mainly unskilled and illiterate and they listed various kinds of manual labour as their main occupation.

## HOW THE MIGRATION SITUATION HAS CHANGED OVER THE LAST SIX YEARS: GROWING CIRCULAR MIGRATION

The census from the first survey (2001–2) showed that more than half the households in four out of six study villages in Madhya Pradesh had at least one person who was a circular migrant (Deshingkar and Start 2003). The proportion was as high as 75 per cent in the most remote and hilly tribal village (PT) with infertile soils. This corroborated the findings of other studies in the state which have also found very high levels of migration. Another study in this volume, of a tribal village in Betul district (Chapter 8), shows high migration rates among poor households with rainfed land. There, migration to brick kilns represents the single largest contemporary migration stream. Similarly, high migration rates have been noted among Sahariya tribals from Shivpuri by a group of NGOs (the Right to Food Campaign, Freedom from Hunger and Fear initiative, and Action Aid). Roughly 60 per cent of the 450,000 tribals in the area who used to be able to make a living from forests are now completely dependent on migration for their livelihoods. The tribals migrate

with their families to locations in Rajasthan leaving behind only
children and the elderly.

Table 4.2: Mobility Patterns in 2001–2

| MP | | Temp. Migration | Commuting | Perm. Migration |
|---|---|---|---|---|
| Ujjain | PR Semi arid, tubewells (WC) | 59 | 16 | 5 |
| | LJ Semi arid, dry (RM) | 50 | 6 | 3 |
| Mandla | GG | 43 | 10 | 10 |
| | PT Forested (RM) | 75 | 13 | 5 |
| Tikamgarh | SM | 21 | 8 | 12 |
| | MB | 64 | 10 | 5 |
| | Overall | 47 | 10 | 7 |

*Source*: Authors.

Data for the next round consisting of 108 migrants and commuters
drawn from a sample of 302 households, showed that the proportion
of households with at least one person working outside the
village was 36 per cent in 2003–4. This included circular migrants,
commuters, and permanent migrants. The last round included only
five villages and comparing the situation in these five villages in
2003–4 and 2006–7, it is seen that the proportion of households with
at least one person outside the village had increased to 52 per cent
by 2006–7 from 40 per cent in 2003–4 (Table 4.3).

Table 4.3: Frequency and Percentage Distribution of Households With
Migrants by Village, 2003–4 and 2006–7

| | Numbers | | | Percentage | | |
|---|---|---|---|---|---|---|
| 2006–7 | Yes | No | Total | Yes | No | Total |
| LJ (Poorly connected) | 51 | 13 | 64 | 79.7 | 20.3 | 100.0 |
| GG (Well connected) | 27 | 13 | 40 | 67.5 | 32.5 | 100.0 |
| PT (Poorly connected) | 23 | 17 | 40 | 57.5 | 42.5 | 100.0 |
| SM (Well connected) | 18 | 60 | 78 | 23.1 | 76.9 | 100.0 |
| MB (Poorly connected) | 17 | 25 | 42 | 40.5 | 59.5 | 100.0 |
| Total | 136 | 128 | 264 | 51.5 | 48.5 | 100.0 |
| 2003–4 | | | | | | |
| LJ (Poorly connected) | 18 | 46 | 64 | 28.1 | 71.9 | 100.0 |
| GG (Well connected) | 24 | 16 | 40 | 60.0 | 40.0 | 100.0 |
| PT (Poorly connected) | 22 | 18 | 40 | 55.0 | 45.0 | 100.0 |
| SM (Well connected) | 16 | 62 | 78 | 20.5 | 79.5 | 100.0 |
| MB (Poorly connected) | 26 | 16 | 42 | 61.9 | 38.1 | 100.0 |
| Total | 106 | 158 | 264 | 40.2 | 59.8 | 100.0 |

*Source*: Authors.

With the exception of MB, all villages showed an increase in the proportion of households with migrants. The increase was especially sharp in the remote village of LJ which showed a jump from 28 per cent to 80 per cent. Focus group discussions and key informant interviews provide insights into why this might be and a detailed discussion is presented in the following paragraphs.

A significant finding is that circular migration is by far the most important form of mobility and has grown faster than commuting and permanent migration. Table 4.4 shows that while the number of households containing at least one migrant or commuter had increased from 106 to 136 between the last two rounds, the total number of *individuals* who migrated or commuted had increased from 169 in 2003–4 to 232 in 2006–7. Commuting was undertaken for work of all kinds—in the formal sector as well as informal skilled and unskilled work, farm and non-farm work. Although the absolute number of commuters increased, their relative proportion fell because of a greater increase in the number of circular migrants. A significant proportion of commuters were travelling to nearby towns. There were just two permanent migrants in 2006–7.

Table 4.4: Frequency and Percentage of Different Types of Mobility, 2003–4 and 2006–7

| Mobility type | 2003–4 | | 2006–7 | |
| --- | --- | --- | --- | --- |
| | Number of individuals | % | Number of individuals | % |
| Commuters* | 44 | 26.0 | 53 | 22.8 |
| Circular migrants | 122 | 72.2 | 177 | 76.3 |
| Permanent migrants | 3 | 1.8 | 2 | 0.9 |
| Total | 169 | 100.0 | 232 | 100.0 |

*Source*: Authors.
*Notes*: * Work of All Kinds.

## Destinations, Distances, and Sectors

The nature of migration has changed in terms of distances and sectors worked in: although migration to large towns continued to be the most common type of migration, migration to smaller towns showed an increase in 2006–7 possibly due to the development of small urban centres. Rural–rural migration had become the least important kind of mobility across the entire sample by 2006–7 as the total number fell from 24 to only 17 rural–rural migrants. The decrease appears to have occurred because many migrants from the remote tribal village of PT who were previously migrating for agricultural work had started migrating to nearby towns.

Table 4.5: Distribution of Migrants by Location of Work in the Villages of MP, 2003–4 and 2006–7

| Village | | Location of work (frequency) | | | Total |
|---|---|---|---|---|---|
| | | Commuting | Migration (rural to rural) | Migration (rural to urban– small town) | Migration (rural-urban– large town) | |
| 2003–4 | LJ | 6 | 3 | 0 | 24 | 33 |
| | GG | 31 | 1 | 6 | 2 | 40 |
| | PT | 6 | 18 | 0 | 18 | 42 |
| | SM | 0 | 1 | 1 | 19 | 21 |
| | MB | 1 | 1 | 6 | 25 | 33 |
| | Total | 44 | 24 | 13 | 88 | 169 |
| 2006–7 | LJ | 26 | 8 | 9 | 49 | 92 |
| | GG | 24 | 1 | 11 | 11 | 47 |
| | PT | 0 | 8 | 7 | 22 | 37 |
| | SM | 3 | 0 | 10 | 15 | 28 |
| | MB | 0 | 0 | 11 | 17 | 28 |
| | Total | 53 | 17 | 48 | 114 | 232 |

*Source*: Authors.

Inter-state migration is very important in MP now probably because growing opportunities across the border in Gujarat and Maharashtra: in the 2006–7 sample, nearly 47 per cent of circular migrants went to destinations outside the state, 36 per cent migrated within the state, 14 per cent migrated within the district, and 3 per cent within the block.

INCOME FROM MIGRATION

Whether migration historically has contributed significantly to incomes has been disputed: Connell *et al.* (1976) and Lipton (1980) for example, argued that migrant remittances were insignificant. Our research shows that migration is the most important source of income for households with at least one member working outside the village. Table 4.8 shows the income shares of different activities that the households were engaged in during 2006–7.[5] This was done by summarizing household income data by activity and then calculating the share. Circular migration accounts for the largest share (31.4 per cent) and is twice as important as cultivation which accounts for only 15.9 per cent of the annual household income

(Table 4.6). Next in importance are salaried jobs and local non-farm wage labour. Commuting was at the 8th position accounting for a mere 5 per cent of total annual household income.

Table 4.6: Proportionate Share of Household Net Income (Gross Income—Enterprise Cost) from Migration and Other Sources, 2006–7

| Activity | % share of net annual income |
|---|---|
| Circular migration | 31.4 |
| Local wage labour (farm and non-farm) | 17.9 |
| Cultivation | 15.9 |
| Salaried Jobs | 11.7 |
| Other elementary | 7.0 |
| Local service, craft & trade related | 5.2 |
| Commuting | 5.1 |
| Forest product/CPR related | 2.5 |
| Sharecropping/leasing | 1.0 |
| Local construction work (unskilled) | 1.0 |
| Livestock | 0.9 |
| Unclassified work | 0.4 |
| Remittance | 0.2 |
| Total | 100.0 |

Source: Authors.

If the same table is broken down by caste, it is seen that circular migration earnings account for a higher proportion of household income among the lower castes and tribes namely, the SC, BC, and ST. In the case of SCs, migration accounted for almost 47 per cent of the household income. In the case of the STs and BCs it accounted for over 27 per cent. The OCs derived the least income from circular migration (19 per cent) as for them cultivation and commuting were more important and provided 25 per cent and 22 per cent respectively of the annual income. For the STs local labouring either on-farm or off-farm were the second most important source of income and only 3 per cent was derived from cultivation owing to their poorer asset base. However, they derived considerably more (8 per cent) from forest products and CPRs thereby confirming the dependence of the poor on the commons.

The results by landholding (Table 4.8) present an interesting picture: migration earnings account for 30–3 per cent of total household income across classes with small differences between them: land-less and marginal farmers derive a slightly lower

Table 4.7: Proportionate Share of Household Net Income (Gross Income—
Enterprise Cost) from Migration and Other Sources by Caste Category,
2006–7 in Households with One Person Working Outside the Village

| Activity | % share of net annual income | | | |
|---|---|---|---|---|
| | Schedule Tribe (ST) | Schedule Caste (SC) | Backward Caste (BC) | Other Caste (OC) |
| Circular migration | 27.3 | 46.8 | 27.8 | 19.1 |
| Commuting | 2.5 | 4.7 | 5.1 | 22.6 |
| Remittances | –* | –* | 0.3 | 0 |
| Local non–farm wage labour | 19.9 | 2.5 | 13.9 | –** |
| Local agricultural labour | 19.2 | 9.8 | 3.0 | 13.5 |
| Salary | 13.8 | 8.2 | 12.3 | 12.4 |
| Forest product/CPR related | 8.9 | –** | 2.0 | –** |
| Cultivation | 3.1 | 4.7 | 21.7 | 25.5 |
| Service, craft & trade related | 2.9 | 2.8 | 6.3 | 6.9 |
| Other elementary | 1.7 | 17.7 | 5.0 | –** |
| Unclassified work | 0.4 | 0.7 | 0.3 | –** |
| Livestock | 0.3 | –** | 1.1 | –** |
| Sharecropping/leasing | –** | 2.1 | 0.9 | –** |
| Total | 100 | 100 | 100 | 100 |

*Source*: Authors.
*Note*: *STs and SCs hand–carry money home and do not send remittances.
**There were no migrants in these categories and therefore no income.

proportion of their overall income from migration compared to
small, medium, and large farmers. However, the proportions of
other components of their portfolio show marked variations across
classes. While the landless and marginal farmers derive nearly
a quarter of their income from local labouring, this proportion is
lower for small farmers and while salaried jobs accounted for 24 per
cent of the income in the case of small farmers this figure was lower
in other classes either because they did not need jobs due to secure
incomes in farming as in the case of medium and large farmers or
because they could not get salaried jobs as in the case of marginal
farmers. The category of landless included some households where
levels of education were high and occupations had diversified away
from agriculture.

## Determinants of Migration Income: It's Not What You Are but Who You Were Born As That Counts

Variations in daily earnings were associated with socio-economic
factors more than human capital variables (Table 4.9), suggesting
substantial segmentation in labour markets. The exception was skill,

Table 4.8: Proportionate Share of Household Net Income (Gross Income—
Enterprise Cost) from Migration and Other Sources by Land Holding,
2006–7

| Activity | % share of net annual income | | | |
|---|---|---|---|---|
| | Landless | Marginal | Small | Medium & large |
| Temporary migration | 30.5 | 29.9 | 33.0 | 32.8 |
| Non-farm wage labour (local) | 14.5 | 16.7 | 2.9 | 11.4 |
| Agricultural labour (local) | 11.7 | 7.6 | 4.0 | 2.8 |
| Government or private sector salaried job | 10.7 | 3.0 | 23.8 | 13.2 |
| Other elementary | 8.3 | 6.8 | 7.0 | 6.0 |
| Service, craft & trade related | 8.2 | 6.0 | 4.6 | 1.2 |
| Commuting | 5.5 | 6.8 | 3.3 | 4.1 |
| Cultivation | 4.7 | 18.1 | 16.9 | 24.4 |
| Forest product/CPR related | 3.6 | 0.8 | 3.4 | 2.7 |
| Livestock | 1.7 | 1.3 | 0.6 | -** |
| Unclassified work | 0.6 | -** | 0.2 | 0.8 |
| Remittance | -* | 0.6 | -** | -** |
| Sharecropping/leasing | -** | 2.5 | 0.3 | 0.6 |
| Total | 100 | 100 | 100 | 100 |

*Source*: Authors.
*Note:* * hand-carry money home and do not send remittances
**There were no migrants in these categories

which was significantly associated with higher income. According
to the analysis, a skilled person's probable earning is 36 per cent
higher than an unskilled person's. Skilled persons in the poorer
quintiles also earn higher than unskilled persons by 27 per cent but
their probable higher earning is less than the skilled persons in the
less poor quintiles who earn 49 per cent higher income than the
unskilled persons. In the absence of education data for migrants,
household level aggregate schooling years collected in 2001–2
census survey was used as a proxy but it cannot be interpreted for
the individual. However, it can provide an indication of the family
background. Ideally education should be associated with higher
earning so the negative sign is incorrect and may be due the use of
an inappropriate proxy. Migrants in the kharif season earned less
than in other seasons. Women were more likely to earn less. Females
were more disadvantaged in the poorer quintiles.

The results of the most recent year confirm that socio-economic
factors are more important than human capital variables, except for
skill (Table 4.10). The effect of skill became weaker and the gender
differential became wider. Caste and village specific differences were

also stronger. A striking result is the lower earning of professionals but FGDs (Focus group discussions) revealed that this is because of the inclusion of poor priests in the sample.

Table 4.9: Determinants of Migration Income in MP, 2003–4

|  | All sample | | Quintiles 1–3 | | Quintiles 4–5 | |
|---|---|---|---|---|---|---|
|  | Coefficient | p–values | Coefficient | p–values | Coefficient | p–values |
| (Constant) | 3.757 | .000 | 3.725 | .000 | 3.027 | .000 |
| Age (years) | .000 | .882 | −.003 | .426 | .012 | .321 |
| Migration experience | .001 | .828 | .000 | .982 | −.013 | .450 |
| Years of schooling in household[a] | −.006 | .018 | −.003 | .389 | −.007 | .391 |
| Gender (female = 1) | −.096 | .079 | −.135 | .025 | −.096 | .471 |
| Skilled worker = 1 | .361 | .000 | .273 | .009 | .492 | .056 |
| Commuters = 1 | −.018 | .837 | .076 | .531 | −.107 | .701 |
| Migration to large town = 1 | .058 | .496 | .158 | .147 | −.231 | .346 |
| Migration at kharif season = 1 | −.061 | .260 | −.073 | .255 | −.038 | .821 |
| Migration at summer season = 1 | .029 | .666 | −.010 | .889 | .366 | .084 |
| Landless = 1[b] | .062 | .308 | .010 | .886 | .215 | .255 |
| Medium, small and large farm = 1 | .084 | .196 | .124 | .157 | .050 | .782 |
| Service, craft & trade jobs = 1[c] | .248 | .058 | −.062 | .704 | .140 | .708 |
| Construction job = 1 | .161 | .047 | .047 | .611 | .381 | .249 |
| Industry/machine operator = 1 | .109 | .282 | −.077 | .519 | .583 | .102 |
| Elementary job = 1 | .161 | .104 | .043 | .775 | .415 | .050 |
| Schedule tribe=1 | −.192 | .525 | −.032 | .914 | .191 | .486 |
| Schedule caste = 1 | .036 | .910 | .286 | .362 | −.067 | .760 |
| Backward caste = 1 | −.143 | .631 | .006 | .984 |  |  |
| GG = 1 | .020 | .851 | .083 | .537 | −.277 | .599 |
| PT = 1 | .180 | .100 | .053 | .704 | .337 | .434 |
| SM = 1 | .213 | .028 | .111 | .352 | .298 | .359 |
| MB = 1 | .326 | .002 | .306 | .008 | .222 | .607 |
| N | 167 |  | 112 |  | 49 |  |
| F value | 5.98 | 0.00 | 4.49 | 0.00 | 3.61 | 0.00 |
| R-square | 0.48 |  | 0.52 |  | 0.74 |  |
| Adj R-square | 0.40 |  | 0.40 |  | 0.53 |  |

*Source*: Census survey 2001–2, Panel survey 2005.
*Note*: Dependent Variable: Natural log of daily migration earnings.
a) These household level data are taken from the 2001–2 census survey; b) Base is marginal farm; c) Base occupation is agriculture (includes forestry and fishery).

Table 4.10: Determinants of Migration Income in MP, 2006–7

| | All sample | | Quintiles 1–3 | | Quintiles 4–5 | |
|---|---|---|---|---|---|---|
| | Coefficient | p–values | Coefficient | p–values | Coefficient | p–values |
| (Constant) | 3.933 | .000 | 4.042 | .000 | 4.184 | .000 |
| Age (years) | .002 | .361 | .002 | .611 | .000 | .928 |
| Migration experience | .001 | .781 | .003 | .581 | .007 | .153 |
| Years of schooling in household[a] | .001 | .591 | .003 | .456 | .002 | .544 |
| Gender ( female = 1) | -.254 | .000 | -.238 | .003 | -.247 | .000 |
| Skilled worker = 1 | .143 | .061 | .180 | .123 | .219 | .025 |
| Commuters = 1 | .011 | .867 | .054 | .571 | .055 | .561 |
| Migration to large town = 1 | .023 | .657 | .074 | .372 | .070 | .286 |
| Migration at kharif season = 1 | -.214 | .001 | -.194 | .034 | -.210 | .026 |
| Migration at summer season = 1 | .000 | .995 | .107 | .170 | -.024 | .782 |
| Landless = 1[b] | .110 | .069 | -.126 | .203 | .197 | .020 |
| Medium, small and large farm = 1 | -.023 | .663 | -.063 | .388 | .068 | .343 |
| Professional job = 1[c] | -1.008 | .000 | -.001 | .998 | -1.723 | .000 |
| Service, craft & trade jobs = 1 | .049 | .612 | .064 | .662 | .043 | .738 |
| Construction job = 1 | .144 | .038 | .058 | .545 | .234 | .022 |
| Industry/machine operator = 1 | .080 | .491 | -.327 | .064 | .406 | .005 |
| Elementary job = 1 | .197 | .004 | .219 | .021 | .308 | .002 |
| Unclassified job = 1 | -.177 | .448 | -.207 | .541 | -.507 | .128 |
| Schedule tribe=1 | -.301 | .054 | -.516 | .042 | -.685 | .003 |
| Schedule caste = 1 | -.342 | .021 | -.438 | .046 | -.890 | .000 |
| Backward caste = 1 | -.214 | .131 | -.303 | .148 | -.698 | .001 |
| GG = 1 | .092 | .254 | .146 | .229 | .124 | .297 |
| PT = 1 | .276 | .001 | .239 | .097 | .300 | .011 |
| SM = 1 | .721 | .000 | .513 | .001 | .872 | .000 |
| MB = 1 | .375 | .000 | .422 | .001 | .447 | .000 |
| N 228 | | 133 | | 95 | | |
| F value | 9.49 | 0.00 | 4.47 | 0.00 | 10.87 | 0.00 |
| R-square | 0.53 | | 0.50 | | 0.79 | |
| Adj R-square | 0.47 | | 0.39 | | 0.72 | |

Source: Census survey 2001–2, Panel survey 2006–7.
Note: Dependent Variable: Natural log of daily migration earnings.
a) These household level data are taken from the 2001–2 census survey; b) Base is marginal farm; c) Base occupation is agriculture (includes forestry and fishery).

From this analysis we conclude that earnings from migration are influenced mostly by skill allowing entry into better paid jobs. In the absence of education data, precise conclusions on the effect of human capital on migration earnings cannot be drawn, and this would merit further investigation.

HAS MIGRATION REDUCED POVERTY?

In the literature on migration, the evidence of the impact of migration on poverty reduction is mixed. While the studies by Mosse and others (cited earlier) emphasized the exploitation of migrant workers and their continued poverty, more recent studies have shown that the economic returns of migration are substantial and the prevalence of recruiting agents is going down. In the Shivpuri study, although many migrants said that they spent more than 60 per cent the wage on living at the destination, they still felt it was an accumulative option. Similarly, a survey of 550 households across 60 villages in Jhabua district by Narain *et al.* (2005) found that income from wage employment was the largest source of income for households in *all* income quartiles. For the first three quartiles, 65–70 per cent of the wage income came from migration. There is also evidence that migration has helped households to smooth consumption. Qualitative data collected by Shah and Sah (2004) from 212 households in a village in Bhadwani district shows that migration helped landless households to maintain their standard of living over a decade. The researchers assessed the change in wellbeing rank over ten years and found that 180 households had retained their original well-being status (including those that were already poor), 7 per cent experienced an improvement, and the remaining 38 per cent deteriorated in status. The analysis suggested that (a) improvement was generally associated with access to irrigation through private sources or obtaining a salaried job; (b) deterioration was largely due to division of landholdings and at times, due to indebtedness, and (c) some households, especially the landless, could retain their well-being status in the better-off or medium categories due to migration.

Daily consumption, that is, spending on day to day needs which are mainly food, was listed as the most important use of migration earnings by 58 per cent (Table 4.11) of the respondents in 2003/4

Table 4.11: Distribution of the Responses on Purpose of Spending
Migration Income  (2003-04)

|  | Rank 1 | | Rank 2 | |
| --- | --- | --- | --- | --- |
|  | N | % | N | % |
| HH daily consumption/expenses | 99 | 58.2 | 20 | 17.4 |
| Paying off debt | 32 | 18.8 | 21 | 18.3 |
| Purchase of agricultural inputs | 27 | 15.9 | 26 | 22.6 |
| Paying for medical treatment | 8 | 4.7 | 39 | 33.9 |
| Hiring in labour | 2 | 1.2 | | |
| Buying lift irrigation pump/drilling tube well | 1 | .6 | | |
| Marriage expenses | 1 | .6 | 1 | .9 |
| Education of HH member | | | 4 | 3.5 |
| Savings | | | 3 | 2.6 |
| Buying land | | | 1 | 0.9 |
| Total | 170 | 100.0 | 115 | 100.0 |

*Source*: Authors.

---

BOX 4.1: MIGRATION FOR REPAYING DEBT

Har Prasad is a 30 year old man belonging to the Dheemar
(fisherman) caste. He migrates twice in a year. He has less then
one acre of land for cultivation. Other members in his family are
involved in fishing and agricultural labour work in the village. He
used to work as a farm labourer but he was so heavily in debt
that he started to migrate in 2004 to earn money to pay off the
debt. He started by migrating for mustard harvesting and later
migrated to Delhi for unskilled construction work with other
villagers. After five years of doing this and after repaying his debts
he stopped migrating. He now cultivates his land and does some
labouring locally.

---

and 54 per cent 2006/7 (Table 4.12) and this finding is consistent
with the wider migration literature.

The second most important use of migration earnings was to
pay off debts (see Box 4.1) followed by the purchase of agricultural
inputs. Paying for medical treatment was fourth. Among secondary
uses, paying for medical treatment and buying agricultural inputs
were the most important.

The situation was unchanged in 2006–7 with respect to the order of
importance of spending on consumption and paying off debt (Table

4.12). However, interviews indicate that the relationship between debt and migration is changing. Migrating through *mukkaddams* often meant that migrants were in a continuous debt cycle. But now migrantion is helping people to repay debts and borrow more if they need to. Group discussions show that some households have become more creditworthy as a result of having more money and therefore take out greater loans which they repay through migration. The former situation would mean that migrant households are in greater debt but are able to eat and live better. Indeed, Ghate (2005) argues that migration improves the creditworthiness of households and they are able to borrow more because of that.

However, spending on health was ranked above investing in agriculture in 2006–7 and may reflect the general trend in rural India of escalating health expenditure among the poor. Spending on health has been linked to greater indebtedness (Farrington *et al.* 2006) but may also be a sign of an enhanced ability to purchase medical treatment with higher disposable incomes. In the 2006–7 round, more migrants said that they were using their earnings to buy assets and land.

Table 4.12: Frequency and Percentage Distribution of Commuters and Migrants by Source of Expenses of Migration Earnings, 2006–7

| | First Rank | | Second Rank | |
| --- | --- | --- | --- | --- |
| | N | % | N | % |
| Household daily consumption/expenses | 79 | 54.1 | 30 | 24.0 |
| Paying off debt | 44 | 30.1 | 16 | 12.8 |
| Paying for medical treatment | 13 | 8.9 | 53 | 42.4 |
| Purchase of agricultural inputs | 3 | 2.1 | 4 | 3.2 |
| Buying assets[b] | 3 | 2.1 | 2 | 1.6 |
| Acquiring land[a] | 2 | 1.4 | 3 | 2.4 |
| Marriage expenses | 1 | .7 | 8 | 6.4 |
| Education of HH member | 1 | .7 | 1 | .8 |
| Hiring in labour | | | 1 | .8 |
| Other[c] | | | 7 | 5.6 |
| Total | 146 | 100.0 | 125 | 100.0 |

*Source*: Authors.
*Notes:* a. Include buying and leasing land.
b. Include buying livestock and irrigation machine.
c. Include death expenses, expenses for obtaining a job, savings, investment in shop/enterprise, and 1 response for building/renovating house.

Repaying Debts More Important For Tribals

For STs paying off debt is the most important use of migration money and this suggests that most of them borrow to migrate and the earnings are spent repaying this debt (Table 4.13) but as we discussed above, paying off debt is not limited to the poor. Investing and saving or spending on education and health accounts for a much smaller proportion of the spending in the case of STs. On the other hand, the SCs spend most of their earnings on consumption. For the BCs too the main uses of migration earnings are consumption and paying off debt but the proportion spent on consumption is less than SCs and more than STs. The OCs also use migration money for consumption and paying off debt but spend proportionately more on education.

Table 4.13: Percentage Distribution of Households Using (or Planning to Use) Mobility Earnings by Purpose, Rank, and Caste Category, 2006–7

|  |  | Caste category | | | | Total |
|---|---|---|---|---|---|---|
|  |  | ST | SC | BC | OC |  |
| Use group rank 1 | Consumption | 26.3 | 70.4 | 56.0 | 50.0 | 54.5 |
|  | Health and education* | 10.5 | 14.8 | 6.0 | 25.0 | 9.0 |
|  | Investment and savings | 5.3 |  | 9.5 |  | 6.7 |
|  | Paying off debt | 57.9 | 14.8 | 28.6 | 25.0 | 29.9 |
| Total |  | 100.0 | 100.0 | 100.0 | 100.0 | 100.0 |

Source: Authors.
Notes: * Only one household reported use on education as rank1.

PROSPECTS FOR UPWARD MOBILITY

Comparing the situation in 2003–4 with 2006–7 indicates that although skill levels have improved over time, a majority of migrant workers from the study villages still see themselves as unskilled. Migrant workers provided their own assessments of skills, which we verified through triangulation. Most migrants were in informal occupations in 2003–4 with construction occupying top rank as it employed 70 workers accounting for more than 41 per cent of migrants in the sample.[6] This was followed by agricultural labourers in second rank, and industrial workers and mechanics in third place. Under 10 per cent of the workers had regular jobs, that is, with contracts in government or the private sector. By 2006–7 the relative proportion of construction workers had decreased (although numbers had increased), that of agricultural workers had remained the same (although numbers had increased), and the relative proportion as well as numbers of workers in services, trade, and craft had increased. This includes occupations such as rickshaw pulling, work in small hotels, drivers, conductors, grocery shop workers, sawmill, and factory workers. The relative proportion and number of industrial workers had fallen sharply. Focus group discussions indicated that this was because workers from other states were being preferred over workers from MP. Indeed key informants from industry and government in Madhya Pradesh confirmed that workers from other states (Bihar, Uttar Pradesh, West Bengal, Orissa, and Tamil Nadu) are preferred in industry because they are more skilled.

Table 4.14: Frequency and Percentage Distribution of Migrants and Commuters by Type of Work

| Type of work 2003–4. | N | % | Skilled% | Unskilled % |
|---|---|---|---|---|
| Construction workers | 70 | 41.4 | 1.4 | 98.6 |
| Agricultural labourers (including forestry and fishery) | 41 | 24.3 | 2.4 | 97.6 |
| Industrial workers and machine operators/assemblers | 22 | 13.0 | 22.7 | 77.3 |
| Salaried jobs in govt and pvt sector | 16 | 9.5 | 75.0 | 25.0 |
| Other unskilled workers (rickshaw pullers, hotel boys , grocery shop workers, sawmill workers, and unskilled factory workers, etc.) | 13 | 7.7 | 30.8 | 69.2 |
| Service, craft, trade, and related | 7 | 4.1 | 57.1 | 42.9 |
| Total | 169 | 100.0 | 16.0 | 84.0 |

| Type of work, 2006–7 | N | % | Skilled/ semi skilled % | Unskilled % |
|---|---|---|---|---|
| Construction workers | 79 | 34.2 | 7.6 | 92.4 |
| Agricultural labourers (including forestry and fishery) | 56 | 24.2 | 7.1 | 92.9 |
| Other unskilled workers (excluding agriculture, construction, and industry) | 54 | 23.4 | 18.5 | 81.5 |
| Service, craft, trade, and related | 23 | 10.0 | 78.3 | 21.7 |
| Industrial workers and machine operators/assemblers | 14 | 6.1 | 42.9 | 57.1 |
| Professional | 3 | 1.3 | 100.0 | 0.0 |
| Other | 2 | 0.9 | | 100.0 |
| Total | 231 | 100.0 | 20.3 | 79.7 |

Source: Authors.

COPING AND ACCUMULATIVE MIGRATION

Qualitative methods highlight the subtle differences within the broad categories of unskilled and skilled. While being a skilled worker was definitely associated with higher incomes, being unskilled did not necessarily always result in poorly paid work as the case studies show.

Two broad kinds of migration can be identified:

*Coping Migration*

One is the kind that involves the poorest, the least educated, and the least skilled migrants. These migrants often belong to the lowest social strata and do not have the assets or the social capital to bear the risk of searching for work themselves, nor the costs of living at the destination. Recruitment is often through a labour market

---

BOX 4.2: LABOUR MARKET INTERMEDIARIES

In certain occupations, especially those that involve the poorest and most vulnerable migrants, recruitment is done by a labour market intermediary or a recruitment agent. The agent often belongs to the community that he or she recruits from. In MP such an agent is known as a *mukkaddam* and is usually a young male who is slightly better educated and socially connected than the labourers he recruits. Historically *mukkadams* played an important role in bringing migrants to the *havelis* (see Box 4.3) from the Mahakaushal region. These days they recruit workers for telephone cable work, road construction, canal construction, building construction, sugar mill work, brick kiln work, and bamboo cutting work (in Maharashtra). *Mukkaddams* typically give the labourers an advance so that they can buy supplies that they need to take with them. The advance also provides the family in the village with some security while the migrant is away. The advance is repaid through migrant wages and the length of time that this takes depends on the payment that the migrant receives at the destination. The *mukkaddam* recruits migrants in groups who stay together at the destination. He takes care of other needs as well including small health expenses, travel expenses, shelter, and communication with the family in the village.

intermediary or recruiting agent locally known as a *mukkaddam*. Examples include migration by tribals and scheduled caste people for the lowest paid unskilled work in construction. Recruiting agents play an important role; offering labourers a hefty advance in exchange for several months of hard work with few breaks and a remuneration rate that is below the market rate. While *mukkaddams* are notorious for exploiting workers in many ways, they also provide them with a degree of protection against the risk in finding work, travelling, finding medical assistance when needed and finding a place to stay. However our interviews indicate that this seems to be changing and the incidence of labour intermediaries is going down because of growing confidence among workers and improving knowledge of the job market.

Another example is migration by tribals for harvesting grain (Box 4.3). Payment is in kind and if translated into cash would amount to a daily wage that is well below the legal minimum. Such migration is commonly known as 'haveli' migration because it is to the agriculturally prosperous belt around Jabalpur, Narsimhpur,

---

BOX 4.3: HAVELI WORK

Malti Bai Bairagi, a 31 year old widow migrates from the village PT to the Haveli region and for non-farm work at different times of the year. This has helped her to survive since the death of her husband when she was thrown out of her in-laws house. She lives in a one room mud house with her school-going son. She migrates alone twice a year for haveli work. She is paid in kind and comes home with roughly 100 kg of wheat, some gram and lentils, and about 80 kg of paddy for two months of work. At other times she works in stone quarries near Kanha Tiger Sanctuary (80 km from PT) for 1–2 months a year where she earns Rs 30 a day. She migrates there with some other people from the village under a labour recruiting agent. The agent is well known and manages all the travelling expenses. She tries to do some farm work locally but it is not always available and is not an important source of income for her. She earns around Rs 1000 from tendu leaf collection in the months of May and June. She says she has no hopes for her own future but continues doing all of this hard and dangerous work for the sake of her son.

Hoshangabad. Haveli is the term for old stately homes owned by zamindars who had large farms.

### Accumulative Migration

The second kind involves people from a slightly higher social background and with more assets and better social networks. They may or may not have higher education levels than the poorer survival or coping migrants and may or may not have more skills. But their contacts in distant locations (relatives and neighbours from the village) provide them with information on job availability and wage rates, and offer them a place to stay when they first go to the city. In this way they are able to manage the risk of having to incur expenses at the destination and the uncertainty of finding work. This group usually includes BCs and upper castes who migrate to work in the construction sector in larger cities, as industrial workers, carpenters, plumbers, drivers, conductors, restaurant waiters, and security guards. Interviews indicate that this kind of migration can lead to substantial earning, saving, and investment in poverty reducing activities and assets in a relatively short time (2–3 years). However, the numbers of migrants in this category are still relatively small.

### NEW TRENDS IN MIGRATION

Interviews and case studies show that migration patterns are changing rapidly in response to new opportunities emerging in high-growth areas and the spread of social networks. Three new phenomena have been identified and these are discussed below.

### Growing Migration of Higher Castes for Manual Work

Groups that were not migrating 3–4 years ago are now engaged in long-distance inter-state migration. An illustrative example is that of the remote village LJ. There has been a sharp increase in migration in this village recently and key informant interviews indicate that this is mainly due to migration spreading among the higher castes. The village is populated mainly by Sondhiya Thakurs[7] who, being relatively upper caste farmers, have historically shunned manual work. Previously only a few SCs (Chamars) would migrate to Kota in Rajasthan. But the drought of 2000–3 changed this. It hit soybean farming badly and farmers had to explore other options. Some Thakurs began to migrate with Chamars and found that the returns were good (Box 4.4). Thereafter they started to migrate regularly and continue to do so despite better rains in recent years.[8]

## Long Distance Migration Of Children

More migration streams involving long distance migration of children have been recorded. But it is not entirely clear whether this is due to increased sensitization of the research team, greater trust on the part of villagers that has caused them to divulge sensitive information, or new work opportunities. It is probably a mix of all three factors. For example, a new migration stream began in village LJ in 2006 when some migrants from LJ learnt from other migrants while working in Kota that wood-cutting work in Kutch (Gujarat) was better paid. Twelve boys and youth (aged 15–20) migrated from

---

BOX 4.4: UPPER CASTES MIGRATING FOR MANUAL WORK

Case 1: In 2003, Raju a Sondhiya Thakur landlord (29 years, LJ village) migrated to Kota with Harijans from his village in search of wage work. This was a major break with tradition as the Thakur caste is superior to the Harijans in the Hindu hierarchy. Raju did this as a last resort in the face of prolonged drought and crushing debts. Very little cash was coming into the house and the family had to sell its cattle and mortgage a large part of the ancestral land. Even that money ran out after a while. Raju started working as a *beldar* (unskilled construction worker) in Kota (Rajasthan) for Rs 50–80/day. He did this for two months in the first instance. He went back again and sends money home through other labourers from LJ. He continues to migrate when he can even though his farming has improved.

Case 2: Bherulal (SC) is a marginal farmer from LJ. During the drought of 2002, his elder son (Jeevan) started migrating to Kota and got work in a food processing factory as a porter during the summer months. Later his younger brother (Bhagwaan) also started migrating to Kota for manual work. There he met a tribal from Ratlam district (MP), who mentioned wood cutting work in Kutch (Gujarat) which paid better. Bhagwan and his friends from LJ went to Gujarat with the tribal man and worked for a month. They were paid Rs 100/day.

LJ to Kutch in 2007. There is also evidence of girls migrating to work as domestic maids in larger cities (see Box 4.5)

## The Discontinuation of Certain Migration Streams

Some migration streams have ceased to exist and others have shrunk: an example of a migration stream that does not exist any more is seen in PR where the Chamars (SCs) used to migrate for brick-kiln work. They have stopped migrating now and have set up small shops with their savings. They combine this activity with working in nearby farms as labourers. In village MB which is only 2 km from the main road, Dheemers (fishermen) started migrating for harvesting paddy, wheat, and mustard to neighbouring districts in about 2000. Then, in 2003 they started migrating to Delhi when their crops failed. But now migration rates have dropped again as more jobs have been created by the National Rural Employment Guarantee Scheme (NREGS) road construction, and new stone crushing units. Similarly, village PT, which had the highest levels of migration in 2001, has shown a decrease in rural–rural *haveli* migrants. PT has poor soils; nearly 60 per cent of the land is rocky and barren on which only maize and minor-millets are grown. FGDs indicate that *haveli* migration has decreased because of greater work availability in the village due to the NREGS. But at the same time there has been an increase in migration to smaller and large towns for a range of occupations including construction work, rickshaw pulling, work in small hotels

---

BOX 4.5: GIRLS MIGRATING FOR DOMESTIC WORK

The migration of girls to Delhi to work as domestic maids was mentioned often in the latest round of data collection. These girls go through placement agents/agencies. According to an NGO working in the area, around 1250 girls have left the area. They earn Rs 1500–2000 per month and send most of the money back home through money orders or through the placement agents. This kind of migration has received negative coverage in the press recently[9] due to cases of sexual exploitation, abuse, forced prostitution and cheating. It is not clear whether efforts are being made to stop this migration and whether this is the right approach given the poverty and lack of employment opportunities that these families face.

---

as hotel boys, drivers, conductors, grocery shop workers, sawmill, and factory workers.

## The Difficulties Faced by Migrants

Whether or not migration is poverty reducing, it is a tough undertaking. Migrants travel and live in very difficult conditions. They work long hours in the most difficult and dangerous conditions; occupational hazards such as injuries and exposure to toxic substances are commonplace and hardly any one is insured or properly treated. Access to clean water, sanitation, and shelter is inadequate. Migrants are often the victims of theft and violence and women and girls face the added risk of sexual abuse. DISHA, an NGO in Ahmedabad, Gujarat surveyed migrants in the city (many of whom were from MP) and found that over half the migrants slept in the open and the rest had makeshift accommodation. Vipul Pandya of DISHA observes, '96 per cent of the seasonal migrants in Ahmedabad, work without protective clothing, 90 per cent carry more than they should, 95 per cent have no safe drinking water, crèches, sanitation, first aid, or adequate lighting at work, 98 per cent are without proper shelter, women are sexually harassed, 14 per cent are harassed by criminals, police and local development authorities, 86 per cent need to look for clean water, 88 per cent bring their children and 58 per cent of the children have no access to schools.'

Migrants are not able to send their children to state schools at the destination and do not have access to subsidized healthcare. According to the Human Development Report for Madhya Pradesh (HDR 2002) migration was the fourth most important reason for keeping boys out of school: about 86 per cent boys remain out of school due to the following five reasons that is, engaged in economic activities (21.6 per cent), cattle grazing (22.4 per cent), sibling care (15.6 per cent), migration (11.5 per cent), and weak financial condition (14.4 per cent). It was the fifth most important reason for keeping girls out of school: about 80 per cent girls remain out of school due to the following five reasons, that is, sibling care (24.6 per cent), engaged in economic activities (18.5 per cent), cattle grazing (13.6 per cent), weak financial condition (13.6 per cent), and migration (9.3 per cent). Migrants are treated as illegal residents and are generally harassed by the police. Although entitled to 'patta' rights under MP law (see Box 4.6) they are discouraged from staying at the same place.

Besides all these difficulties migrant dwellings are vulnerable to being demolished during anti-slum drives and they are often perceived as criminals by the police because they have no fixed abode. Other vulnerabilities are uncertainty in the job market and high expenditure at the destination particularly related to health.

---

BOX 4.6: THE MP STATE PATTA ACT

MP has a State Patta Act that offers tenure security to slum residents. (MP *Nagariyon Kshetra ke Bhumiheen Vyakti, Pattadhruti Adhikaron ka Pradan Kiya Jana, Adhiniyam,* 1984, popularly known as the Patta Act) decrees that all landless people residing in areas less than 50 sq. m. are entitled to leasehold rights on lands occupied by them or on another site. Only residential use is permitted. All land developers set aside 15 per cent land for housing the service sector or alternatively pay the government Rs100 per sq. m. as shelter tax in lieu of land. Through this policy, (*Nirbandhan tatha Sharte Niyam,* 1998 incorporated in Municipal Act under Section 291), Bhopal has been able to generate large amount of resources which can be used for constructing housing for the poor. It issues two types of pattas: a 30 years-patta (patta 'kha') is given to those who are living in settlements that are to be improved and rehabilitated and an annual patta (patta 'ga') that is given to those who are living in settlements that are to be relocated. The patta can be inherited but not transferred. In reality the patta is a formal recognition of the slum for purposes of receiving municipal services. No effort has been made to integrate these areas within the city and to network them into the city systems. Planned resettlement of slum dwellers with pattas is underway in Bhopal. The BMC follows a two-pronged strategy on resettlement: a) providing serviced land, and b) constructing houses for slum families. Nearly 2,500 slum families are being shifted to 7 newly developed sites on the city fringes. (Source: Ribeiro E. F. N. and Renu Khosla, 'Urban Spaces and the Poor', paper presented at India Urban Space Conference, February 2006.)

CONCLUSIONS AND IMPLICATIONS FOR POLICY

In situations where both agriculture and the rural non-farm economy have been stagnant, circular migration and commuting have become major livelihood options. Circular migration is by far the most important form of mobility in Madhya Pradesh and has grown faster than commuting and permanent migration. Migration is ever more complex and diverse than before and is constantly changing in response to new opportunities. While some new migration streams have emerged, others have disappeared. A majority of mobile workers have little or no education and are broadly in the category of unskilled workers. The construction sector continues to be the largest employer. Those who belong to traditionally disadvantaged groups (SCs, STs, and women) and those who are relatively powerless (children, widows) tend to be employed on exploitative terms and are vulnerable in a number of ways. Others with a higher social standing and better social networks are able to play the migrant labour market to their own advantage. Migration is critical to livelihoods providing money for day-to-day consumption and in many cases, money for repaying debts.

Nearly all migrants live and work in difficult and dangerous conditions and require social protection which includes access to subsidized food, education, health, and insurance. While rural employment programmes such as the MP Rural Employment Guarantee Scheme (see Chapter 9 for a detailed discussion of its impacts on migration) as well as the newly created Special Economic Zones will provide some jobs, these will not be able to stem the tide of circular migrants. There is an urgent need to reduce the risks and costs associated with migration and protect the most vulnerable migrants. It remains to be seen whether the Unorganized Sector Workers Social Security Bill will provide access health insurance, old age benefits, and other forms of social security. There are also civil society efforts such as the employment exchange being proposed by Samarthan in collaboration with the World Bank funded District Poverty Initiatives Project (see Chapter 12 for details). In addition, the Government of Madhya Pradesh has recently introduced an employment-oriented skills upgradation programme for poor workers which aims to provide a range of services and ID cards to poor migrants. The momentum of such efforts must be maintained through advocacy, policy research, and grass-roots level initiatives.

NOTES

1. BIMARU is the term used for the erstewhile backward states of Bihar, Madhya Pradesh, Rajasthan, and Uttar Pradesh. The literal translation of this term in Hindi is sick. But in 2006, the Union Minister of State for Commerce Jairam Ramesh said that BIMARU is passe, because of the progress of Rajasthan and M.P. on account of better governance. He coined BU, the new sobriquet for the backward States of Uttar Pradesh and Bihar (*The Hindu*, 9th Sept. 2006).

2. An *India Today* survey in 2006 called 'The State of the States' identifies MP, UP, and Orissa as the fastest movers, i.e., those where the most rapid improvement has been seen over the last year in certain areas. MP was the fastest mover in agriculture (area under cash crops, farm GDP divided by rural population, per capita farm power consumption, farm loans, food grain productivity, percentage of irrigated area), and infrastructure (% of hh with electricity, LPG, % villages with *pucca* roads, per capita road length, bank branches, density of post offices, and teledensity). This contrasts with other states such as Bihar, Assam, and Jharkhand that have not performed that well.

3. Kleih, U., R. Som. Y. Kumar, S. K. Jena, A. Singh, and L. Singh, (2003), 'Household Access to Rural Non-farm Livelihoods Synthesis of Participatory Rural Appraisals and Questionnaire Surveys in Four Blocks of Madhya Pradesh', NRI Report no: 2378, Natural Resources Institute, U.K.

4. The names of villages have been abbreviated in order to protect their identity

5. Total income data were not collected in 2003–4.

6. Similar findings were reported by Mosse (2005) based on a survey covering 2,588 households in 42 villages in the WIRFP project area for the year 1995–6. Roughly 65 per cent of the 4,170 migrants surveyed were involved in urban construction work, often in the regional cities of Baroda, Ahmedabad, Surat, or Kota. Almost all work was provided by the building industry in its widest sense—including ground preparation, earthwork for pipelines, electricity and telephone cables, quarrying and brick work— and only 11 per cent of migrants were agricultural labourers.

7. The Sondhiya Thakurs regard themselves as upper caste Rajputs but they are officially classified as OBCs.

8. It is interesting to note that the newly migrating Sondhiya Thakurs were unskilled in non-farm work compared to the more experienced Chamars.

9. *The Week* 10 September 2006, 'Where is My Daughter', Deepak Tiwari. 5000 girls missing Dindori, Balaghat, Seoni, and Mandla.

REFERENCES

Catalyst Management Services 2006, Baseline Information for the Madhya Pradesh Rural Livelihoods Project (MPRLP).

Connell, J., B. Dasgupta, R. Laishley, and M. Lipton, *Migration from Rural Areas: The Evidence from Village Studies*, Delhi: Oxford University Press, 1976.

Deshingkar, P., and D. Start, 'Seasonal Migration For Livelihoods, Coping, Accumulation And Exclusion' Working Paper no, 220, London: Overseas Development Institute, 2003.

Farrington, J. P. Deshingkar, C. Johnson, and D. Start, *Policy Windows and Livelihoods Futures*, New Delhi: Oxford University Press, 2006.

Ghate, P., 'Serving Migrants Sustainably: Remittance Services Provided by an MFI in Gujarat', *Economic and Political Weekly*, 23 April 2005, pp. 1740–46.

Kleih, U., R. Som, Y. Kumar, S. K Jena, A. Singh, and L. Singh, 'Household Access to Rural Non-farm Livelihoods: Synthesis of Participatory Rural Appraisals and Questionnaire Surveys in Four Blocks of Madhya Pradesh', NRI Report no: 2378, May 2005.

Lipton, M., 'Migration from Rural Areas of Poor Countries: The Impact on Rural Productivity and Income Distribution', *World Development*, 1980, pp. 227.

Mosse, D., S. Gupta, M. Mehta, V. Shah, and J. Rees, 'Brokered Livelihoods: Debt, Labour Migration and Development in Tribal Western India', *Journal of Development Studies*, 38(5), June 2002, pp. 59–87.

——, S. Gupta, and V. Shah, 'On the Margins in the City: Adivasi Seasonal Labour Migration in Western India', *Economic and Political Weekly*, 9 July 2005, pp. 3025–38.

——, S. Gupta, M. Mehta, V. Shah, and J. Rees, 'Seasonal Labour Migration in Tribal (Bhil) Western India', Report to DFID–India, New Delhi, KRIBP Working Paper, Centre for Development Studies, University of Wales, Swansea.

Shah A. and D.C. Sah, 'Poverty among Tribals in South West Madhya Pradesh: Has Anything Changed over Time?', *Journal of Human Development*, 5(2), July 2004, pp. 249–63.

Virgo, K., R. Yadav, Y. Kanugo, and R. Bond, 'Agriculture or Livelihoods? Experiences of Practitioners and Beneficiaries of the DFID-funded Western India Rainfed Farming Project', Paper presented at Tropical Agriculture Association Seminar, University of Bath, 3 July 2003.

# 5

# Circular Migration Streams from Southern Rajasthan
## Brick Kiln Work, Work in Textile Markets, and Ice Cream Vending

*Bharati Joshi and Rajiv Khandelwal*

## INTRODUCTION

Within the diverse ecological and human landscape of Rajasthan, the southern region occupies a unique niche. The region is traversed by the rugged Aravali ranges and is a concentrated pocket of Rajasthan's tribal communities—the Bhils, Garasias, and Meenas. Poverty is a dominant feature of the area with mean household incomes substantially below the national average and poor scores on virtually all quality of life indicators (Aravali 2003).[1]

Agricultural production is low with limited land available for cultivation, low rainfall, and inadequate irrigation cover. Agricultural productivity is also related to access to information, technologies, and markets—all of which have been poor in the case of tribal cultivators. Pockets of agriculture intensification do exist in the region but are led by non-tribal farmers who have access to irrigation. Despite considerable efforts to improve soil and water management through a succession of donor-supported programmes, the collective impacts on the quality of natural resources and community livelihoods has been modest. Livestock are also a significant feature of livelihoods, but again productivity is considerably below potential. Significant forest resources in the area have been degraded and make only small contributions to income and employment.

With the exception of mining and construction, virtually no other activity in the region generates significant local employment outside the farm sector. Government drought relief programmes do provide daily labour opportunities in drought years but these opportunities are limited. Migration has thus become the predominant source of income for the region as a whole and for tribal households in particular.

This chapter examines the social and economic opportunities and costs of migration from southern Rajasthan, which is one of the poorest tribal dominated regions of the country. Three little-studied migration streams are discussed: ice cream vending in south and west India; brick kiln work in north Gujarat; and work in textile mills and shops in Gujarat. The evidence is drawn from studies undertaken in early 2007 by the Aajeevika Bureau, an agency providing support to rural migrants from southern Rajasthan. The chapter provides insights into the nature of migrant labour contracts, the role of social networks, and power relations in shaping the outcomes of migration.

The chapter begins by setting out the overall context of migration from southern Rajasthan before turning to a discussion of the three migration streams, recruitment practices, living and working conditions, and economic returns. The final section examines the constraints which migrant labourers, in general, face, and goes on to highlight the nature of interventions that will help them overcome these constraints.

## MIGRATION FROM SOUTHERN RAJASTHAN

A study conducted by the Aajeevika Bureau indicates that migration now accounts for nearly half of the household income for all households in the region and for tribal households it is over 65 per cent. The incidence of migration is not only large but is spreading rapidly to new destinations and sectors in response to opportunities created by economic growth.

Construction and mining engage the largest number of tribal migrants. There is indeed a highly skilled group of construction technicians among the Rajasthani migrants—plumbers, carpenters, masons, and painters. However, the presence of tribal labour at these more remunerative levels is limited. Mining and quarrying enterprises have thrived on the availability of cheap tribal labour. Brick kilns across Gujarat engage large groups of Rajasthani tribal labourers. One of the case studies in this chapter concerns brick kiln workers.

The hotel and restaurant establishments across towns, cities, and highways of the states of Gujarat and Maharashtra are the other major employers of migrant labour. Often child labourers from Rajasthan enter this sector working as helpers, sweepers, cleaners, and waiters while only a few enter the more skilled tasks of cooking. Thousands of tribal and other poor migrant workers find work as domestic help in the cities of Gujarat.

In the industrial areas, factories, and commodity markets of Gujarat, tribal labour is engaged in headloading or pushing carts. This is a physically punishing form of wage labour but employment is steady and the wages are relatively higher. Small manufacturing and processing units are the other major sector which tribal labourers work on a seasonal basis. For example, the textile market of Surat, covered in detail in this chapter, attracts thousands of young tribal migrants, but few find long-term employment.

Large numbers of tribal families seasonally migrate to farms in Gujarat to work as share tenants, usually for a paltry share of the harvest. Over the past five years there has been a huge upsurge in the movement of tribal children from south Rajasthan to work as cotton pollinators on cotton farms across the vast tracts of north Gujarat.

GROWING NUMBERS, CHANGING DESTINATIONS, AND OCCUPATIONS

Migration from southern Rajasthan is not only large in terms of the number of people it involves but also in terms of targetting newer destinations and sectors, especially in response to the opportunities created by rapid urban growth in Gujarat and Maharashtra. While Gujarat is the key destination for Rajasthani migrants, mega cities like Mumbai and Pune are also attracting more Rajasthani migrants. Workers from this region are now found in cities as distant as Bangaluru (the new official name of Bangalore) and Chennai. A few have also migrated to the Gulf.

BRICK KILN WORKERS OF KOTDA

The Context

The vast, remote block of Kotda in the south of Udaipur district has long been considered an intractable development challenge despite its ample forests and natural wealth. Kotda has a population of nearly 183,000 of which 90 per cent is tribal. It is amongst the poorest blocks of Rajasthan on many counts such as literacy, health, infrastructure, and services. The terrain is mountainous and the potential of cultivation very limited. Landholdings are less than one hectare on average and most farmers take a single crop for home consumption.

The block headquarter is 120 kms from Udaipur, and is very poorly connected. The block is very near the border with Gujarat and towns in north Gujarat such as Khedbrahma, Idar, and Palanpur are more accessible than the district headquarters.

## Migration Streams from Kotda

With very little local employment available, the economy of Kotda depends heavily on migration. The principal destinations for tribal migrants from Kotda are prosperous towns and villages in north Gujarat. Unlike other blocks of Udaipur district that send workers to urban and industrial areas, Kotda's labour export is mainly to agricultural pockets, although there are other streams as listed below. Low literacy levels and lack of skills have pushed the migrating tribals towards unskilled and low paying work.

The major migration streams from Kotda include:

- Migration of families from July to March for sharecropping in north Gujarat (known as *bhagiyas*);
- Migration of children and adolescents for work on cotton farms in north Gujarat; and
- Migration for semi-skilled stone work within Rajasthan (to Pindwara, Sumerpur, Falna).

Seasonality is evident in all the streams: agricultural labourers migrate during July (*kharif* sowing) and again in November (harvest) and then November (*rabi* sowing) and March. Many work as share-croppers and in that case, migrate for the entire cropping season, other wage labourers from October to June, and brick kiln labourers from November to May every year. During other times of the year, these people till their own small and marginal lands or work locally.

The cluster of panchayats around the Mandwa region of Kotda block is the main source of migrant labour for the brick kilns of Gujarat as well as for those in the neighbouring districts of Pali and

Sirohi in Rajasthan. Migration to brick kilns began 25 years ago and has grown to a major stream.

## A Profile of Brick Kiln Workers

Typically groups of families from the same hamlet or village work in a brick kiln. They leave as a group, live on the site as a makeshift community and return after the cycle is over. Young and able-bodied men, in the age group of 20–30 years, are considered most suited for this hard work and men outnumber women by 5:1. Almost 78 per cent of the migrant brick kiln workers encountered during the study were less than 30 years of age. The entry age for a brick kiln labourer is only 17 years.

Clearly a lack of local employment options drives the largest number of youth (60 per cent) to brick kiln work. A few (21.6 per cent) have followed their relatives and acquaintances into the kiln fields, while others (15 per cent) have taken the advice of brick kiln mates/contractors. In the initial years, all migrants toil as mere labourers in the kilns. Some later become labour contractors or mates.

## The Recruitment Process

Brick kiln workers are usually recruited by a mate or contractor. He belongs to the same village or panchayat as the labourers. The contractor and kiln owner estimate the number of workers needed and the contractor recruits them from the village. Many kiln owners are potters by caste. These days other castes are also entering the business because of its high profit margins.

The process of scouting and hiring begins about 15–20 days before the start of the brick-making season. Typically the labour contractor pays an advance to the labourers in order to 'book' them for the cycle. This payment is usually around of Rs 3,000.

## Economic Returns

Wages are paid either on the basis of pieces of bricks prepared or the number of days of labour, depending on the kind of task being performed by a brick kiln labourer. The average earnings of a brick kiln worker are Rs 50—60 per day or roughly Rs 900–1800 per cycle of 16–30 days.

The earning from *patla* work ranges from Rs 180 to Rs 200 per 1000 bricks prepared; while that from *khadkan* work is in the range

Table 5.1: Nature of Tasks and the Corresponding Wages
of Brick Kiln Labour

| Task | Nature of Work | Daily Work Hours | Wage Rate(in Rs.) |
| --- | --- | --- | --- |
| Brick making | Skilled | 13 – 15 | 90 – 95 |
| Headloading of bricks | Unskilled | 09 – 10 | 50 – 60 |
| Arrangement of bricks as | | | |
| *patla* or *khadkan* | Skilled | 09 – 10 | 70 – 80 |
| Coal and kiln firing work | Unskilled | 09 – 10 | 60 – 70 |

*Source*: Authors.

of Rs 100 to Rs 120 per 1000 finished bricks (see Table 5.1) Hence, if 100,000 bricks have been prepared, the patla workers are paid between Rs 18,000 to Rs 20,000, while the khadkan workers receive between Rs 10,000 to Rs 12,000.

## Prospects For Upward Mobility among Brick Kiln Workers

The earliest job of each new recruit in a brick kiln involves loading-unloading of bricks and coal-breaking. They gradually move on to more responsible and better paying, *khadkan* and *patla* work. Kiln workers usually continue until the age of 40–5 years. Only a few of the more enterprising labourers turn into labour contractors after completing two-three migration cycles during which time they acquire a better understanding of the intricacies of the labour recruitment process. When a labourer first becomes a mate, he does not automatically or immediately win the trust of the kiln owner. Hence, he continues working under the guidance of an established contractor who takes labour contracts on the former's behalf until the newcomer has become established in the trade.

## Living Conditions at the Destination

The contractor provides extremely basic accommodation to the workers. The dwelling units are usually within the kiln compound and are made of bricks and plastic sheets. Three to four labourers occupy each room. The rooms have low ceilings and living conditions are cramped. Tough living conditions at their destination often drive the new recruits back home mid-way through the brick-production cycle.

Migrating labourers bring part of their grain requirement from the village and buy the rest at the destination. This is the main expenditure, while at the brick kilns grocery shops sell grain at more

BOX 5.1: WHO DOES WHAT IN A BRICK KILN

There are two kinds of kiln workers:

(i) *Patla workers:* Patla refers to the systematic arrangement of raw or ready-to-be-fired bricks in a brick field. Each such arrangement usually has about 100,000 bricks. Raw bricks are prepared by the patla workers using moulds. Usually, all workers at a patla arrangement belong to one family; alternatively, five to seven close friends or distant relatives form a work-group to accomplish the task of raw-brick making.

(ii) *Khadkan:* Khadkan is that stage in the production process of bricks during which raw bricks from the patla arrangement, that is, the previous stage, are arranged along with coal, fuelwood, and other fuel to form a kiln and fired to make finished bricks.

Both men and women work as labourers in the brick kilns. However, jobs are segmented by gender. Women carry bricks as head-loads within the kiln field, break coal into smaller pieces, and cook food for groups of labourers at the work site. Men, on the other hand, make bricks, arrange them into stacks, prepare and fire the kiln, transport finished bricks as headloads, and also engage in breaking coal into smaller pieces. Since both male and female members of the migrating families can engage in the brick manufacturing process, it is common for them to bring their children to the destination. Children are also involved in both the stages, wherein they work as headloaders, carrying from five to seven bricks between patla and khadkan arrangements in the kiln fields. They usually do not go to school when they are at the kilns.

than the market price. Being migrants from outside the state, these labourers do not have access to subsidized ration supplies under the Public Distribution System (PDS) in Gujarat, even when they are entitled to access PDS supplies in their source villages in Rajasthan.

## Working Conditions of Brick Kiln Workers

Kiln work is tantamount to bonded labour: working hours are long (15–16 hours a day), safety and hygiene is non-existent and movement is restricted. Injuries are common especially for those who carry bricks and fire the kilns. First aid is seldom available at work sites. When paid a piece-rate, the labourers try to load and carry as many bricks as possible at a time, increasing the chances of being injured. Any medical expenses or hospitalization charges incurred by injured labourers are initially paid for by the mate, but later on cut from their wages. Such unforeseen expenses can eat into 20 per cent of the season's earnings of a labourer, not including the number of work-days lost due to the injury.

Final wages are settled only after the manufacture of bricks has been completed. Although the minimum estimated daily wage of a brick kiln worker is Rs 60, nearly 45 per cent of the workers contacted were found earning less than the minimum wage. The difference is on account of variance in work completed, specific tasks, and unexplained cuts in the wage payments to these informal sector workers.

## Specific Vulnerabilities and Policy Implications

A major cost of brick kiln work which has long term implications for the perpetuation of poverty, is the inability of the workers to send their children to school while they are at the kilns. None of the kilns in our study had any kind of arrangement for educating the workers' children. Apart from that, the living and working conditions of kiln workers and their families are dirty and dangerous with a high risk of personal injury. Hardly any of them had saved anything even after years of migrating to the kilns and were trapped in a continuous cycle of borrowing and repayment.

The educational needs of brick kiln workers' children must be given top priority (this is discussed in the concluding chapter). As of now there are no interventions in this area. However, other NGO initiatives could provide a model for intervention for the migrants from southern Rajasthan.

There is a need to create public awareness and put pressure on government agencies to ensure that working and living conditions of brick kiln workers are improved. Although this issue has been in the public eye for a while now, it has proved to be notoriously difficult to change. The labour department in Karnataka, for example, has raided several brick kilns but with very disappointing results.

Other needs include access to the PDS so that workers do not have to purchase grain at market rates, registration of workers and contractors, and written agreements between them.

TEXTILE MARKET WORKERS FROM GOGUNDA

The Context

Gogunda is a hilly block in Udaipur district. Almost 44 per cent of Gogunda's population belongs to the scheduled tribes. Only 13.09 per cent of its total geographical area is cultivable, of which only 18 per cent is irrigated. As per current estimates of the Aajeevika Bureau, close to 83 per cent of the total 30,133 households in Gogunda derive a major share of their income from labour; 63 per cent of these households have one or more persons migrating. Furthermore, 60 per cent of this migration is outside the state of Rajasthan.

Migrants from Gogundas are found everywhere in cities such as Ahmedabad, Rajkot, Surat, Mumbai, Pune, and beyond. More than 75 per cent of Gogundas in Gujarat are engaged in unskilled or semi-skilled jobs such as working at construction sites, in hotels, running tea stalls, or working in the textile market town of Surat.

According to the Aajeevika Bureau's estimates there are over 60,000 labourers from Rajasthan in the textile markets of Surat (Aajeevika Bureau 2004). Surat is the largest market for synthetic cloth in Asia. More than twenty million metres of cloth is produced and traded in Surat every day (Breman 1996). It is also one of the main industrial towns of the country, with other important industries such as diamond cutting and polishing, construction businesses and a well-established chemical industry all of which employ immigrants.

Profile of Textile Market Workers

The workers engaged in the textile markets of Surat are mainly wage labourers hired through labour contractors. More than 60 per cent of these labourers belong to the scheduled tribes (Bhil Gametis from Udaipur and Rajsamand)—the others are Rajputs, Meghwals, and even Brahmins indicating that migration cuts across all social groups. This is due to the fact that there is hardly any local work available. More than 40 per cent of the labourers contacted during the study confirmed having entered the market as labourers while they were between 10 to 14 years of age. More than 15,000 of the 60,000 workers in Surat are younger than 14, making it one of the main child labour-intensive industries in the region (Aajeevika Bureau 2004). These young labourers are described as ideal workers by shop owners. In the words of a labour contractor from south

Rajasthan, they are 'energetic, pliable, easy to control and have low costs of maintenance'. Many of the migrant labourers are unmarried at the time of their entry in the textile market.

The textile industry includes four kinds of factories and establishments:

(i) Yarn mills: Yarn is manufactured here and the main jobs are machine operation, packing yarn, and transporting yarn;
(ii) Looms: These manufacture cloth. There are 700,000 looms in Surat; the main job is operating the machines;
(iii) Cloth mills: The grey cloth obtained from the looms is bleached and coloured here to make finsihed cloth which is, then, sold on the textile market;
(iv) Textile market: There are more than 30 textile markets in Surat. This is where fabric cutting, and folding are done before sale to retail outlets and wholesalers.

Migrants from Gogunda work mainly in the textile market (see Box 5.2 below) and rarely find jobs in other parts of the textile industry where jobs are better paid.

---

BOX 5.2: WHO DOES WHAT IN THE TEXTILE MARKET

There are three different kinds of workers in the textile market: (i) the non-tribals, mainly Jains, who are the traders; (ii) contractors who are mainly STs; and (iii) skilled and unskilled textile workers. The first migrants to Surat from southern Rajasthan were non-tribals who established themselves as traders. They later hired tribal workers from Gogunda to expand their trade in Surat. The rising demand for skilled and unskilled labourers in the textile markets of Surat gave rise to the system of labour contractors who then started recruiting children and young labourers from their own villages. Despite a long history of working in the textile market, tribal workers from Gogunda have remained in unskilled work on highly exploitative terms.

---

Interviews revealed that more than 60 per cent of the new migrants work as unskilled workers performing simple tasks like saree folding, saree-stitching and packing, and cleaning the shops for the first few weeks. On the other hand, non-tribal entrants are employed in better paid jobs on the shop floor.[2]

## The Recruitment Process

The recruitment of textile market workers is a multi-staged process that starts in the villages. Relatives and acquaintances provided links to the contractors in about 55 per cent of the migrants interviewed, followed by labour contractors and local shopkeepers (36 per cent). In fact, the former serve as informal labour agents for the textile traders in Surat and each labour-sourcing relative or acquaintance gets paid Rs 70 to Rs 80 per worker supplied.

## Career Progression in the Surat Textile Market

Only about 5 per cent new migrant labourers are able to make a direct entry into the semi-skilled work such as cutting sarees and fully skilled tasks such as embroidery. These tasks are also better paid than the unskilled ones (Table 5.2). None of these skilled labourers interviewed were tribal, and all were educated and experienced. In fact, there is a direct correlation between a labourer's educational level and the type of work he is given in the textile market.

Table 5.2: Tasks and Monthly Earnings of Labourers in the Textile Market

| S. No. | Work | Skilled (S)/Semi-Skilled (SS)/ Unskilled (US) | Average Monthly Wage (in Rupees) |
|---|---|---|---|
| 1 | Saree cutting | SS | 2,500 |
| 2 | Saree folding | US | 1,500 |
| 3 | Stitching a folded saree | US | 550 |
| 4 | Saree packing | SS | 2,000 |
| 5 | Embroidery | S | 5,000 |
| 6 | Salesman on shop-floor | S | 3,000 |
| 7 | Other shop-based assistance | US | 950 |
| 8 | Cooking food for other labourers | SS | 1,000 |
| 9 | Middle men in the industry | S | 3,500 |
| 10 | Loom or mill worker | S | 3,000 |

*Source*: Authors.

## The Migration Cycle

Surat's textile market functions throughout the year; hence migration occurs round the year. A majority of the workers migrated for six months or more. Since a majority of these workers are child labourers, the contractor pressurizes them and their families to keep them at the textile market for as long as possible.

Although some workers moved to other contractors and traders within the first year, roughly 90 per cent remained attached to the same employer in successive migration cycles.

Upon nearing the age of 30, these workers are either laid off or they seek employment in other areas, because of the demanding and poor working and living conditions in Surat. A small proportion moves to more skilled and better paying jobs in the textile market of Surat.

### Living Conditions of Migrant Textile Labourers

Textile workers share small, dingy, poorly-ventilated, and dirty rooms (6–10 to a room) Each room measures about 10 ft × 12 ft. The rent and all other expenses including water and electricity charges, and food are borne by the contractor. He tries to skimp on these expenses as much as possible and provides the most basic food.

### Working Conditions

The working conditions vary by task: the worst off are child labourers who are assigned unskilled tasks, who often have to work long hours in dark and cramped shop basements (to escape legal action for hiring child labour). Those working on the shop floor or in the open are better off.

Working days are long—usually 10–12 hours for sari folders. On average, four to five labourers are employed in each sari shop and they cut, measure, fold, stitch, and pack 2,000 to 2,500 saris everyday. Coupled with this, they often have to walk more than an hour to and from work every day. The labourers are served tea once or twice a day, and are also given an hour off in the afternoon. Corporal punishment is common, even for small faults.

It is hardly surprising that many children give up the work and return to their villages without collecting their wages. It is not uncommon for children to hitch rides back because they have no money to pay for the journey and this puts them at considerable risk.

### Managing Finances

Workers in Surat are generally employed on a monthly wage basis and only 23 per cent of the labourers received a daily wage. In the absence of a written agreement between the contractor or trader and the labourer, underpayment, delayed or irregular wage payment is the norm. Since most are child labourers, formal contracts cannot be entered into. Added to this, child workers face the problem of not being able to save and this puts them at the mercy of the contractor who keeps their money and settles the payment at the end of the migration cycle in the village. This leaves the child with very little control over his or her earnings.

Workers return home up to four times in a year. Regular remittances in such a situation are ensured through friends and relatives (in 84 per cent cases), and less frequently through contractors (9 per cent) and demand drafts/money orders (6 per cent). The lack of education and the fear of complicated government procedures prevent these labourers from accessing formal remittance channels. However, their preferred medium of sending money (that is, through friends and acquaintances) is also risky, as there have been several cases of theft and delayed/under payment. Theft is rare when the contractor keeps the money, because he cannot risk the erosion of social networks and relationships in the source villages.

Unskilled migrants often take advances from their employers for health and other expenses. These advances bond the workers to their bosses year after year. But skilled and better paid embroidery workers and loom operators find it difficult to obtain advances from their employers because they are considered as a 'mobile' workforce without any loyalty to the employer. There is a huge demand for skilled workers in Surat.

## Specific Vulnerabilities and Policy Implications

Although NGOs and government officials working in the area are aware of the high levels of child labour in the textile markets of Surat little has been done to address the issue There is a need for systematic assessment of the magnitude of this phenomenon and development of policy responses for improving their working and living conditions. There is also a need to address the structural barriers faced by tribals in moving beyond unskilled and poorly paid work. This would require a combination of advocacy, awareness creation, legal action, and capacity building among migrants.

Specific interventions include:

- Helping migrant workers to voice their concerns and realize their rights;

- Helping them to form groups for mutual support and collective action;
- Registering migrant workers and contractors;
- Providing workers with access to microfinance;
- Improving transport links between source villages and destinations in Gujarat.

## ICE CREAM VENDORS OF RAILMAGRA

### The Context

Railmagra is a block of Rajsamand district in southern Rajasthan. In contrast with the more hilly and tribal inhabited areas, Railmagra is an OBC (Other Backward Caste)-dominated block of Rajsamand district. The OBCs (40 per cent of the total population) include people of Ahir, Jaat, Salvi, Kumawat, Mali, Prajapat, Gadari, Banjara, Kir, Kumhaar, Nai, and Dhobi communities. The block has 29 *panchayats* covering 99 revenue villages and a population of 113,238.

Despite a past of prosperous agriculture, Railmagra has witnessed many adverse changes including persistent drought, overexploitation of groundwater and population pressure on limited land resources. With land-based livelihoods becoming more difficult to sustain, migration has replaced farming as a major income source in the block. At the time of this study, 49 per cent of the families in Railmagra were found to depend primarily on migration, while only 21 per cent depended mainly on agriculture.

Migrant occupations are often linked to specific castes and this has shaped migration streams from Railmagra. The Jats work in the cloth mills of the Malwa region which has traditionally been a major destination for migrants from the region for a number of years. The Rajputs found work as security personnel, drivers, and recovery agents for moneylenders. These choices were determined not by traditional skills but by the social group's perception of what constitutes menial work. Slowly, they established themselves in stable occupations in bigger cities of the region. Sensing a business opportunity in the rising demand for dairy products in cities, migrants from Railmagra entered into the trade of sweets, snacks, and ice cream production. The Gadarias set up milk businesses, the Kumawats and Telis started manufacturing and selling *namkeen* (savoury snacks). Their employers are, more often than not, themselves the natives of Railmagra, who are willing to provide work and support the livelihoods of their old acquaintances, whom they can trust more than the workers from other places.

Ice cream vending has emerged as the most important occupation for youth from Railmagra. Ice cream vendors from Railmagra can be found manufacturing, hawking and selling their produce all over the country, from Jammu and Kashmir to Tamil Nadu, and from Gujarat to Orissa.

## Profile of Ice Cream Vendors

The typical ice cream vendor is a male who is under 26 years of age. Many ice cream vendors start working when they are around 15 years old. Railmagra has around 2,500 ice cream vendors belonging to different castes. Most work for a businessman, locally known as the 'cart owner', who owns a number of carts (locally called lorry). The cart owners are responsible for mapping vending routes, recruiting vendors, and manufacturing ice cream. Both the owner and the vendors sell ice cream.

Most ice cream vendors covered in the study were the eldest sons in their families and almost 70 per cent of them were married. OBCs—Jats, Gujjars, Ahirs, Gadariyas—are in a majority and constitute 55 per cent of the total vendor workforce from Railmagra. Youth from the scheduled castes (SCs 30 per cent) also work as vendors. Education up to the eighth grade seems to be the unwritten educational qualification needed to enter the trade because vendors are expected to record, and report their daily sales and earnings at the end of the day.

The migrant ice cream vendors from Railmagra can be divided into three broad skill categories, depending on their age and the number of migration cycles (or years) completed in the ice cream vending trade, as explained in Table 5.3. While the skilled (that is, the more experienced) ice cream vendors also manufacture ice cream on their own, the semi-skilled ones assist their cart owners in the process every night after the vending is over. The unskilled workers are entrusted only with the task of selling ice cream and their finances are more closely monitored by the cart owner. The study found almost 78 per cent of vendors to have less than three years of experience in this trade; 18 per cent had been in the trade for four to eight years; and only about 4 per cent had stayed for over eight years.

Table 5.3: Skill Categories of Migrant Ice Cream Vendors

| Skill category | Age Group(in Years) | Migration Cycles/Years in Trade |
| --- | --- | --- |
| Unskilled labour | 14—17 | < 3 |
| Semi-skilled labour | 18—23 | 3—5 |
| Skilled labour | > 23 | 5 and above |

*Source*: Authors.

## The Recruitment Process

The cart owners look for vendors in and around their own village. The cart owner typically makes an advance payment of Rs 2000–2500 to the head of the household. This payment is later adjusted against the final payment to the vendor. It is only the more skilled and experienced migrants who are paid a monthly wage on a regular basis at the destination. There is no written contract or agreement between the cart owner and the vendor to formalize the terms and conditions of this association.

A majority of youth sign up for ice cream vending during school vacations. They are initiated into this trade through their friends, relatives, or a well-acquainted local cart owner. Once recruited, ice cream vendors migrate for six to eight months at a time. They usually drop out of school.

## Destinations

Railmagra sends the largest number of ice cream vendors to Ahmedabad, Rajkot, Surat, Vapi, and Anand in Gujarat; to Pune, Solapur, Wardha, Nasik, and Mumbai in Maharashtra, and Hyderabad and Vishakhapatnam in Andhra Pradesh. Ice cream vendors from Railmagra are also reaching many small towns of Karnataka and Tamil Nadu. The long summers in south India mean that the ice cream has an uninterrupted demand. Many a times, the vendors are asked by their cartowners to move directly from their current destination in one state to another state, or they do so on their own, depending on demand.

The migration cycle usually lasts for 6–8 months. Most venders return home with the onset of the monsoon in June–July, first from the south Indian states, followed by others.

## Living Conditions of Ice Cream Vendors

More than 90 per cent migrant ice cream vendors from Railmagra live with their cart owners; the remaining form groups and live in rented premises. In both the cases, six to seven men share a small room. The same room also accommodates the raw material and equipments required for manufacturing ice cream. There are usually no facilities such as running water or toilets. The rent is paid by the cart owner who also pays for their food and other essentials like soap. Some cart owners also provide clothes to their workers.

Food is cooked once a day by one of the workers. Working days are very long and ice cream for the next day has to be prepared in the evening. Ice cream vendors rarely develop any kind of relationship with the communties at the destination and work and live on their own.

## Not Such a Cool Job

Ice cream vendors start their day at 5 am. Ice cream is stocked in the cart for the day and after a meal they are on the streets for the rest of the day. They work up to 16 hours in a day, pushing the cart through predetermined routes. Apart from the physical discomfort associated with standing long hours or pushing the ice cream cart through busy city roads, the vendors face several other problems in their day-to-day job. These include:

- Free ice cream demanded by local policemen;
- Harassment at the hands of drunkards and other anti-social elements;
- Underpayment by cart owners; and
- Sudden termination of duty without payment of arrears if there is a dispute with the cart owner.

Despite these problems, over 79 per cent of the ice cream vendors contacted as part of this study expressed a willingness to stay on in this trade with the dream of becoming a cart owner one day. However, only a few are able to become cart owners. By their second migration cycle, new recruits become competent in ice cream preparation and can be assigned that task as well.

Ill health is a major complaint among ice cream vendors. Congested and unhygienic living conditions, and poor nourishment make them vulnerable to infections and respiratory disorders. Further, there is a high incidence of sexually transmitted diseases (STDs) among them. Many tire of the physical demands of the trade and this is one of the most common reasons for ice cream vendors coming back home half-way through the migration cycle.

## Economic Returns

Ice cream vendors migrating to Gujarat and other parts of central India earn approximately Rs 800 to Rs 1500 per month. Those migrating to the distant south earn slightly more, but never more than Rs 2000. Since the boarding and lodging of the vendors are paid for by their employers, the ice cream vendors can theoretically save their entire wage every month. However, this seldom happens, because:

- The cart owners never pay the vendors in full; some or the other unaccountable deductions are made from the labourers' wages every month;
- The cart owners often deduct randomly determined amounts from the labourers' wages to pay for a broken glass or spoilt milk/ice cream;
- The wages retained by labourers in cash are prone to theft or these get spent on day-to-day living and recreation.

There are many circumstances in which the vendor can have his earnings entirely forfeited—for example, if he returns from the destination mid-way on account of poor health or a family emergency or decides to shift to another employer at the destination, he may lose most of his wages. To prevent sudden drop outs, cart owners hold back some part of the wage, even after a cycle is satisfactorily completed, as a surety for the next season's attachment. Those vendors who frequently change their destinations and/or cart owners fail to accumulate savings and remain poorer than those who stay on to complete the annual migration cycle.

Final payment for a cycle is settled by the cart owner in the migrant's source village, in the presence of his guardians. Very few vendors have a formal bank account. Most save in gold if there are accumulated savings. Some migrants also lend money on interest to their fellow workers and relatives at the destination. Formal remittance mechanisms are rarely used. It is not uncommon for a migrant ice cream vendor to borrow in his source village to enable his household to tide over at least one migration cycle, before his first earnings from migration come home.

## The Cart Owners—Are They Any Better Placed?

Most cart owners belong to a slightly higher class and social group than vendors. Many were engaged in traditional occupations (like pottery), or they managed family businesses (like running sweet shops) or worked in cloth mills before becoming cart owners. During the first migration cycle, the cart owner recovers his costs. But in subsequent cycles they are able to earn Rs 20,000 to Rs 25,000 per cart per cycle.

Though better placed than the migrant vendors, the cart owners bear the risk of losses of raw material (spoilage, spillage, etc.), loss of business during rainy and winter seasons, competition with other cart owners and bribing local police and officers. The cart owner has also to bear the losses or make-do with diminished earnings if a vendor leaves suddenly.

## Specific Vulnerabilities and Policy Implications

The working and living conditions of vendors are difficult and far from any kind of definition of decent work. Besides this, the job does not offer prospects for upward mobility to most vendors barring a few who make it as cart owners.

There is a need to recognize the importance of ice cream vending as an occupation for the rural poor in policies and documents related to small scale enterprise development in the region and develop interventions to support them. Specific policies and interventions that could help vendors are:

- Financial services including savings and credit schemes so that vendors stand a better chance of investing in purchasing carts and starting their own businesses;
- Organizing migrants into common interest groups to enable them to access institutional support from the government and other donors;
- Legal support such as facilitating a written agreement between the cart owners and ice cream vendors; registration of both the parties; settling work related disputes between them;
- Pre-migration counselling on health risks and management, legal issues, and occupational safety matters.

CONCLUSION

The migration process in each of the migration streams studied is such that only a few relatively powerful individuals who have the right social networks, some education and/or capital are able to control the market and take a major share of the profits. Such people are either labour contractors or proprietors of businesses. For a vast majority of illiterate and poor tribals who come from families with few assets and contacts with powerful people, work is on highly exploitative terms with few prospects for accumulation and exiting poverty in the longer term.

Nevertheless, migration does help the family to cope with the shortage of employment locally and provides them with cash that is critical for their survival. The importance of such migration should therefore not be underestimated and policy should aim to reduce the hardship and risks faced by poor tribal migrants.

The case studies provide evidence of the many market imperfections that permeate rural labour markets and render the simplistic demand and supply analyses of neo-classical economics meaningless. Common to all four occupations is the critical role played by market intermediaries, who are often from the same social background. These intermediaries provide the link between poor, unskilled migrants from disadvantaged social groups and their employers in cities and industries. However, intermediaries are well-placed to play the market to their own advantage and can exploit cheap labour in a number of ways illustrated by the case studies. On the whole, migrants are paid irregularly, often underpaid and cheated in a variety of ways which include giving them poor food and not providing adequate housing and sanitation.

The case studies also provide information on the rough living conditions of migrants and the lack of adequate health and safety measures at work which are the result of callous action by intermediaries and the flouting of labour laws by employers. They do so in the knowledge that they are very unlikely to be caught and punished.

While many of the problems are common to the occupations studied, there are also important differences. Notable are the high incidence of child labour in the textile industry and in brick-kilns, and the high risk of injury in loading and unloading. These require focused attention and interventions and a number of suggestions for practical steps that can be taken by government and civil society organizations have been made.

The Aajeevika Bureau is grappling with many of these issues. So, are technical support, human resource development, and counselling enough to enable and empower the migrant communities to stand up and get counted, or to move out of the poverty trap? Will short term migration ever bring about significant and sustainable improvements in the livelihoods of those households? Is complementing the existing livelihood systems of migrants enough or is a more comprehensive and multisectoral approach required? What kind of an agency or a coalition of agencies will be required to improve the lot of migrants? These issues require constant deliberation, discussion, and reframing through learning from grassroots experiences. Some of these questions are revisited in Chapter 10 which details the Aajeevika Bureau experience.

## NOTES

1. Aravali is a state-level development research organization in Rajasthan.
2. However this privilege is reserved for males. Girls and women are excluded from working on the floor in textile shops and are relegated to lower paying and more physically demanding jobs.

## REFERENCES

Aajeevika Bureau, 'Status of Rajasthani Migrant Labour in Key Destination Areas of Gujarat', 2004.

Aravali, 'Aajeevika—Livelihoods in Rajasthan: Status, Constraints and Strategies for Sustainable Change', Discussion Paper Series 6, Human Development Report Centre, UNDP, 2003.

Breman, J., *Footloose Labour—Working in India's Informal Economy*, Cambridge: Cambridge University Press, 1996.

# 6

# Circular Migration in Bihar
## The Money Order Economy

*Priya Deshingkar, Sushil Kumar, Harendra Kumar Choubey,*
*and Dhananjay Kumar*

## INTRODUCTION

The incidence of out-migration from rural Bihar is greater than anywhere else in India. A combination of circumstances, both natural and societal, has created a situation in the state where sending a family member out to earn is a basic survival strategy. While migration from flood and drought prone areas is not new, the closure of industries as well as law and order problems added to the outflow of people, with a marked increase in migration after 1990.

This chapter is based on a month long study conducted in six districts of Bihar namely Nalanda, Gaya, Muzzaffarpur, Purnia, Madhubani, and Sitamarhi. Of these, four are among the poorest districts in India.[1] A minimum of two multi-caste villages were studied in each district, one remote and the other well-connected in order to examine any effects of connectedness on migration patterns. In addition, one extra village was studied in Muzzaffarpur and Purnia each to ensure that we captured the dynamics of migration among Muslims.

Despite numerous studies of migration in Bihar, aspects of its complexity, diversity, and impact on different groups of people remain poorly understood. This chapter aims to fill some of these gaps. It is based on a consultancy on migration for the World Bank funded Bihar Rural Livelihoods Project (BRLP) and the IFAD funded Women's Empowerment and Livelihoods Project in the mid-Gangetic Plain (WELFMGP) (Deshingkar et al. 2006).

The chapter consists of three parts. The first describes the context in which migration occurs and provides background information on the rural economy, farm and non-farm employment trends, agricultural productivity, infrastructure, and education. The next part contains the main findings of the study by district focusing on variations in migration and remittance patterns by social group, occupation, and destination. Part three discusses sources of risk and vulnerability and how these are being addressed by various migrant support programmes. The final part discusses the way forward and practical steps that can be taken to support migrants.

A description of the villages studied is provided in Appendix 6.1. The main sources of primary evidence are key informant interviews and focus group discussions. We would like to stress that figures provided in the chapter (related to number of migrants, earnings, remittances, and savings, etc.) are best estimates made by highly experienced professionals as well as migrants themselves and should therefore be regarded as reasonably accurate. A number of secondary sources have also been used including research studies on migration, poverty, and rural development in Bihar as well as data from the Indian Post Office and government officials. Information collected through interviews and group discussions has been

Map 6.1: District Map of Bihar
*Source*: http://gov.bih.nic.in/profile/Districts.htm

triangulated and cross checked with other reliable sources and this has been indicated in each instance through referencing.

## THE CONTEXT

Bihar is the poorest state in India with the lowest per capita income amongst the major states. In 2004–5, the real per capita gross state domestic product (GSDP) was Rs 4,435 while the nominal per capita GSDP was Rs 7,080 which were less than half that of the neighbouring state of Jharkhand. More than 40 per cent of the population lives below the poverty line. It is also the third most populous state with a total population of 83 million. The state's performance lags seriously behind others. Although moderate progress was made during the 1990s (1993–4 to 1999–2000) in reducing poverty by nearly 7 percentage points, the rate of poverty reduction was well below the national average. Current projections are that Bihar is likely to fall well behind on most of the Millennium Development Goals (MDG) targets for 2015. Bihar's rank for human development index (HDI) among the Indian states has remained unchanged at 15 since 1981, while its score has increased marginally from 0.237 in 1981, to 0.308 in 1991, to 0.267 in 2001. It fares very badly on a number of indicators. In the 1990s Bihar had the lowest Gender Equality Index in India, and had witnessed a decline in absolute terms over the earlier period. In the 2001 census, it had the lowest literacy rate in the country—48 per cent against a national average of 65 per cent, and it is the only state where primary enrolment fell between 1993 and 1999, and 80 per cent of the household heads in the bottom income quintile have no education (World Bank 2005).

Bihar is a predominantly agrarian economy with a small manufacturing base. According to the NSS, cultivation and farm labour together account for 80 per cent of employment. Crop productivity has been below the Indian average for most cereals. The causes for the large yield gap include: low investment rates, lack of water management with annual flooding of the Gangetic plain, weak transport and marketing infrastructure, as well as severe fragmentation of land holdings. 31 districts are flood prone and 11 are drought prone.

Poverty is predominantly rural in Bihar and is associated with limited access to land and livestock, poor education and healthcare, as well as low-paid occupations and social status. NSS data show that

75 per cent of the poor were landless or near landless in 1999–2000, and the land reforms introduced in 1950 have been largely ineffective. North Bihar and the Chhotanagpur Plateau are significantly poorer than southern parts of the region, the differences being explained in part by infrastructural and geographic factors such as agro-ecology, population density, infrastructure and transport, but there are also important societal differences: SCs and STs are likely to be three times poorer than other castes. They are also three times more likely to be landless, and their status on these two counts has remained virtually unchanged since 1993–4. Among Muslims, the prevalence of poverty is also higher than among other groups, at 49.5 per cent in rural and 44.8 per cent in urban areas (ADRI 2006).

Bihar has a poor record on government service provision and poverty alleviation programmes, including serious mis-targeting in the Public Distribution System (PDS) and chronic teacher absenteeism. Electricity supplies have been erratic: in 2003–4, per capita consumption of electricity was 44.85Kwh as compared to 606Kwh at the national level. Less than 8 per cent of the 81,655 km of roads in Bihar are national or state highways, with some 45 per cent of the road network unpaved.

The History of Migration in Bihar

There is a long history of migration in Bihar and this has been studied in depth by a number of scholars. According to the 1998 Uttar Pradesh-Bihar Living Standards Survey conducted by the World Bank,[2] 95 per cent of migrants from Bihar are male, migration is highest in the richest and poorest quintiles, and the poorest migrate for shorter durations. The ratio of remittances to household consumption was reported to be 4 per cent on average and lower for SCs and STs (though there may be some under-reporting here, as estimates reported below are much higher).

Studies in north Bihar (Karan 2003) show an increase of migration rates from 28 per cent to 49 per cent in a 17-year period. All caste groups, as well as Muslims, migrate and the recent increase has been most marked in OBCs, SCs, and Muslims. Remittances account for approximately one-third of total average annual income in sample villages. As expected, higher castes remit more, and the amount remitted by Muslims is disproportionately high. The most common use of remittances was to cover consumption needs and medical expenditure.

A study of 36 villages across six districts (Nalanda, Rohtas, Gopalganj, Gaya, Madhubani, and Purnia) in north and central Bihar by Dayal and Karan (2004) found that roughly 12 per cent of males in the sample households were seasonal migrants and 9 per cent permanent migrants. In general, poor and marginal farmers migrated seasonally or commuted and the rich migrated permanently. It was found that poorer Forward Castes (FC) were also engaged in seasonal migration due to the stigma of working as manual workers locally. The study, while highlighting the vulnerability of migrants and migration as a coping strategy also shows that young people are now consciously opting to migrate to explore other areas and, in the case of lower castes, to break away from caste oppression in the village.

As regards the socio-economic status of Muslims, a study conducted by the Patna-based Asian Development Research Institute (ADRI)[3] in 2004 found that two out of every three Muslim households in rural Bihar send at least one of its working members away to earn. Only men, generally in their 20s or 30s, migrate and there is a very high percentage of *de facto* female-headed households. International migration is found only among Muslims: more than 40 per cent of rural Muslim migrants from Siwan and Gopalganj district head for Gulf countries. The average annual remittance by migrants from rural areas is about Rs 1,350 per month, and from urban migrants is Rs 1,840 per month.

However, scholars differ in their conclusions on the drivers and impacts of migration. For example, de Haan's study of migrants from Saran to the industrial areas of Kolkata[4] argues that early out-migration was not necessarily the result of underdevelopment—rather, early development contributed to out-migration. He also suggests that the income that was derived from this migratory work helped to maintain a high population density and high out-migration and population density reinforced each other. He differs from others (Iyer et al. 2004)[5] who have emphasized the distress-nature of migration. De Haan views migration as a potentially accumulative household strategy that builds on existing migratory links and traditions.

## MIGRATION PATTERNS IN THE STUDY DISTRICTS

There is no doubt that migration in all six districts has shown a marked increase within the previous decade.[6] The reasons include the closure of local industrial units, reduced local employment opportunities due to law and order problems or political unrest, and the emergence of new opportunities in industries mainly outside Bihar where members of the village have contacts. It is also evident that migration among lower castes is a relatively recent phenomenon in many locations. In Madhubani, for example, migration began with the BCs and OBCs. SCs followed later using their connections with the early BC and OBC migrants.

Long distance migration rates do not appear to be affected by the level of connectedness of the village. For example, there are very high rates from remote as well as well-connected villages. But well-connected villages have more commuters. Migrants are usually single men, in the age group of 15–45. However, brick kiln migrants and intrastate rural–rural migrants often take their wives and children with them.

Women, older children, and the elderly are left behind. We often heard accounts of entire villages where hardly any young men were seen. Although many upper caste and BC women staying behind do not work outside the home, those belonging to poorer households (SC and EBC) work in farms locally.

Table 6.1 summarizes the major features of migration in the study districts. All have high migration rates driven originally by a combination of worsening poverty caused by flooding, water logging, land fragmentation, low farm productivity,[7] law and order problems, and industrial closures. But the situation has been changing. While some new migration streams have emerged, others that were widespread in the 1980s and 1990s are now waning. For example, migration for farm work to Punjab was a major migration stream a decade ago. But many migrants who were previously migrating to the farms in Punjab and Haryana are now migrating to major towns and cities all over India. We cover this in some detail at a later point in the chapter. Similarly, migrants who were once going to Nepal and the north-east are also migrating to urban centres in mainland India because of the political problems in Nepal and attacks against Biharis in Assam and Manipur. Migration to brick kilns[8] has grown in many locations and has offered some of the poorest social groups access to work outside the village but at a heavy price as we show later.

## MAJOR MIGRATION STREAMS

The main kinds of migration by social groups, occupation, and destination are discussed below. The first four are more common among the lowest castes and least educated people. These jobs also pay less than industrial work that has been captured by better connected and better educated OBCs, BCs,[9] and FCs. Under each broad heading we provide location specific information to highlight variations by district and social group.

### Farm Work within the State and Uttar Pradesh

The poorest (but not the very poorest who cannot migrate) SCs and EBCs with no land and no education, especially the Musahars[10] are often engaged in seasonal farm work in other districts within the state. This work is accessed through contacts. One person with good contacts finds work for a group of friends, neighbours, and relatives from the same village but no commissions are paid. Living and working conditions are basic—the farmer's main responsibility is to provide workers with a source of water and a roof over their heads. Payment is often in kind. Paddy workers are given food and 1/16th–1/12th of the crop for harvesting. Each family is able to bring back 8–10 quintals of paddy. The wage for weeding is 3.5 kg rice/day and for threshing it is Rs 30/day. Such farm work helps the family to smooth consumption and prevent downward slides into poverty. Trips are short and children are rarely brought along.

### Migration to Nearby Urban Centres for Rickshaw Pulling and Manual Work in the Lean Season

Poor SC, EBC, and BC households migrate for rickshaw pulling independently or through contacts during the lean season for 8–9 months in a year. A rickshaw can be hired for Rs 15–20 a day and the earnings can be anywhere between Rs 150–250 a day. A rickshaw puller can save up to Rs 100 a day after expenses. For a majority, the earnings have made the difference between a hand to mouth existence and being able to eat well. If work is available regularly and if the migration cycle is relatively long then this can become

## Table 6.1: Major Trends and Features of Migration in the Study Districts

| District name and characteristics | Caste, skill, and asset base of migrants | Type of work and when | Who migrates | Coping or accumulative and wage rate |
|---|---|---|---|---|
| Gaya: Gaya has the largest SC population in Bihar. Migration is highest in the blocks of Atree, Parahia, Kochas, Tekari, Imamganj, Bara Chattee, and Dumaria. | More than 50% of the landless or functionally landless SC and OBC households have one or more migrants. | Migration to brick kilns in UP, Jharkhand, MP, or within Bihar. rickshaw pulling in Patna, Ranchi and Jamshedpur are major streams. Brick kiln work for 7–8 months from October – July.<br><br>Rickshaw pullers make several trips of 7-15 days each earning Rs 50–80/day. | Musahar (SC) families migrate for brick kiln work and single men migrate for rickshaw pulling. 80 per cent migrants unskilled and poorly educated, in the age group of 17–35 years. Upper caste Bhumihar also migrating because they will not do manual work locally. | Brick kiln workers earn roughly Rs 175 per 1000 bricks. Rickshaw pullers earn up to Rs 2000/month. Both coping in most cases but accumulative for those who work in longer trips and spend little at the destination |
| Nalanda: Land is owned mainly by the upper castes: Brahmin, Bhumihar, Rajput, and Kayasth. | Migration is especially high among the SC castes (Ravidas/Chamar, Paswan, Pasi, Dhanuk, Dom, Rajak, and Musahar) who are mainly landless, near landless or marginal farmers. | Work in paddy fields, rickshaw pulling, brick kiln work and construction work are the major migration streams.<br><br>Migration increased sharply after 1995 due to law and order problems, caste conflict, poor electricity supply, and political unrest. | Musahars (SC), Paswan (SC), and Mallah (EBC) migrate with families for farm work within the state and brick kiln work in UP and West Bengal, stay there for 7–8 months/year.<br>BC and SC migrate to Bihar Sharif and Patna for rickshaw pulling.<br>Daily commuting to Nalanda and Bihar Sharif from nearby villages. | Paddy workers are given food and 1/16th–1/12th of the crop for harvesting. Each family is able to bring back 8-10 quintals of paddy. Helps the family to smooth consumption and in coping.<br>Wage for weeding is 3.5 kg rice/day and for threshing Rs 30/day. Coping. |

| Muzzaffarpur: The blocks of Gayghat, Katra, Aurai, Sakara, Gochaha, Kanti, Marwan, Runi Ghat, and Gai highly prone to floods and water logging. | About 80 per cent of the population of these blocks is either landless or near landless. Most of these households have at least one migrant. | Brick kiln work is the main migration stream. Roughly half the households migrate for 4–6 months and the remaining migrate for 9–10 months/year. | 5 per cent of the migrants mainly SC/STs work in nearby brick kilns. Women are not involved in this kind of work in this district.<br><br>Commuters work as construction labourers and rickshaw pullers. | Rickshaw pullers earn Rs 100 and are able to save about Rs 50–60/day. Coping but can become accumulative with regular work.<br><br>Construction workers earn Rs 60 – 100/day. Coping but can become accumulative with regular work.<br><br>Brick kiln workers earn Rs 70–80/day. Spending is usually high so they come home with Rs 1000–2000 at the end of the season. Coping for most. |
|---|---|---|---|---|
| Purnia: Acute unemployment and extreme poverty are widespread. The blocks of East Dagarwa, Baisee, | SC and EBCs comprise 75 per cent of the migrant population. They are mainly illiterate, unskilled, and landless or small and landless or small | SCs and EBCs go to Punjab and Haryana for seasonal farm work where they stay for 6 months. 15–25 per cent of migrants | More than 50 per cent of the households in have at least one migrant. | Brick kiln workers earn around Rs.50-70/day on a piece rate basis. Coping.<br><br>Farm workers in Punjab earn Rs 100–200/day. Accumulative if spending at destination not high. Industrial workers earn |

Contd...

Table 6.1 (contd.)

| District name and characteristics | Caste, skill, and asset base of migrants | Type of work and when | Who migrates | Coping or accumulative and wage rate |
|---|---|---|---|---|
| Amaur, Baisaa, Kasba, and Jalalgarh are flood prone, and K-Nagar, Shree Nagar, Dhamdaha, Bhawanipur, Rupauli, and Banmakhi are water logged. | and marginal farmers. Migration higher in Muslim blocks. | are employed in industries in Delhi, Mumbai, Surat for 9-10 months/year. Muslims work in embroidery and tailoring. | | Rs 2500–5000/month depending on their skills and experience. Accumulative in 5–10 per cent of the cases on average. |
| Madhubani: Many blocks are flood prone. | 60–75 per cent of SC households have migrants and 40 per cent of OBC households have migrants. Overall about 70 per cent of the households are engaged in migration. Unlike Purnia the rate of migration among the Muslims in the villages visited is almost half that of the Hindus because many have local businesses. | Migration to brick kilns is another major stream. Roughly 3000 workers who used to go to Nepal to work in the construction industry have now started migrating to major cities across India. | Women do not migrate and a few work on farms locally. Mallah, Muslim, Tatma, Paswan, and Musahars migrate for brick kiln work from Oct.- Mar. Migrate to Punjab and Haryana for farm work Nov-June. SCs and OBCs migrate to cities for work in small industrial units and construction work. Children migrate to Kolkata to work as domestic servants and in tea shops and restaurants. | Brick kiln workers are paid roughly Rs 170/1000 bricks made. Coping for most. Farm workers are paid Rs 10 per quintal of sugarcane cut and cleaned or Rs 600–800 per keela (local measure of area) for planting it. Paid Rs 1200/keela for harvesting paddy and Rs 800/keela for harvesting wheat. Accumulative if expenditure minimal at destination. Industrial workers are paid between Rs 2000 and |

| Sitamarhi: Land is concentrated among the Yadav, Kurmi, Sahu (OBC), Rajput, Bhumihar, and Brahmin (forward castes). | 50–60 per cent of the households have at least one person migrating. Mainly among the SCs and OBCs who are landless or nearly landless. The blocks of Dumra, Sonbarsa, Sursand, Parihar, Malangwa, and Majorganj were named as high migration blocks. | Migration increasing every year due to the growing population and divided farms. 2–3000 people used to migrate and commute to Nepal for construction work (Rs 50–100/day) but this source of work is no longer available. | Roughly 40 per cent of the migrants are employed in Mumbai, Kolkata, Punjab, Delhi, and Surat for 4–6 months. They make 1–2 trips back home in a year. SCs and EBCs work as casual labourers in construction or in industries. They also migrate to Punjab for farm work. Muslims migrate to industries in Mumbai, Delhi, Ludhiana, Kolkata, Jorhat, and Hyderabad for tailoring and embroidery work. | 4000/month depending on the skill and amount of work done. Accumulative for 5–10 per cent. Construction workers earn about Rs 75–150/day but work may not be found immediately, and there may be a waiting period of 10–12 days before they get a job. Coping. Tailoring and and embroidery work is accumulative. |
|---|---|---|---|---|

*Source*: Authors.

an accumulative option. Indeed, there were some cases where the earnings had helped them to lease in land which seemed to be a popular way of spending surplus money.

## Migration to Brick Kilns within Bihar, Uttar Pradesh, and Nepal

By all accounts migration to brick kilns has grown in the last five years especially in the districts of Madhubani, Gaya, and Nalanda. Although the earnings in this kind of work are comparable or even better than casual non-farm labouring, workers return with few savings. Cheating is common and spending on liquor at the destination is high. The living and working conditions of brick kiln workers are notoriously poor with long working days, crowded make-shift dwellings, and physical isolation and this has attracted attention in a number of Indian states. Workers are recruited by an agent who gives their families an advance of Rs 2000–5000, making it tantamount to bondage. Payments are settled at the end of the season and cases of underpayment are common. Provisions have to be purchased in shops which have a monopoly in the area and so tend to charge more than the market price. The overall improvement in household well-being is limited. What makes migration to brick kilns from Bihar especially problematic is the high incidence of child labour. Bihari workers tend to be employed in the least skilled task in brick kilns—moulding—and this is where the contribution of child labour is highest (ILO 2005, Srivastava 2005, see also Chapter 7 in this volume). The children of kiln workers often drop out of school and carry on in the same occupations as their parents.

## Farm Work in Punjab and Haryana

Poor and unskilled SC, EBC, and OBC from Bihar have been migrating to Punjab and Haryana since the late 1960s when the green revolution began. Hundreds of thousands of workers migrated seasonally for farm work—in 1981 there were roughly 400,000 workers in the two districts of Hoshiarpur and Ludhiana alone (Singh 1997). Although this kind of work has been regarded as a form of bonded labour by many analysts (see for example, Iyer 2004) the interviews and discussions show that this work has given many poor and lower caste workers an opportunity to earn reasonable wages which they could not do easily in local markets. Migrants work in paddy, wheat, cotton, sugarcane, and vegetable farms. They usually migrate in November and return in May–June. Workers are paid Rs 10 per quintal of sugarcane cut and cleaned or Rs 600–800 per keela (local measure of area) for planting it. They are paid Rs 1,200/keela for harvesting paddy and Rs 800/keela for harvesting wheat. Some are paid in cash (roughly Rs 3,000/month with food and accommodation).

Unlike farm work within the state, migration for farm work in Punjab is often through friends and relatives although it was once through labour contractors as is the case in many other states (see Chapters 3 and 4 for an account of recruitment practices in Andhra Pradesh and Madhya Pradesh). This kind of migration has many characteristics of chain migration (Box 6.1) but differs in the important aspect of being circular.

---

BOX 6.1: FARM WORK IN PUNJAB—CHAIN MIGRATION

Hariharpur village, Dumra block, Sitamarhi[11] is a multi-caste village with a population of 4,000. Nearly half are BCs: Kushwaha, Yadav, Badhai, Luhar, Baniya. Another 40 per cent are SCs, EBCs, and Muslims. Upper caste Bhumihars and Rajputs account for another 7–8 per cent of the population. Most of the BCs and almost all upper caste families own some land. While a majority are small and marginal farmers (1–10 bigha), about 25 households have larger holdings.

Migration has been increasing every year. Every youth wants to leave the village. Nearly 80 per cent of BC, SC, and Muslim families of the village have 1–4 migrants in the age group of 17–45 years. Altogether around 1500 people from this village migrate to a particular location in Ludhiana along a migration stream that has existed for the last 10–12 years. That place has come to be known as Hariharpur village in Punjab. Almost 70 per cent of migrants are unskilled and take up any manual wage work that is available. They earn Rs.70–250/day in/around Ludhiana through contractors, labour contractors, and local labour markets. Wage work is available 20–5 days/month.

The first migrant from Hariharpur went to Punjab in the late 1990s after learning about work possibilities from other migrants in the region.

Despite being relatively well paid, farm work is seen as a dead-end job with few prospects for upward mobility. Although a few workers have diversified into non-farm work in Punjab (cloth mills and garment industries or casual construction workers), they are now looking to find work in larger cities where wages are higher. Work in cloth mills and garment industries are paid Rs 4,000–5,000/month and casual labourers are paid Rs 100–120/day.

In the last five years farm workers from Bihar in Punjab have begun moving into industrial work again through contacts. It appears that Nepali labourers are taking their place in Punjab and Haryana. There are migrants from Bihar in small and large towns in Gujarat, Delhi, Mumbai, Kolkata, Chandigarh, and Surat.

Inter-State Migration to Large Cities and Urban Centres for Casual Labouring in the Non-Farm Sector and 'Factory' Work

Although migration to Kolkata, Assam, and Punjab is not new, migration to the cities of Delhi, Mumbai, Bengaluru, Surat, and Hyderabad is relatively recent. Here migrants undertake a range of non-farm work as casual workers or more regular 'employees' in 'factories'.[12] In general those who have some education (up to matriculation) or traditional skills that are in demand (e.g., the Muslims with tailoring and embroidery skills) have been able to get relatively well-paid jobs in industry. Social networks in the village and the destination are also critical in accessing industrial work in distant locations. Others who have fewer skills and fewer contacts work as casual labourers and may not get work as regularly.

Take the case of Purnia where roughly 15–25 per cent of migrating men are employed in industries in Delhi, Mumbai, and Surat where they earn Rs 2,500–5,000/month depending on their skills and experience. Many work in woollen garment industries. They are away for 9–10 months/year. Muslims have found work in export units making clothes, bags, and zari items (a specialized kind of embroidery using metallic thread and sequins which is in great demand in fashion houses in India and abroad). Embroidery workers can earn Rs 400–50 in a day if working over time, otherwise Rs 250 if only working 8 hours. Payment is settled at the end of the season. They are given some money every week to buy food etc. and get half a day off on Sunday. Those in iron rod work earn Rs 80–90 a day (workers), and Rs 100–50 (head man) and get work all year round in

Mumbai. Muslims work in a variety of other non-farm occupations (rarely farm work) including working as vendors, rickshaw pullers, porters, boot polishers, mechanics, and tailors. They earn between Rs 50 and 200/day in Kolkata, Mumbai, and Delhi.

Migration to factories appears to be equally high from both well connected and remote villages (see Box 6.2) because it is social networks that matter more than road connectivity. Migrants are prepared to make long distance journeys on verbal guarantees of

---

BOX 6.2: MIGRANT 'FACTORY' WORKERS

Chopra is a well connected village in Bysec block, Purnia and lies on the national highway about 25 km from Purnia. It has 300 Muslim families and 20 Harijan (SC) families. The village is well connected. All households have at least one migrant. Migration started in 1970 first for iron rod and centering work, then for farm work. Earlier migration was through labour contractors but these days people migrate through their own contacts. Now, work in stitching and embroidery is growing. While the SCs go to Punjab for farm work, the majority of the Muslims work in the non-farm sector either as labourers or factory workers. There are no big landlords in this village and nearly all Muslim families have a small plot of land but this is prone to flooding. Most have some education through madrasas (Islamic schools) but no one is educated beyond school. Mohammad Ansar (26) has been migrating to Delhi since the age of 10. His work involves stitching bags and embroidery. The first year was training during which time he was given food and accommodation only and no wages. His brother Akbar (22) also migrates to Delhi now. Each saves around Rs 10–12,000 in a season (Jan.—July). When they come back they work in farms locally. His father Mohammed Jahid (52) owns a tea shop in the village. Another brother Anwar (7) studies in the village.

Badalpur is a remote village in Bycee block, about 37 km from the Purnia district headquarters.[13] There are 600 Muslim families in this Muslim dominated village which has a population of 3,000. There are 25 farmers with more than 10 bigha of land while 50 Yadav families own about 1.5 bigha land. Nearly all young people in the age group 16–45 years migrate while elderly people are engaged in own farming/sharecropping, animal husbandry, and business. Punjab is the main destination for about 400 men of the village. They are engaged in paddy work for 60 days and wheat work for another 60 days at Rs 100–200/day. Another 350 migrants are involved in tailoring and zari work in Mumbai and Delhi. The number of migrants from both these villages and surrounding villages is increasing every year. Barhi is a large and remote village in Madhubani dominated by Yadavs, Muslims and Mallahs with 470 households. Hardly anyone is educated beyond high school (matriculation). Migration rates are very high among the BCs and SCs. While some continue to go to Punjab and Haryana, a majority are now working in various industries in Mumbai, Delhi, Gurgaon, Surat, Ahmedabad, Kolkata, Arunachal Pradesh, Trivandrum, Kathmandu, and other places in Nepal (Siraha, Lahan, Janakpur). They work in shifts of 8 hours but try to get as much overtime work as possible. Earnings were in the range of Rs 2,000–3,500 depending on experience, skills, and over time worked. Industries included mattress factories, autorickshaw workshops, wire and coil industry, bag and shoe making, and welding units. In all the cases discussed, migration was through contacts at the destination who were usually from the same village or neighbouring village. These were relatives or neighbours and the process had all the characteristics of chain migration. Fresh arrivals in the city would be offered a place to stay for 2–3 weeks while the migrant looked for work or finalized verbally the job that he had been promised through his contact (all are men).

finding accommodation and work from friends and relatives in the city.

OCCUPATIONAL AND SPATIAL MOBILITY

Along with interstate migration to cities for factory work has become a kind of occupational mobility that has not been seen before and this is especially marked in the case of the OBCs. Some migrants try out several jobs before they settle into one that they like (Box 6.3).

Social networks are crucial for new migrants arriving in the city to find a place to live, to obtain job and market information, to contact

---

BOX 6.3: CHANGING JOBS AND BECOMING UPWARDLY MOBILE

Bhola Prasad Bharti (45) a resident of Barhi, migrated from 1993 to 1998 to Delhi with others from the village to work in a plastics factory where he earned Rs 1,200–1,800 a month. He then went to work in Kolkata in a sweet shop for Rs 1,700–2,200 for a couple of years and later started working in a gas plant in Surat where earned Rs 1,500–1,800. The plant manager then posted him at Pune as a supervisor for Rs 2,400 per month. He has recently returned to the village for good and plans to send his grown up sons to a factory somewhere. He will manage the family farm.

---

prospective employers and to obtain the necessary certificates. They are also critical for moving up the job ladder by changing jobs. Many migration decisions are based on information gained through contacts in the village. Successive migration can be to different and far away places—the case of a family from Gaya (Box 6.4) shows how jobs in destinations as far apart as Punjab, Delhi, coastal Andhra Pradesh, and Gujarat were accessed through friends and other migrants bringing back information to the village.

But for those with fewer connections finding work in distant locations is not as easy. For instance, key improvement interviews indicate that while a majority of Musahars in Gaya go to brick kilns, 2–3 per cent migrate to Surat, Mumbai, Kanpur, Agra, Kolkata, and Delhi looking for work. They do not have contacts in the cities like BCs and OBCs and usually end up as manual labourers working for Rs 30–60/day for 20days/month. However, there are other reasons for the Musahars not being able to find work in cities including caste based discrimination, lack of skills, and capital needed to pay bribes and pay for food and accommodation immediately after arriving in the city.

## Migration as a Stage in the Household Life Cycle

Migration is viewed as a finite stage in the life cycle of many households: as sons approach an age where they can be sent away to earn, the head of the household stays in the village to look after the farm and other enterprise. This is a form of relay migration (see Box 6.5).

---

Box 6.4: Exploring Opportunities Using the Village as a
Base and Village Social Networks for Information

Manoj Kumar Sharma (OBC, 32 years, 10+2 educated, 5 brothers):
Jhikatiya village, Gaya.

    Manoj first migrated in 1995 to Ambala (Punjab) with a friend
who had worked there for several years. He worked there in a
small scale bicycle manufacturing unit for Rs 1,500/month. After
working there for six months he returned to the village with no
savings. He migrated again in 1999 to Delhi for work in another
factory through some other friends and came back soon without
any savings. He then learnt about jobs in Vishakhapattnam, a
coastal town in Andhra Pradesh, and went there to work for a
public sector petroleum company where he was paid Rs 80 per
day. But he came back to the village after six months as the work
was finished. He heard about work in Daman, Gujarat through
some friends and migrated once again in February 2000 to work
in a PVC pipe producing factory for Rs 55/day with the possibility
of working 4 hours overtime every day. The factory provided
accommodation and food. The factory moved to another town
in Gujarat and he went to work there. He found work there for
all three of his brothers in 2005. Now together they send home Rs
1,000–2,000 each month. Although much of this money is spent
on consumption, some is left over. This year they are converting
their village house into a *pucca* house and have invested some
money in their farm as well. They plan to drill a tube well next
year.

---

The Importance of Skills

In each district roughly 5 per cent of the migrants were skilled
and belonged mainly to the OBC castes. This includes carpenters,
masons, welders, electricians, plumbers, tailors, drivers, mechanics,
etc. However, migration of skilled workers may or may not follow
a seasonal pattern. Skilled migrants earn considerably more than
unskilled workers, that is, roughly Rs 3,000–7,000/month. Skills may
be acquired through apprenticeship or on-the-job training. There
is a growing demand for skilled workers ( for example, Lalhariya
migrants were able to secure jobs in plywood industries in Ludhiana

---

**BOX 6.5: RELAY MIGRATION**

Mohd Salim Ahmed (50) started migrating to Delhi in 1985. He started as a construction worker and progressed to being a *mistri* (mason) in a few years but stopped migrating when his sons were old enough to migrate. He has two sons and three daughters aged 12, 7, and 5. Ahmed (25) has been stitching bags in Chennai for the last five years. Two years ago, the younger son (20) joined him in the same factory. Each son earns around Rs 3,000 a month and saves around Rs 2,000 after spending. They are away for 8–9 months and work 12 hour days. They come back 2–3 times in a year. Both together remit about Rs.20,000–25,000 a year. Ahmed still works as a mistri but around the village (at Rs 100 a day and gets 10–15 days of work per month, mainly in the block headquarters).

---

because they used to work in a local plywood factory in Kasbah). Skill enhancement is clearly an area where interventions are needed.

Migrants also bring back a range of skills, which in the right circumstances could foster local development and household incomes. For example, Muslims in Chopra were able to establish garages, mechanic shops, bicycle repair centres, and tractor repair centres with the skills that they had learnt in Punjab. Those with highly specialized traditional skills have been able to occupy a well paid niche in the labour market, for example, Muslims in embroidery and Brahmins from Madhubani as cooks in Bangalore. The sweet makers from Sitamarhi are well known across India (Box 6.6).

Another example is the *makhana* processors from Madhubani. A small number of Mallahs (EBC) from Madhubani migrate to Assam, UP, Kashmir, and Orissa to work in the specialized job of harvesting and processing *makhana*, a nut that grows in water bodies and is used widely in sweet preparations in north India. In a season one migrant is able to save Rs 10,000. Travelling expenses, accommodation, and food are provided by the *makhana* farmers. But not all specialised jobs are well paid—Doms (SC) migrating to Patna to work as sweepers for government departments and private hotels get paid only Rs 900/month with accommodation, breakfast, tea, and meals.[14]

---

BOX 6.6: THE *HALWAIS* AND SNACK VENDORS FROM SITAMARHI

Sursand block in Sitamarhi is famous for quality halwais. In the marriage season (December–July) around 500 halwais with their helpers migrate to urban centres in Delhi, Bihar, Rajasthan (Jhunjhunoo, Kota, Jaipur), Maharashtra (Mumbai), and Gujarat (Ahemdabad, Surat, Rajkot). *Halwais* are paid on a contract basis (Rs 1,000–3,000/contract for 1–2 days) while helpers get Rs 100/day with food. This is a traditional skill but demand for it has increased in the last 5–6 years. Destinations lack skilled *halwais*. When not migrating, these people work locally as snack vendors in Sursand block and earn Rs 100–50/day. Siya Ram Rajvanshi 65 years, illiterate, landless snacks vendor has four sons and all are vendors for the same earnings in the same block. He has used migration money for buying land and converting his *kutcha* house into a *pucca* house. He inherited 2 bighas of land 40 years ago and bought another 4 bighas in the last 10 years. One brother works as a *zari* worker in Mumbai for last 10–12 years for Rs 100–50/day. But the brother does not have sons who earn well and has not been able to build assets like him. Most of his remittances are used by his family living in the village for every day expenses and social functions.

---

MIGRATING CHILDREN

The autonomous migration of children appears to be on the increase. The terms under which they are employed are very poor and conditions often dangerous, and in many cases such migration would be more appropriately called trafficking. But, for their families this is clearly an important source of income and for the children, the job may bring food security and in some cases, prospects for better work after a few years.

Roughly 2,000–3,000 children from poor Muslim and SC families in Madhubani and at least 1,000 children from Purnia have migrated to Uttar Pradesh and Gujarat for carpet weaving. This kind of migration began in 1990. They stay there for 8–9 months earning Rs 2,000–3,000/month. Children from Madhubani, Sitamarhi, and Purnia in the age groups of 8–16 years also migrate to Kolkata and towns in UP, Punjab, MP, Chhattisgarh, and Bihar to work in sweet

> BOX 6.7: MIGRATION OF POOR SC AND BC CHILDREN FROM GAYA[14]
>
> A new trend that has gained momentum over the last 3–4 years is the migration of children aged 13–17 years belonging to Musahar and Maanjhee castes from Maanpur and Bodh Gaya blocks to cities in Uttaranchal and Himachal Pradesh (Shimla, Kulloo, Dharmshala, Leh, Laddakh, Dehradoon) and Kolkata. They are taken to work as domestic servants. So far about 500 children have migrated of whom a few were girls. They are promised Rs 1,000–2,000/month with food but are generally not paid this much. There are 20–5 middlemen who are active in the district. There have been cases of sexual exploitation and physical abuse and overall, 10–20 per cent of the children have faced problematic situations. Some have come back with diseases (in the case of one 14 year old boy with HIV/AIDS). Their earnings are used by their families to buy food and other essentials and repay debts.

shops, restaurants, and as domestic servants. These are children from SC families. They earn Rs 1,000–2,000 per month and are given food and accommodation. When these labourers grow up they move to other cities for better jobs. Finally, the trafficking of girls from Madhubani was also mentioned. But it appears to have decreased because of improved awareness and border police efforts in last 3–4 years.

## REMITTANCE PATTERNS AND THE IMPACTS OF MIGRANT EARNINGS ON HOUSEHOLD WELL-BEING

### Quantum of Remittances

No formal data on the total value of remittances exist but some idea can be gained from post office data on money orders. Although not all MOs are sent by migrants they do account for much of the money sent in this way to rural Bihar. According to post office officials the total value of MOs sent to Bihar from other parts of India was Rs. 450 crores in 2005–6. However, this represents a fraction of the total money sent and carried to Bihar by migrants. The rate of increase of MOs has slowed down recently as other remittance mechanisms have become popular: it slowed from 13 per cent in 2004 to just under 4 per cent in 2005. But there are seasonal fluctuations which reflect the seasonality of migration, as the flows to north Bihar show below (south Bihar not provided) (Figs. 6.1 and 6.2).

A chart showing the number of MOs received in rural areas in Bihar by place of origin shows that Delhi is at the top (Figure 6.3). Punjab is some way behind now, followed by West Bengal, other

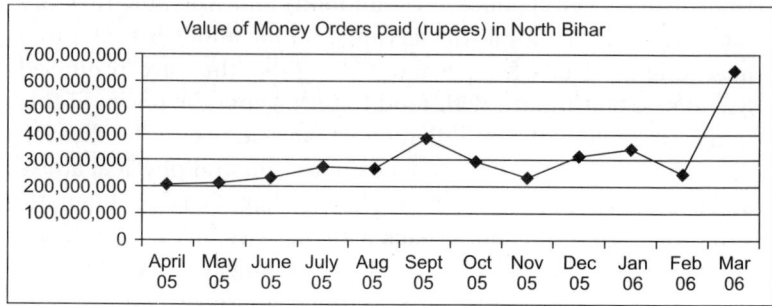

Figure 6.1: Value of Money Orders Paid in North Bihar

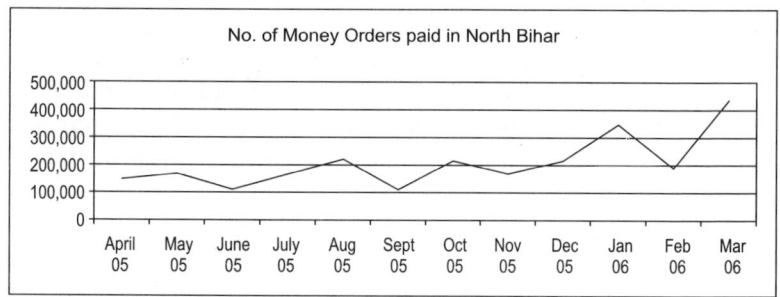

Figure 6.2: Number of Money Orders paid in North Bihar

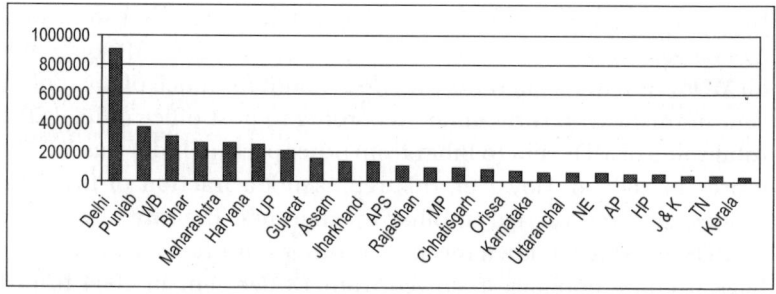

Figure 6.3: Money Orders Received in Rural Bihar by Place of Origin

parts of Bihar, Maharashtra, Haryana, UP, and other states. The figures for Bihar probably relate to MOs sent by salaried permanent migrants in urban centres rather than poor migrants.

A breakdown by major sending areas (Figure 6.4) shows that nearly all dip in the month of May. The explanation lies in the fact that most migrants return to their villages in March for the festive season and rabi crop harvests. They stay in the village for 3–4 weeks and migrate again in mid/late April. Since the month of May is a start-up period they usually do not send money to their villages then. They are paid a month or six weeks after arrival and usually send money orders to their families in June and July.

Indeed data for Delhi show a sharp increase in June (Figure 6.5).

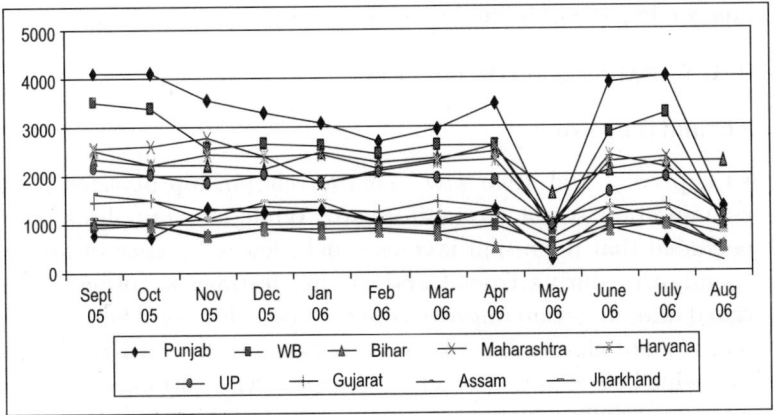

Figure 6.4: Money Orders by Major Sending Areas

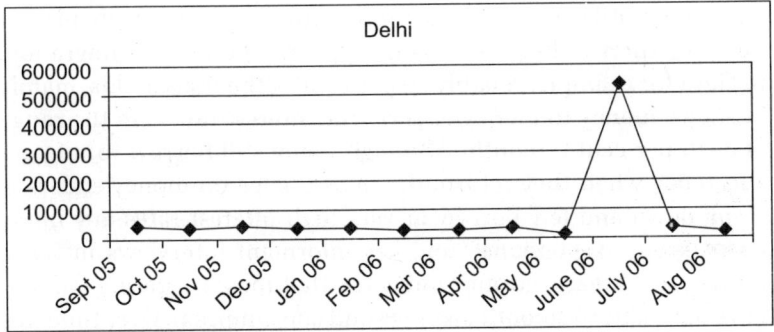

Figure 6.5: Remittances from Delhi

## Remittance Mechanisms

Until very recently migrants used to send remittances through MOs, friends, and relatives or carry the money themselves. But MOs are slow and inefficient[16] and sending through friends or carrying money on one's person is risky. Private agents who transfer money electronically through social contacts are becoming more popular. The use of bank drafts has also increased as more and more migrants become familiar with the workings of the system and set up accounts of their own. However, a majority of poor migrants still hand carry money. In Sitamarhi for example, migrants visit their families every 4–6 months and hand carry (up to Rs 3,000–5,000). Few families have postal identities so very few remittances are sent through MOs. The situation in parts of Nalanda is similar.

IMPACT OF MIGRATION ON POVERTY

### Debt and Borrowing

In Chapters 3 and 4 we saw that the relationship between debt and migration is not straightforward. While some analysts have concluded that migration increases debt levels because of higher expenditures during transit and at the destination, others have argued that migration improves the creditworthiness of households and they are able to borrow more because of that (Ghate 2005). Borrowing before migration and repaying after returning continues and is especially widespread among poorer migrants.[17] However, several respondents mentioned that borrowing food grains from the rich to tide over the lean season (which was commonplace in Sitamarhi until a few years ago) and borrowing at very high interest rates for survival had virtually disappeared because of migration. In Gaya for example, roughly 30 per cent of the households, mainly SCs, owe money to moneylenders. The interest rate is in the range of 3–10 per cent a month. Although many still borrow to migrate and repay when they return, the dependence on moneylenders is going down and few borrow at very high interest rates any more. Focus group discussions[18] and key informant interviews in Gaya, Purnia, and Muzzarfarpur[19] indicated that most migrating families have been able to smooth incomes and consumption. Over time this has led to an improvement in living standards. Mohammed Islam,

---

BOX 6.8: MIGRATION HAS IMPROVED LIVING STANDARDS

Poor Yadav households from Gyan Dob Tola in Badalpur village say, '*Bahar jaane ka maqsad hai kamana aur bachat karna. Baahar jane se pahle ki tulna me khan-paan aur rahan-sahan me sudhar hua hai, bhukhmari khatm ho gai hai, ab koi karze me nahhee hai*' (The main purpose of migration is to earn and save. Migration has improved our standard of living and we can eat better. Hunger and indebtedness are gone). Migrants have been using remittances mainly to repair old *kutcha* houses or to convert them into *pucca* houses. Around 10–12 have bought land for housing or farming. Another 25 Yadav families of the village have shared in 1–2 *bigha* using migrant remittances for last 5–6 years.

---

a 40 year old illiterate farmer from Badalpur village in Bycee block Purnia district says, '*Palayan se fayada ye hua hai ki jin gharon me pahle time se chulha nahee jalta tha ab who thhek se kha-pee rahen hain*' (The main advantage of migration has been that families that were not able to eat regularly before now have enough to eat).

### Investing in Housing and Agriculture

Migration money is being used to invest in agriculture—for leasing-in land, drilling tubewells and purchasing inputs. Better established and higher earning migrants are able to spare money to invest in housing and farming. For example, migrants from Gaya who work in cast iron industries of Agra and Kanpur are able to save about Rs 3,000/month which they send home for investment in leasing land, farm inputs, or to start a petty business. In Badalpur village, Bycee block, Purnia roughly 50 families have started petty businesses such as small village shops in and around the village using remittances.

Roughly 5–10 per cent of migrating households have invested in land (buying, sharing-in, or leasing-in) through migration. These appear to be mainly OBCs from large families who have more than one person working in relatively remunerative work (especially 'factory' work). For example, in Hariharpur village, Dumra block, Sitamarhi, remittances were used previously for loan repayment and consumption. But as the families became wealthier they have started investing in land. More than 50 per cent migrants have acquired some land in the last 7–8 years. In Gaya remittances

---

BOX 6.9: USING MIGRATION MONEY TO IMPROVE AGRICULTURE

Bisundhari Yadav (55) is a farmer in Itra, the well-connected village in Gaya. He has not studied beyond primary school. He and his wife Raiee Devi (50) live with their 3 sons and the sons' wives and 8 children. Yadav also has three daughters, all married and living in another village. The eldest son Rajkumar (35) has studied up to V standard and manages the farm. The second son Kameshwar (30) has studied up to Xth (failed) and has been migrating to Surat to work in a *zari* factory for the past 10 years. He earns Rs 3,500 a month. Rampati the younger brother (18), educated till VII standard, has also been there for the last year earning Rs 2,600 a month. Both get 7 days off a month not because they want them but because there are now too many workers in the factory. They also never manage to work over time now. They take turns coming back for festivals and to supervize the sowing and harvesting in their farm. Both together send Rs 10,000–12,000 2–3 times a year through Money Order (MO) and also hand carry some money when they come home. This money is used for the farm, savings, and consumption. They had 3 bighas of ancestral land and bought 3 more *bighas* 2–3 years ago from Muslims in the village who left because of Naxal harassment. They bought another 9 *katthas* (20 katthas make a bigha of land) two years ago for Rs 20,000. They have also bought land to build a house for Rs 60,000. They also lease-in 5 bighas of land from Muslims. They are now growing paddy, vegetables, onions, tomatoes, potatoes, chillies which they sell in the local market. They also own 2 buffaloes, 2 bulls, and 3 calves and sell *khova* (thickened milk cake) and milk. They say that there is much improvement in their situation because of remittances. They spent lavishly on their 3 sisters' weddings.

---

have allowed people to lease in land and buy inputs for growing vegetables. Vegetable farming is growing in the region and this will eventually create local jobs.

THE NEGATIVE IMPACTS OF MIGRATION

There are heavy costs associated with migration too—long separation from one's family brings isolation and loneliness; many are engaged in dirty, dangerous, and degrading occupations that affect their health and others engage in high-risk sexual behaviour and fall prey to STDs or HIV/AIDs. Women and children who are left behind also suffer from loneliness, anxiety, and vulnerability to sexual exploitation. Children who migrate with their parents miss school.

## Health Problems

- Migrants in Nalanda have reported coming back with respiratory illnesses (asthma, TB), hepatitis, and STDs. Four men who were migrating to Mumbai tested positive for HIV. Health problems are a major reason for discontinuing migration.
- According to staff at Adithi, nearly 300 HIV + cases have been detected in Sitamarhi in the last 2–3 years and these are mainly migrants. However, residents from Hariharpur village which has very high levels of migration to Ludhiana said that strong social networks and policing of their behaviour at the destination prevented them from engaging in high risk sexual activity and this had protected them against diseases.
- About 5–10 per cent migrants from Madhubani working in cities have come back with diseases including asthma, TB, AIDS, and hepatitis.
- Staff at Adithi in Muzzaffarpur say that migrants' families have no idea about health risks in relation to HIV/AIDS and STDs and how they might be exposed to these diseases.

## Labour Shortages

Labour shortages arising from the mass exodus of young able-bodied men were mentioned in a number of places. While rich farmers have invested in tractors and harvesters to replace them, smaller farmers have to make to do with their own family labour (if there is no stigma attached to doing this in their caste) or leave their land fallow. In Sewdah village for example, no bulls are visible in the village. Instead of oxen, there are 12 tractors and 10 power tillers in the village. In Jhikatia village, OBC farmers are not able to get labourers in peak seasons as they are no longer interested in local wage work. They prefer going to Punjab and Haryana. One farmer in Purnia commented, *'Pahle ek mazdoor bulane par bees aate the, ab 20 bulane par ek aa jaaye to badee baat hai Purnia mein'* (In the old days, if you called one labourer there would be bees willing to work for you but now if you call bees and if only one turns up that is an achievement in Purnia). In Gaya too mechanization has increased for these reasons.[19] Migration appears to have pushed up local wages. In Purnia social taboos related to upper castes doing manual work have started to break down because of the shortage of labour. Now upper castes are occasionally seen ploughing their own fields, but with a tractor. Apparently ploughing with a tractor doesn't carry the same shame as using a traditional plough.

CONCLUSION

Rural people in Bihar have become ever more mobile especially in the last decade, with deteriorating employment prospects locally and emerging opportunities elsewhere. With the exception of the poorest, the largest landowners, and successful businessmen, nearly all others including medium farmers, and forward castes, are migrating. While the most educated and wealthy (usually upper castes and BCs but not always) migrate for secure and well-paid jobs on a more permanent basis, the vast majority of migrants go for periods ranging from 3 to 9 months.

SCs and EBCs are engaged in both short distance and long distance migration but usually in the lowest paid jobs. Farm labouring work, casual labouring work in construction, work in brick kilns and rickshaw pulling are the four most important categories of work for the poorest, unskilled landless, and lowest caste migrants. This includes (but is not limited to) the Musahar, Majhi, Dom, and other SCs. They are prevented from breaking away from such jobs because of their limited skills, education, and social networks. Discrimination at the destination is also a factor in keeping certain castes in certain jobs.

There are strong indications that many migrants belonging to the diverse category of BC have become upwardly mobile, at least in economic terms, graduating from farm work to working in a variety of industries where earnings are higher. At the same time, they have also become more spatially diversified, using their social networks to switch between destinations that are often quite far from each other in order to move up the job ladder in occupations that require similar skills. The choice of destination is strongly determined by social networks—people from a particular caste and village tend to go to the same destination and into similar occupations—and this may constrain the range of economic opportunities available. Distance and transport facilities are not as important in determining the choice of destination.

The attractions of city life have become a major factor in shaping migration decisions especially for young people and this explains, in part, high migration rates among the better-off. It is clear that migration and remittances have improved the standard of living of thousands of families in the poorest districts of Bihar. Among the poorest unskilled labourers, even though the accumulation of assets is minimal and the costs in terms of children's education are high, migration helps to smooth consumption, improve food security, and reduce reliance on moneylenders.

There has also been an increase in child migration from this class of migrants, especially from the northern districts and this has many exploitative aspects. Even if it brings in additional cash to poor households, such migration has many aspects that are akin to trafficking and require urgent attention.

For the better educated and connected migrants working in industries, migration money is an important way of financing agriculture and the accumulation of assets. Such migrants remit a sizeable proportion of their incomes and often work overtime to earn as much as possible during their time at the destination. However, the costs of such migration may be high in social and health terms: long periods of separation cause loneliness. Working in industries with poor labour standards exposes workers to numerous hazards. Health complaints are common. Migrants are not fully aware of the health risks at work and are often not in a position to demand protection. Being alone and away from the family may also result in more risky sexual behaviour at the destination and migrants are not fully aware of the risks of exposure to STDs, HIV/AIDS, and other diseases.

Even if more employment is generated locally through NREGS and new policies put in place to promote industry and agriculture, it is important to move away from simplistically negative views of migration as mainly a symptom of distress, and to start to develop ways of maximizing its benefits for poverty reduction.

There is a need for comprehensive migrant support programmes which aim to:

- Create awareness among migrants about their rights so that they can better protect themselves against exploitation (on work time, wages).
- Create awareness among migrants about health risks and occupational hazards, especially in relation to the industries where Bihari workers are most commonly employed.
- Improve their bargaining power through skill enhancement programmes and certification through partnerships with NGOs and government.
- Reduce uncertainty in the job market by providing information on job availability, wages, and duration of work.
- Recognize the vulnerability of those who are left behind in migrating households and devise ways of supporting them. The need for communication, representation in village institutions, and remittance mechanism is greatest.
- Improve the understanding of migration in terms of its patterns, drivers, and impacts by building up a comprehensive database on migration by caste, gender, asset holding, occupation, duration, and returns in their own project districts.
- Help migrants to save and remit money to their families safely and efficiently.
- Help in creating the conditions for better investment of remittances in agriculture. This should be built into plans for developing agriculture, livestock, and enterprise.

Many of these issues are picked up again in the last four chapters which discuss existing support systems, their successes, and future challenges.

NOTES

1. According to a recent survey by Rajiv Gandhi Foundation, out of the 100 most poor districts in India, 26 districts are from Bihar: Araria, Banka, Begusarai, Darbhanga, Gopalganj, Jamui, Kaimur, Khagaria, Kishenganj, Lakhisarai, Madhepura, Muzaffarpur, Nalanda, Navada, achim Champaran, Purvi Champaran, Purnia, Saharasa, Saran, Shekhpura, Sheohar, Sitamarhi, Siwan, Supaul, and Vaishali.
2. 2250 rural households in south and eastern Uttar Pradesh, and north and central Bihar.
3. Sponsored by Bihar State Minorities Commission.

4. A. De Haan, 'Migration and Livelihoods in Historical Perspective: A Case Study of Bihar, India', *Journal of Development Studies*, June 2002.

5. G. Iyer (ed), *Distressed Migrant Labour in India*, New Delhi, Kanishka, 2004.

6. However it needs to be borne in mind that major changes are occurring now that may alter migration patterns: the 2005 change in government is introducing policies to improve the law and order situation, intrduce the NREGA, and revitalize industry and agriculture.

7. Farm productivity deterorated in Bihar through 1990s due to a dombination of climatic factors, Naxalism, caste conflict, poor electricity supply, and the collapse of Irrigation canals in many locations.

8. The destination and season for brick kiln work are similar in all the study districts.

9. Backward Castes (BC) is a broad category including other Backward Castes (OBCs) and Extremely Backward Castes (EBCs).

10. The Musahar are classified as a scheduled caste. They are spread across the Districts of Madhubani, Muzaffarpur, Darbhanga, Champaran, Hazaribagh, Santhal Parganas, Bhagalpur, Munger, Purnea, and Gaya. There were 13,91,000 Mushars in Bihar in 1981. They are thought to be an offshot of the Bhuiya tribe of Chhota Nagpur and are in fact referred to by that name in Bihar as well. The name translates into rat-taker or rat-eater, Musahars are mainly landless agricultural labourers. The Musahars have largely remained on the periphery of society (Mukul, 'Everyday Life of Musahars in North Bihar', *EPW*, Special Article, 4 December, 1999.

11. FGD, 5 men-3 migrants and 8 women with 3 Adithi coordinators.

12. Employees in the sense that they have a regular and fixed monthly income with fixed over time rates. Many of the industries are small scale units that may or may not be legally registeres with government and may operate without adhering to labour standards or hygiene and safety regulations. Contracts are often verbal, based on mutual trust.

13. Mohd Islam (40 years, illiterate), medium farmer.

14. Aasmani Devi; Malik (Dome/SC), 45 years , illiterate, panchayat member-Dullipattee, ainagar block, Madhubani.

15. AVS, Bodh-Gaya.

16. according to the WELPMPG the transaction is reportedly 5-6 per cent and the transaction time is on an average 30 days for some of the interior villages.

17. BRLP, Birjoo Milki.

18. FGD, 25 people from general SC, BC, OBC, and minority communities.

19. Mr. Chhedi Prasad, Secretary, Samagra Vikas Sansthan, Bara Chattee, Gaya; S.K. Jha, DDM, NABARD, Purnea; *NIRDESH*, Muzzaffarpur.

20. DRDA, Gaya.

## REFERENCES

ADRI, *The Socioeconomic and Educational Status of Muslims in Bihar*, Patna: Asian Development Research Institute, 2006.

Dayal, H., and A. Karan, 'Migration from Rural Bihar and Jharkhand', in G. Iyer, (ed.), *Distressed Migrant Labour in India : Key Human Rights Issues*, New Delhi, Kanishka, 2004.

De Haan, A., 'Migration and Livelihoods in Historical Perspective: A Case Study of Bihar, India', *Journal of Development Studies*, June 2002.

Deshingkar, P., S. Kumar, H. K. Chobey, and D. Kumar, *The Role of Migration and Remittances in Promoting Livelihoods in Bihar*, Report of the study commissioned by World Bank funded Bihar Rural Livelihoods Project (BRLP) and the IFAD funded Women's Empowerment and Livelihoods Project in the mid-Gangetic Plain (WELPMGP), India, 2006.

Ghate, P., 'Serving Migrants Sustainably: Remittance Services Provided by an MFI in Gujarat', *Economic and Political Weekly*, 23 April 2005, pp. 1740–6.

Karan, A., 'Changing Patterns of Migration from Rural Bihar', in K. G. Iyer, (ed.), *Migrant Labour and Human Rights in India*, New Delhi: Kanishka Publishers, 2003, pp. 102–139.

*ILO Report on Brick Kiln Workers*, New Delhi: International Labour Organization, 2003.

Iyer, K. G. (ed.), *Distressed Migrant Labour in India : Key Human Rights Issues*, New Delhi: Kanishka, 2004.

——, Veer Singh, and P.P. Arya, Distressed Migration: Causes. and Consequences', in G. Iyer, (ed.), *Distressed Migrant Labour in India: Key Human Rights Issues*.

Singh, 'Bonded Migrant Labour in Punjab Agriculture', Economic and Political Weekly, 32(11), pp. 518–19.

Srivastava, R., 'Bonded Labour in India, Its Incidence and Pattern', Working Paper 43, Geneva: International Labour Office, 2005.

APPENDIX 6.1 DESCRIPTION OF STUDY VILLAGES

## Madhubani

*1. Barhi Village, Block Jayanagar Remote 30–40 km away from Madhubani.*

| Caste | Households | Migrating individuals |
|---|---|---|
| Yadav | 250 | 200 |
| Sahni | 200 | 200 |
| Muslim | 200 | 250 |
| Paswan | 60 | 50 |
| Chamar | 25 | 30 |
| Teli | 20 | 0 |
| Tatma | 15 | 20 |
| Lohar | 10 | 5 |
| Thateri | 10 | 15 |
| Sonar | 10 | 10 |
| Dhobi | 10 | 10 |
| Khatwe (BC) | 8 | 10 |
| Nai | 7 | 4 |
| Gaderiya (shepherd) | 6 | 5 |
| Baniya | 5 | 4 |
| Koyri | 5 | 4 |
| | 841 | 817 |

*2. Paraul Village, Beni Patti Block, Madhubani. 17–18 km from Madhubani and 4–5 km from Block. 2–3 km from Main Road. 2900 Voters.*

| Caste | Households | Migrating individuals |
|---|---|---|
| Mushahar | 250 | 300 |
| Rajput | 100 | 100 |
| Brahman | 100 | 125 |
| Yadav | 75 | 100 |
| Paswan | 70 | 35 |
| Kyot (BC) | 40 | 50 |
| Muslim | 40 | 40 |
| Chamar | 25 | 50 |
| Mallah | 25 | 10 |
| Kayastha | 25 | 50 |
| Tatma | 20 | 30 |
| Lohar | 20 | 25 |
| Dhobi | 10 | 20 |

| | | |
|---|---|---|
| Nai | 10 | 7 |
| Giri (FC) | 10 | 10 |
| Halwai (BC) | 10 | 10 |
| Teli | 10 | 5 |
| | 840 | 967 |

Farm land possessed by Brahman, Rajput, Yadav, and Kayastha. Mango orchards. Paddy, wheat, maize, some sugarcane.

## Gaya

### 3. Alipur Village, Tekari Block, Gaya. Remote Village 35 km from Gaya and 10–12 from Block HQ. Road Very Bad.

| Caste | Households | Migrating individuals |
|---|---|---|
| Yadav | 60 | 30 |
| Bhumihar | 30 | 10 |
| Kahar | 20 | 25 |
| Ravidas (Chamar-SC) | 20 | 30 |
| Paswan (SC) | 10 | 15 |
| Bhuiyan (SC) | 7 | 9 |
| Majhi | 6 | 10 |
| Dhobi | 5 | 0 |
| Badhaee | 5 | 4 |
| Dom | 4 | 5 |
| Halwai | 3 | 2 |
| Nai | 2 | 3 |
| Teli | 1 | 3 |
| | 173 | 146 |

Cropping pattern—paddy, wheat, masoor, chana, now very little sugarcane, mustard. Bhumihar and Yadav own the land.

### 4. Itra Village, Bodh-Gaya, Block 4 Tolas. District Gaya, Well-connected.

Main tola

| Caste | Households | Migrating individuals |
|---|---|---|
| Yadav | 150 | 40 |
| Muslim | 150 | 135 |
| Badhaee | 3 | 6 |
| Ravidas | 1 | 0 |
| Total | 304 | 181 |

Majhi Bigaha tola

| Caste | Households | Migrating individuals |
|-------|-----------|----------------------|
| Majhi | 100 | 25-30 |

Baijan Bigaha tola

| Caste | Households | Migrating individuals |
|-------|-----------|----------------------|
| Yadav | 25 | 12 |
| Majhi | 40 | 17 |
| Pasi | 15 | 10 |
| Total | 80 | 39 |

Pachanwa tola

| Caste | Households | Migrating individuals |
|-------|-----------|----------------------|
| Yadav | 50 | 20 |
| Majhi | 25 | 10 |
| Badhaee | 3 | 0 |
| Total | 78 | 30 |

## Purnia

*5. Chopra Village Block Bycee, Purnia District. 25 km NH31 from Purnia. 3 km from Bycee. Well connected*

| Caste | Households | Migrating individuals |
|-------|-----------|----------------------|
| Muslim | 300 | All houses many with more than one person |
| Harijan | 20 | – do – |

All land with Muslims and distributed relatively equitably. No very big landlords. Summer paddy and also kharif paddy. Jute. Lowland, lots of flooding during kharif.

*6. Lalhariya Village Connected 10 km from Purnia, Block Kasbah, 1.5 – 2 km from Kasbah.*

| Caste | Households | Migrating individuals |
|-------|-----------|----------------------|
| Chaurasia (Paan) | 150 | 125 |
| Tatma (SC) | 75 | 45 |
| Yadav | 25 | 15 |

| | | |
|---|---|---|
| Badhaee | 15 | 15 |
| Chamar | 12 | 2 |
| Nai | 1 | 0 |
| Total | 278 | 202 |

Land is held by the Chaurasia and carpenters. Paddy, wheat, jute. Some grow sugarcane and make it into jaggery for home consumption. Banana

## 7. Dhamdaha Block, Kurkuron Village, Purnia 40 km from Purnia, 5–6 km from Dhamdaha. No Cars Only Tam-tams and Rickshaws.

| Caste | Households | Migrating individuals |
|---|---|---|
| Muslim | 400 | 500 |
| Sahu (Bania) | 50 | 10 |
| Rishidev (Musahar) | 50 | 100 |
| Yadav | 40 | 12 |
| Chamar | 16 | 8 |
| Gupta | 10 | 8 |
| Dhobi | 10 | 6 |
| Dom | 7 | 0 |
| Kumhar | 5 | 2 |
| Total | 588 | 646 |

Banana farming new. Paddy, wheat, maize, mustard, sunflower.

## Sitamarhi

## 8. Gobindphanda, Block Gumra, Sitamarhi, Connected, 6 km from Sitamarhi but 9 km from Block HQ but Very Near Rega Block (2km).

| Caste | Households | Migrating individuals |
|---|---|---|
| Chamar | 110 | 100 |
| Kanu (Bania) | 100 | 40 |
| Koyri | 75 | 10 |
| Brahman | 50 | 40 |
| Paswan | 50 | 15 |
| Yadav | 35 | 10 |
| Sahar (BC) | 30 | 10 |
| Nai | 20 | 0 |
| Lohar | 10 | 0 |
| Muslim | 10 | 15 |
| Kurmi | 10 | 4 |
| Kalwar | 5 | 0 |
| Amat (BC) | 5 | 0 |
| Mali | 3 | 0 |
| Total | 513 | 244 |

Lots of sugarcane here. Work all year round. Yadav and Kanu hold the land.

## 9. Pathanpura, Block Sursand, Sitamarhi, Remote, 23 km from Sitamarhi and 3 km from Block.

| Caste | Households | Migrating individuals |
|---|---|---|
| Muslim | 400 | 350 |
| Koyri | 65 | 10 |
| Chamar | 50 | 50 |
| Nonia (SC) | 35 | 45 |
| Sahu | 30 | 5 |
| Bhumihar | 10 | 12 |
| Dhobi | 10 | 20 |
| Kumhar | 8 | 10 |
| Halwai | 6 | 3 |
| Lohar | 6 | 4 |
| Khatwa | 5 | 5 |
| Paswan | 5 | 3 |
| Sonar | 4 | 3 |
| Nai | 4 | 5 |
| Total | 638 | 525 |

## Muzzaffarpur

## 10. Mohammadpur Khajir Village, Muzzaffarpur. Marhwan Block, Well Connected, Near Muzzaffarpur.

| Caste | Households | Migrating individuals |
|---|---|---|
| Muslim | 100 | 150 |
| Sahni/Mallah | 100 | 300 |
| Yadav | 70 | 90 |
| Lonia | 45 | 22 |
| Bania | 40 | 50 |
| Nai | 20 | 5 |
| Chamar | 20 | 20 |
| Kurmi | 15 | 30 |
| Kanu Bania | 15 | 10 |
| Lohar | 7 | 4 |
| Paswan | 6 | 5 |
| Koyri | 6 | 3 |
| Rajput | 5 | 4 |
| Kumhar | 2 | 1 |
| Sonar | 1 | 0 |
| Total | 452 | 694 |

Jobadih 2.5 km from road . Castes Koyri, Nunia, Tatma, Kumhar. Details of households and migrating individuals need to be completed.

# Nalanda

*Mohanpur Village, Block Hilav, Nalanda, 12 km from Bihar Sharif, 5 km from Silav, Well Connected, Very Near Nalanda, 2 km.*

| Caste | Households | Migrating individuals |
|---|---|---|
| Koyri/Mahato | 100 | 20 |
| Majhi | 80 | 120 |
| Paswan (SC) erst Dusadh | 75 | 40 |
| Ravidas (SC) | 35 | 50 |
| Yadav | 20 | 10 |
| Kahar | 20 | 15 |
| Bhumihar | 20 | 6 |
| Nai | 20 | 7 |
| Pasi (sc) Choudhary | 15 | 10 |
| Brahman | 10 | 4 |
| Dhanuk (BC) | 8 | 4 |
| Dhobi | 5 | 4 |
| Total | 408 | 290 |

*Ajaypur Remote, Block Noorsarai, Nalanda, 20 km from Nalanda, 6–7 km from block, 5 km from main road, transport by tum-tum.*

| Caste | Households | Migrating individuals |
|---|---|---|
| Kurmi | 400 | 100 |
| Majhi | 200 | 150 |
| Yadav | 85 | 30 |
| Parsi Toddy | 40 | 25 |
| Paswan | 35 | 15 |
| Brahmin | 20 | 7 |
| Baniya | 15 | 0 |
| Muslim | 10 | 0 |
| Badhaee | 10 | 0 |
| Kumhar | 8 | 4 |
| Nai | 8 | 3 |
| Kanu (BC) | 4 | 5 |
| Dom (SC) | 2 | 0 |
| Total | 837 | 339 |

Land mainly with Kurmis. Paddy, wheat, mustard, lentils, potatoes.

# 7

# Brick Kiln Workers from Jharkhand

## The Labour of Love [1]

*Alpa Shah*

## INTRODUCTION

The state of Jharkhand was carved out of the southern part of Bihar in the year 2000. More than 26 per cent of the population of the state is tribal.[2] Although rich in mineral resources and industry, many tribal areas of the state have poor irrigation, low agricultural productivity, and low levels of industrialization, making seasonal migration an important livelihood strategy.

This chapter draws on eighteen months of fieldwork (November 2000–June 2001) in an *adivasi* (Scheduled Tribe) dominated village called Tapu in Bero block, Ranchi District, Jharkhand and a one week stay at a labour camp in a brick kiln in West Bengal. It argues that migrants do not understand their movement in economic terms alone. Many see the brick kilns as a temporary space of freedom to escape problems back at home; explore a new country; gain independence from parents; and live out prohibited amorous relationships. It is suggested that Jharkhandi activist and policy makers' construction of such migration as a 'problem' is as much about their vision of how the new *adivasi* state ought to be as about exploitation. Migration to the kilns is seen by them as a threat to the purity and regulation of the social and sexual *adivasi* citizen. This moralizing perspective creates a climate that paradoxically encourages many young people to flee to the brick kilns where they can live 'freely'. In this way, the new puritanism at home helps to reproduce the conditions for capitalist exploitation and the extraction of surplus value, while not focusing on the material issues of how the conditions of labour migration can be improved further for the poorest.

A brief context to seasonal casual labour migration from Jharkhand is followed by an extended story of the escape of Burababa Munda from Tapu to a brick kiln in Uttar Pradesh. This story reveals that Burababa's children also had complex reasons for migrating. The chapter then examines the other side of the picture of unmitigated misery in the brick kilns, and the reasons people give for migrating. These are quantitatively documented in the penultimate section. The conclusion examines the discourses of *adivasi* activists vis-à-vis the perspectives of the migrants to suggest that the representations of the activists paradoxically help to reproduce the conditions for capitalist exploitation and the extraction of surplus value, while leaving aside the crucial issues of improving the conditions of labour migration for the poorest.

THE MIGRANT'S POINT OF VIEW

Clutching a small bag of clothes, Sanicharwa Mundein left Tapu village[3] one frosty January morning to board a bus for Ranchi, Jharkhand's capital, the first leg of a journey to a brick kiln in West Bengal. She walked to a nearby village where she was to join other villagers and the labour contractor, Ganga Yadav. Two months before, after a devastating argument, her husband Rana had fled to a brick kiln with Ganga. Sanicharwa said she was afraid to lose Rana to another woman at the kilns. She had to join him.

Following Meillassoux (1981 [1975]), seasonal casual labour migration of people like Sanicharwa and Rana is usually understood as part of a broader system of exploitation and oppression characteristic of capitalist production (Breman 1985, 1994, 1996; Mukherji 1985; Standing 1985). A result of this analysis is a conflation between the role of migration in the broader social system with the migrant's point of view. The migrant is rarely depicted as opting for departure and is usually assumed to live in extreme poverty with little alternative but to leave the home area for the dry six months of the year to subsist or survive (Breman 1985; Shah *et al.* 1990).

In recent years the migrant has acquired more agency. Yet, most often he/she is seen as a rational actor striving for an economic optimum (Lal 1989), or participating in a defensive coping strategy in the context of debt and extreme economic vulnerability (Mosse

2002 *et al.*). Although some critics object that the migrant is not just *'homo economicus'*, and consider social, religious, and 'ethnic' factors, their accounts argue that it is mainly economic choices that drive such migration (De Haan 1994; Rogaly and Coppard 2003). Those who integrate the social and cultural contexts of migration do so more in their analysis of change in the areas receiving immigration (Appadurai 1996), or creating emigration (Gardner 1995; Osella and Osella 2000; 2003), rather than in their considerations of why people move.

This chapter argues that, from the point of view of those who migrate from Jharkhand to the brick kilns of other states in India, it makes little sense to understand seasonal casual labour migration in economic terms alone. In focusing on such movement, marginal but increasingly important to labour studies (Breman 1999), the aim is to further highlight recent contributions to the study of migration (Osella and Gardner 2004; De Haan and Rogaly 2002). These show that while economic considerations might shape or constrain it, seasonal, casual labour migration is a dynamic socio-political process. The argument here is that the migrants do not see brick kiln migration just in terms of money; nor as the irredeemable torture and drudgery that much of the literature portrays. Rather, they view their migration as a temporary escape from a problem at home and an opportunity to explore a new country, gain independence from parents, and live out prohibited amorous relationships. These are important dimensions of seasonal casual labour migration which, though occasionally hinted at, have generally been neglected in the literature and are rarely projected as a primary impetus for migration. For many migrants, life at the kilns is seen as 'free'. The desire for freedom is historically situated: its motivational force cannot be assumed as self-evident. Even though the kilns do not give migrants complete freedom, it is significant that Tapu migrants often describe the kilns as a place where they can live 'freely'.

The aim here is not to conduct an economic analysis of migration, nor to contest the view of migrant labour at the brick kilns as part of an exploitative system of capitalist production. Indeed, many migrants acknowledge that they are cheap labour for wealthy industrialists and that they expect to be cheated at the kilns. As Willis has proposed with regard to why working class children in England want working class jobs, 'there really is at some level a rational and potentially developmental basis for outcomes which appear to be completely irrational and regressive'.[4] In other words, it is suggested in this chapter that it is not contradictory to view brick kiln labour migration as exploitative, while also understanding that most migrants not only view their movement as a choice but see the brick kilns as an important, if temporary, space away from the social constraints back home.

CONTEXT

Circular migration from Bihar, the state from which Jharkhand seceded in November 2000, is at least a hundred years old (De Haan 2002). In the late 1800s, West Bengal, Andaman and Nicobar Islands, Assam, Bhutan, and even Burma attracted migrants from Jharkhand. Tribal people of Chotanagpur were preferred in railway and road building projects, and especially tea plantations, where they were considered 'more industrious and tractable than other classes'.[5] By 1895, at least 50 per cent of workers in Assam's tea plantations came from Chotanagpur.[6] 'Weiner[7] estimates that by 1921 nearly a million tribals, one-third of Chotanagpur's tribal population, had emigrated. In Tapu there are village memories of migration for road building and tea picking to places near the Chinese border.

With the saturation of tea plantation labour, many of the offspring of Assam and Bhutan migrants went instead to the new brick kilns of West Bengal, Uttar Pradesh, and Bihar. Although it is difficult to estimate Jharkhand's annual migration, most agree the figure is at least several hundred thousand.[8] Of the 100 Tapu households, at least 47 per cent of the adult population have ventured at some stage to the brick kilns in those states. The Yadavs, descendants of the old landlords, do not generally migrate. It is mainly the Munda, Oraon, Maheli, Badaik, and Lohra, all SCs and STs who migrate. In 2000–1, 36 per cent of Tapu's ST and SC population above the age of 16 migrated—a total of 73, of whom 47 per cent were male and 53 per cent female.

It would be easy to conceive this migration as merely a survival strategy, or as the sociologist Jan Breman (1985) puts it, as a defensive coping strategy. At first glance Tapu strikes the outside observer as an economically depressed Jharkhandi village in an underdeveloped region (Devalle 1992; Prakash 2001). All the villagers live in mud houses; there is no electricity, public health facility, or school. Literacy rates are low. Disregarding those still studying, only 15 per cent of Tapu people have attended school up to primary class 8; 8 per cent have passed matriculation, and only 4 per cent have passed intermediate. Although every household owns some land, limited irrigation means that many harvest only one main crop a year. After the November harvesting, livestock rearing and manual labour in the village stone-chipping industry and in nearby government schemes are the main sources of livelihood. Poor people, especially ST and SC families, have little option but to migrate. But in Tapu the situation is more complex: economic motives may be significant, but others also matter. Indeed, it is the latter that the migrants stress most.

ESCAPING TO THE BRICK KILNS

Burababa, Somra Munda's father, had not been seen for two nights. It was August 2001, and Somra had just discovered that Burababa was on his way to the plains of Jonepur, Uttar Pradesh, to join his second son Mangra for the rest of the year at the brick kilns.

Somra was upset that his father had run away. The past year had been frustrating. Against Somra's wishes, Burababa, well over 60 years old, had chosen to work as a *dhangar* (a live-in year-round general manual labourer)[9] in the house of a Yadav, who was a descendant of an old village landlord. Somra had wanted his father to live at home, and to be able to feed and clothe him like any decent son. He also needed him to look after the family's cattle and work in their irrigated fields. Yet Burababa wanted to work and eat at the Yadav's, sleep wherever he liked, and earn a meagre Rs 1,200 for the year. With the beginning of the rains and the rice-transplanting season, Somra had finally convinced Burababa to leave the Yadav and come home.

The rice-transplanting season is a great annual festival period. The village is a hive of activity. All the seasonal migrants return at this time. Mornings are filled with hard work. The men exchange labour to plough and prepare each other's water-logged fields. The women, with their legs coated in oil and sarees hitched up, sing and joke as they sow rice in the fields. The children have mud bath and catch crabs and snails to eat. In the afternoons the high spirits of the fields are carried into the village. The owners of the fields sown that day host a lunch for the men and serve them rice beer and wine from the *mahua* flower. The women are also served the alcohol, as well as nibbles of fried lentils and wild mushrooms. The party begins at noon and continues into the evening. Those with energy to spare (especially youngsters), then move on with their singing and drumming into the *akhra* where the night is danced away. At four in the morning the new day begins with new fields to be ploughed and sown and a new party to be hosted.

For Burababa and others, the rains are a time for merriment and bonding. But his return to his son's house had become a great strain due to the restrictions imposed on him. Several years ago, Somra and his immediate family had become part of a group of Mundas who call themselves Bhagats and who consider themselves a class above the impurity and decadence of the Munda households of their birth. Somra's bitter memories of his childhood are dominated by moving from house to house as a *dhangar*, Burababa's lack of concern about providing his children with an education, and his developing fondness for the local brew. At some point, Somra ended up working as a dhangar in a nearby village where he fell in love with his Munda employer's beautiful daughter, Ambli. To Somra's dismay, after 10 years of living in Ambli's house, her father married her off to a man from a neighbouring village. However, Ambli was soon back with Somra.

Somra now felt the need to prove his worth to Ambli's parents who had given their other daughters in marriage far up the social scale—to armymen and policemen. He decided to emulate Ambli's father and become a Bhagat, training intensively for several months. He joined a group of Mundas living under strict rituals of secret prayers, refraining from food cooked by others and non-vegetarian food (all but sacrificial meat), and giving up liquor (except the foreign or 'English', varieties, beautifully sealed and packed in bottles labelled 'Old Monk' or 'Royal Challenge'). By this cleansing and ritual training they derive secret powers to cure minor illnesses and drive away troublesome spirits. Apart from the whisky and rum, Somra's lifestyle became closer to some Brahmin families in neighbouring villages than to his brother Mangra or his sister Jitia. Somra today thoroughly disapproves of his siblings' and his own former lifestyle.

Somra had for instance arranged the marriage of Mangra to a suitable girl, only to find that Mangra had brought from the kilns a Ho tribe woman from South Jharkhand. Mangra's Ho-speaking partner had difficulty with Nagpuria, the local language, and felt ostracized by other villagers. Unlike most other brick kiln migrants, Mangra has since chosen to live at the brick factory almost all year round, bringing his family to Tapu only occasionally for a few weeks in the rains. He thus chose not to farm the fields that are his share and not to live under the eyes of his watchful elder brother Somra. Jitia, Somra's sister, had also been married off to a man from a neighbouring village, only to return a year later declaring her love and determination to live with a married man, Minktu in her natal village. After one night in the akhra, several years ago, Minktu and Jitia had met secretly. On Jitia's return, Minktu left his first wife and child. The new couple ran away to the kilns to escape the accusations of dishonour and came back the following season, Jitia expecting her first child. As to Somra's remaining sibling, Budhwa: Ambli (Somra's partner) had a paternal cousin, Chotki, who spent all her days at their house and who fell in love with him. Chotki and Budhwa eventually ran away to the brick kilns to consummate their love in peace. After two children, the couple decided to stop migrating, look after their village fields, and follow in Somra's footsteps to become Bhagats.

Although Budhwa's fate was slightly different to that of Mangra and Jitia, what is common in all the stories is that at some point migrating to work seasonally in brick factories provided an escape mechanism from the claustrophobic restrictions of their brother and others in the village. So, Burababa's escape that rainy season was in part only a repetition of what had happened in that courtyard several times before. When Burababa returned to Somra's house, he also returned to a strictly vegetarian, teetotaler life—too restrictive for the old man. Eventually, at a time when few remain at the brick kilns, the old man made a secret arrangement with a labour contractor and left for the kilns.

There is a contrast between scholarly views on seasonal labour migration and what it might have meant for Burababa. Burababa's story might seem exceptional because of his son's puritanism. However, life in the village can be restricting for many people in different ways. The migration stories in the village suggested that scholars might perhaps have overlooked the possibility that many migrants see migration as a liberation from the constraints of village life. A week at the Daisy Brick Factory in Bengal reinforced this suspicion.

## The Misery of the Daisy Brick Factory

The Daisy Brick Factory, apparently the largest of approximately 350 such factories in Hoogly District, produced around 5 million bricks a year. The main entrance to the factory skirted a six-floor mansion. This was one of the factory owner's houses that he wanted to convert into a five star luxury tourist resort with a swimming pool and golf course stretching to the banks of the Ganges. A crowded labour camp of approximately 200 brick shacks lay adjacent to this mansion. Each shack was six by three metres in size with a low tile roof. It housed about four people, had merely a line for hanging clothes, a coal-fired stove, and sometimes a single rope bed. At one end of the compound, three taps supplied water to the camp. There was no sanitation, bathing facilities, or electricity in the camp, although the furnace a few metres away was floodlit at night.

Most labourers worked in the beating heat six days a week on one of three shifts: 5.30–8.00am, 10.00am–noon, and 2.00–6.00pm. While low-caste Bihari labour specialize in moulding bricks and Bengali labourers extract clay, Jharkhandi *adivasi* and low-caste labour load and unload bricks to and from the furnace, trucks, and stores. In the Daisy Factory, Jharkhandi labour accounted for almost half the labour force. Factory owners told me that, unlike Jharkhandis, Bengalis could not endure carrying bricks and considered it a menial task.

Jharkhandi women balance up to eight uncooked bricks on their heads. Men either receive these bricks from women to line the furnace, or carry a greater load of up to sixteen cooked bricks on a bamboo sling across their shoulders. Payment is at piece rates. Labourers expect that, subtracting living costs, hard-working couples will bring home Rs 8,000–9,000 for the six month season. Such couples are, however, rare. It is far more common to hear stories of individuals who managed only Rs 2,000. Although it is likely that the major reason for this shortfall is cheating on the part of employers and contractors, the explanation that labourers give for this low total wage is that the individuals were too busy having fun.

### The Love of Labour

It is difficult to imagine that the motivation to endure such hard working and living conditions could be anything other than the migrants' extreme poverty. But what did migration mean for those who moved? The answer—hardship, torture, and drudgery—often seems so straightforward and agreed-upon that the question itself is rarely seen as worth posing. Were the stories about the fun of brick kiln migration that were heard back in Tapu simply a consequence of the migrants' reluctance to admit that the brick kilns are actually awful and that the only reason for moving is the economic constraint of staying at home? This is unlikely for two reasons.

The first is that although many Tapu people could earn as much at home, they preferred to go to the kilns. Take the Mahelis. Stigmatized as the lowest, filthiest, most drunken caste by other Tapu residents, they had a reasonably profitable business of making bamboo baskets. The work is usually done by husband–wife pairs. A bamboo stick is bought for Rs 10–40. One person skins it making long, thin strips. The other weaves the strips. In a week, the pair make an average of 50 baskets with material costing Rs 200, and a net weekly profit of Rs 400. The baskets are sold in the Bero bazaar twice a week. Peak seasons are between October to December, when large baskets are in demand for harvested husked rice. From December to June, smaller baskets are bought for vegetable-picking and cow-dung gathering, as baskets made in this season are the strongest.

In comparison, what do migrants come back with? Even if we take the salaries of hard working couples at the kilns (Rs 8,000–9,000 for the season), the monthly average is less than what the Mahelis earn at home. Given that very few migrants come back with such money, why do some Mahelis prefer to migrate when they could easily earn more in the village? Etwa Maheli, a young man, and his two brothers usually go to the kilns, though in 2001 the youngest stayed home to look after their elderly parents. Etwa himself had been migrating for seven years, for two of which he had been an assistant contractor. The first year he went with a Maheli woman from the village. They married and had a child, but a few years later she left him for another man. Eventually Etwa 'made another woman'—a Lohra one from a nearby village. Even after the birth of two children, the couple continued to migrate. When asked about the economic logic behind their migration, Etwa simply said, 'money isn't everything'. Life in the factories is fun, and a welcome break from making bamboo baskets, enabling encounters with diverse people. Most significantly, at the kilns all labourers treat each other with respect as 'everybody is equal there'. From a village environment where he and his family are severely stigmatized, this was very important to him.

Undoubtedly carrying bricks is tough, but it would be a distortion to portray life at the brick kiln as unremittingly bleak. In one of the five shacks of migrants from Tapu, were four, unmarried and unrelated girls who, despite their parents' pleas, had all migrated. The eldest, 20 year old Shila, had left the village overnight without her parent's consent. In the winter months, disappearing children were a common phenomenon in Tapu. Although parents were usually upset, they rarely worried. It was assumed that they had gone to some brick kiln and that they would hear from them in due course. In the three months that Shila had been at the kiln she had transformed from a school-skirt-clad girl to a woman dressed in a saree. As with the case, reported by Rogaly and Coppard (2003), of a woman separated from her second husband, who migrated from Puruliya to the rice fields of Bardhaman in order to have an affair with the labour contractor, it also transpired that the relationship between the labour contractor, Jeevan, and Shila was more than platonic. But there were complications in Jeevan and Shila's romance.

Jeevan had been married for twelve years but, though his wife and child were in the village, the other girls did not think him a suitable match for Shila. They had found Shila a quiet young boy from Ranchi whom they referred to as '*bhatu*' (Nagpuria for 'brother-in-law'). One night Shila had served rice-beer to the bhatu and Jeevan had danced with a female labour contractor. A jealous tension thus developed between Shila and Jeevan. Later that week, Jeevan disappeared to the market for a few hours in his shiny new jacket. At around the same time, the female labour contractor, with lipstick and high heel sandals, left the camp. After his return from the market, Shila sarcastically taunted Jeevan saying he ought to leave his door open that night so that his '*mal*', or 'property' could slip in.

The next night Shila invited the bhatu back to the shack where he sat quietly while the other girls giggled and joked. Jeevan got increasingly infuriated. When the bhatu left, Jeevan shouted at the girls to shut up, bellowing that the shack had turned into a 'free zone', and that they were ruining their reputation. He threatened to send Shila's father a message telling him what she was up to. This outburst produced an uncomfortable silence. Shila stopped eating, trying to make the point that Jeevan had hurt her. One Sunday, Jeevan, Shila, and a few others visited a Church in the nearby town of Bandel where Jeevan bought Shila a necklace. In the evening Shila made chicken curry for Jeevan, his brother, the girls, and us. After a few cups of *hadia* (rice beer), relations between Shila and Jeevan seemed to be sunny again.

Shila and Jeevan's affair was only one of the flirtatious relationships between young men and women. As is true of the casual and contract labour in Bhilai, described by Parry,[10] joking and flirting between men and women were common as they worked, but it was in the confines of the labour camp that amorous relationships were expressed more fully. Indeed, unmarried men and women openly flirted with each other there, sat on each other's laps, held hands, lay next to each other on the floor or in rope beds—things that would never be seen in Tapu.

While sleeping arrangements were flexible, food was always consumed in the 'correct' shack, some nights some of the girls slept in Jeevan's in-law's shack and some nights in their own. Tapu villagers say that amorous relationships are pursued with ease at the kilns because most young people choose to go to different kilns from their siblings or other immediate kin. In many cases, having family around is indeed likely to cramp one's style. This explanation resonates with Parry's reports from Bhilai that husbands and wives generally avoid taking work on the same construction site because of the sexual banter and flirting that is characteristic of such work sites and the jealousy that this produces.[11] To some of the youth from Tapu, the brick kilns provide a convenient temporary space away from the authority of, and responsibility to, immediate family.

THE SOCIAL CONSTRAINTS OF THE VILLAGE

To understand why people felt constrained in the village it is necessary to know something of the sexual norms of the ST and SC communities in Tapu. Firstly, intra-clan, inter-tribe, and inter-caste unions are prohibited. Thus, as in Chopra's story of how migration to Punjab allowed an Oraon man from Ranchi district to elope with an unsuitable girl from a lower status family,[12] migration provides the space to explore such prohibited unions. Second, unlike for the Girasias of Rajasthan (Unnithan-Kumar 1997), or the Muria of Bastar (Gell 1992), divorce and post-marital affairs in Tapu are new, if they ever were, not readily accepted. Nevertheless, they do occur and often end in secondary unions. In Tapu, of the 83 married ST or SC men in the village, approximately 30 per cent were not with their first spouse. Affairs after marriage, or continuation of premarital relationships once married, as in Somra's sister's case, are pursued with greater ease at the kilns. In at least 50 per cent of the secondary unions of ST and SC Tapu men, migration to the brick kilns had enabled the development of the second relationship.

Premarital sexual relations were, in general, common in the village. The restriction on such relations, however, is that they must not become permanent. Thus, a third village norm encouraging migration is that marital partners must not be of the boy or girl's choice but must be selected by their parents. Although it was not necessary for a woman to be a virgin, marital partners should not have previously engaged in sexual relations with each other. It has been suggested that this is the main reason why parents prefer brides for their boys from outside the village—to ensure that the potential partners had not had sexual relations. As was the case for Somra and two of his brothers, premarital lovers who want a more permanent relationship commonly deploy the tactic of leaving for the kilns and returning after the woman is several months pregnant. In the village, early pregnancies resulting from illicit affairs are aborted. After childbirth, however, such affairs are legitimized.

Another restriction on premarital sexual relations is that the older generation must not know of them. This is the reason why parents hold contradictory views about their children running away to the kilns. On the one hand they are upset, not just because a child's departure means one less hand in the fields, but also because they know that the kilns provide space for developing amorous affairs. On the other hand, many parents understand the youngsters' desires—they had been in the same situation themselves, and had often met their own marital partners in the labour camps. Thus, when parents express displeasure and hurt when their children take off to the kilns, this is usually because—as parents—they ought not to endorse the sexual freedom that everyone knows brick kiln migration entails. This is not to say, however, that every young person who goes to the kiln engages in amorous relationships. The important point is that the ability to explore amorous relationships more fully in the brick kilns than in the village makes migration attractive.

## FURTHER REASONS FOR MIGRATING

Not all Tapu migrants at the Daisy Factory, however, had come to live out prohibited sexual relations, or for the fun and games of the kilns. In the shack adjacent to that of the four girls lived an old man who had run away from his son under similar circumstances to Burababa, and hoped that on his return his son would treat him better. Pera Munda, in his mid-thirties, his Oraon wife Sanicharwa and their son lived in the third shack. Pera had been coming to the kilns for the past seven years, for various reasons. Initially, migration was a means of escape from his father. Between the age of six and his late teens, Pera had been a *dhangar* in a village near his own. When he returned to live in Tapu, he argued with his father continuously. Migrating to the kilns provided some relief from the tensions at home. When his father died, Pera inherited land and livestock and considered staying in Tapu all through the year. However, soon afterwards, Pera's elder brother, accused of a murder, was jailed. Pera and his brothers mortgaged their lands to pay a zamindar descendent who claimed he could get the brother released. Pera thus continued going to the kilns to pay off the debt. At the kilns he fell in love with Sanicharwa. In Tapu, their inter-tribe union was stigmatized, and this provided another incentive to continue migrating to the kilns.

By 2001 circumstances had changed: Pera not only recovered enough of his family's land to stay in Tapu all through the year, but also Sanicharwa gave birth to a child. As a result, the couple's union became more legitimate. Pera now wanted to settle in Tapu, where they had a bigger house, livestock to look after, and fields to cultivate. But while Sanicharwa recognized the difficulties of looking after a baby in the beating heat in a tiny shack, she was convinced that life at the kilns would be liberating in comparison to the claustrophobic atmosphere of the village where she would be looked down on for her lower caste status. At the kilns 'all people are equal', she said and people forget the rules of 'purity and pollution'. This is clearly not always the case ( for example, Jharkhandis rarely mixed with low caste Biharis), but it is also true that in most kilns there would be only a few people from home for whom the hierarchy of the village and the rules of purity were relevant.

Next to Pera, lived his father's brother's son, forty-five year old Samu, his second wife Anita, and their six-year old son. Anita said that she would continue to migrate as long as she could do kiln work. This was another exceptional family that had been going to the kilns for more than ten years though their reasons had changed over time. Before her first marriage, Anita had gone to the kilns with her sister's husband and other young people, 'for fun'. She subsequently eloped with her first husband to the tea gardens, staying there for four years until her partner was caught having an affair with another Jharkhandi woman. When she returned to her natal village she felt ostracized as a single woman. This, and the fact that she had a daughter to marry off, gave her reason to continue migrating to the kilns, where she eventually became an assistant labour contractor. On 'Karma' festival, Samu (a widower) visited her village. Anita seemed his perfect partner and he took her back to Tapu. Each season they migrated to be 'alone' at the kilns until one year when Samu was able to build a hut for them to live in, thus enabling their separation from the extended family. Puzzled as to why they should continue to migrate, Anita finally confirmed that in Tapu she was accused of witchcraft, and that the brick kilns provided a welcome space of escape from the malicious village gossip.

Fatra, a middle-aged Munda man and his fourteen year-old daughter lived in the fifth shack, while his wife and four other children were back in the village looking after the fields and livestock. He had mortgaged some of his fields as his family in Tapu had suffered recurrent bad luck with malaria and he had to spend much money on sacrificial chickens and on medicine given by the healers. Fatra said he was at the factory that year for the sole purpose of earning money to redeem his land. In some years he would go to the kilns, while in others he stayed in Tapu. He explained that it was not always necessary to migrate, as he could earn enough by tilling his fields and working as contract labour. However, in years when their financial situation was precarious, as in 2001, it was safer to go to the kilns where he was sure to save money. Like many others, he explained that in the village money rapidly flows away into drink and celebration with relatives and friends. At the kilns one saves more, not necessarily because one earns more but because one spends less, since wages are paid only at the end of the season. For him, the brick kilns provided a space away from home where he could concentrate on hard labour without the distraction of kinsfolk.

It is clear that the migrants from Tapu were motivated to come to the Daisy Brick Factory that year for a range of different reasons. However, the most striking feature of all the stories is how rarely migration was seen as *solely* an economic necessity, and how often it was also perceived in terms of the temporary need to be in a space away from the village and from the constraints and obligations of kinship, from domestic disputes and a narrow-minded and oppressive village environment. For six months of the year at the kilns, migrants could lead what they saw as a more autonomous life without disrupting kinship and friendship networks in the village or a long-term connection with their house and land. Brick kiln migration, after all, was almost always seen as a temporary phase in a person's life.

SOME QUANTITATIVE INDICATORS

One hundred and fifty-five persons, that is 47 per cent of the adult population of Tapu, have at some point been to the brick kilns. Of these, 57 per cent say that they migrated the first time for either one or more of the following reasons—to explore and roam, to escape from a problem at home, or to live out a prohibited amorous relationship. Regardless of the compulsion to earn money, the migrants themselves rarely stressed economic motivations. They saw the brick kilns as a space in which they could do certain things and be certain people away from home.

The various reasons people gave for migrating from Tapu in 2000–1 are summarized in Table 7.1.[13] In 2000–1 there were 79 migrants (73 of them above the age of 16). 56 of the total number of migrants for that year, just above 70 per cent, felt that there were sufficient resources in the village (from cultivable land, livestock, forests, and casual labour) and that they did not need to supplement their lifestyle with money from the kilns. More than half of these migrants (accounting for nearly 40 per cent of total migrants) were unmarried youth, who say they went for the fun and adventure of amorous relationships, life away from parents, and visiting new places.

Many young people stressed that the migratory process was an individual, exploratory one. Of course, as Parry (2003) remarks of long distance labour migrants to Bhilai, there is a contradiction between the actor's perception of individual autonomy in the migration decision and what is actually going on.[15] As with the migrants in

Table 7.1: Reasons Given for Migration by the Tapu Migrants, 2000–1[14]

I. Migrants who say they have sufficient resources to stay in the village all year

| | |
|---|---|
| *Number of migrants* | 56 |
| % of total migrants (n.79) | 71 |

*Reasons for migrating*

| | Fun, adventure, amorous relationships | Young families wanting to set up a new household | Escaping after a problem with kin | For a one-off saving |
|---|---|---|---|---|
| Number of migrants | 31 | 13 | 3 | 9 |
| % of total migrants | 39 | 16 | 4 | 11 |

II. Migrants who say they would have difficulty making ends in the village all year

| | |
|---|---|
| *Number of migrants* | 23 |
| % of total migrants (n.79) | 29 |

*Reasons for migrating*

| | Social exclusion (e.g. witchcraft accusation) | Inter-tribe marriage | Old, single man, not wanting to live with kin | Young, separated, single women |
|---|---|---|---|---|
| Number of migrants | 10 | 6 | 3 | 4 |
| % of total migrants | 13 | 8 | 4 | 5 |

*Source*: Authors.

Tirupur in Tamil Nadu described by De Neve (2003), kin did not necessarily form the most important social network in the kiln. The youth usually migrated with people from surrounding villages and socialized with other Jharkhandis in the kiln, repeating the pattern of earlier migration.

More than 20 per cent of the migrants who said there were enough resources at home for them not to need to migrate, that is, 16 per cent of the total, were people with young families who wanted to be independent from joint households. In these cases, paternal land had not yet been divided, precluding their setting up their own households, and the young families did not get on with their parents. While the parents wanted newly married sons to stay in the village and help in the fields, these young couples, like the Darana women in Jaipur (reported by Unnithan–Kumar 2003), rebelled by leaving for the kilns to be free of family constraints and to earn enough money to return and set up their own households. They were not migrating just for 'fun'.

Three of the Tapu migrants in 2000–1 had quarrelled with their relatives and had left abruptly in protest. Like Sanicharwa who followed her husband to the kilns in the aftermath of a marital argument, in 2000–1 one woman, who left the village after a fight with her husband, was followed by him to the kilns. Dupont (2000) also notes the importance of familial tensions and quarrels in explaining why houseless people in Old Delhi had migrated to the city.[16]

Just over 10 per cent of the 2000–1 migrants wanted to get away from kin for a different reason, that is to ensure they saved a certain amount of cash that year. This was usually to pay off a loan (as in the case of Fatra Munda) or to buy some cattle. Although they could earn this money in the village, they said it was easier to save at the kilns.

Twenty three migrants, just under 30 per cent of the total in 2000–1, said they would find it difficult to make ends meet in the village. Of these, four were women whose husbands had left them and who, as a result, felt vulnerable and ostracized in Tapu. They had no land, and as a result of their marginalization had not developed survival strategies to cope with village life all year round. Three were older men, now single, who could not live with their siblings, sons or daughters. They had no desire to productively cultivate their share of land, especially because they could not rely on help from kin. Sixteen were individuals who felt ostracized in the village because they either had inter-tribe marriages or were accused of witchcraft. They felt more comfortable at the kilns and had therefore neither made their land productive, nor developed alternative livelihood strategies to enable them to stay in the village all year round.

It is perhaps possible that, at a practical level, economic imperatives may be more salient than many Tapu migrants allow. Indeed it may well be that without seasonal migration, Tapu people would not have the same standard of living. However, what these figures and the complex stories that lie behind them suggest is that, from the migrant's point of view, the economic motivations are eclipsed by a discourse that stresses the space that brick kiln migration provides for both social and cultural autonomy from the village.

ANTI-MIGRATION STANCES

As Jonathan Spencer has pointed out (2003), social theorists and policy makers tend to perceive migration as 'a problem', and policies and development strategies are often aimed at reducing pressures to migrate (De Haan and Rogaly 2002).[17] Jharkhand is no exception. Not only is this evidenced by development projects in the area, quantifying their 'success' in terms of a decrease in seasonal casual labour migration, but also by Jharkhandi activists who lead a strong anti-migration movement. In November 2001, an activist vehemently arguing for an anti-migration bill to be passed in Jharkhand was quoted in the Ranchi daily newspaper, the *Prabhat Khabar*,

Why should tribal girls ... be oppressed by the brick-kiln owners, contractors and middlemen? Why should they be forced to work as bonded and low-waged workers? These questions are about protecting the reputation of the glorious history of this land and about living freely in a democracy with equality of rights, the protection of human rights, and the right to freedom ... (28 November 2001).

But women interviewed in Tapu were keen to migrate to the kilns and said the newspaper had got it wrong. The contrast between the two viewpoints is striking. Did those who railed against brick kiln migration not know of its non-economic significance for the majority of the migrants, or that many workers find a silver lining in the 'romantic' possibilities of such spaces? In Tapu, everyone was aware of them. This was true even of the higher caste Yadavs who do not migrate to the kilns, despite the fact that some engaged in hard manual labour in the village and are now often less well-off than some of the migrant families. For the Yadavs, such migration signifies an impure life of low bodily self-control in food, drink, and sex—something demeaning for higher castes, if 'natural' to *adivasis* and *dalits*.

For people like the Bhagat and Somra Munda, were on the other hand keen to distance themselves from this representation of adivasi people. One of the main ways in which they did this was by emulating certain higher caste values (in attitudes to food, drink, and sex) and by stigmatizing life at the kilns. Most of the ST and SC older generation in Tapu had more ambivalent views on brick kiln migration. On the one hand they respected Somra, but on the other they also quietly appreciated that, as adivasis or lower castes, their values were different from the higher castes.

The most vehement protestors against brick kiln migration we.., however, well-meaning middle-class adivasi activists in Ranchi city, like the one writing for *Prabhat Khabar* (quoted above). These activists are generally urban-based and highly educated—even having PhDs from foreign universities. Some are educated *adivasis* from Christian convert backgrounds. Others may often use only their first names to hide their upper caste identity.[18] They say that seasonal migration is compelled by extreme poverty and that migrants not only leave behind their home traditions but are also exploited and oppressed at every stage, starting from the labour contractor at home to the managers and bosses at the kilns. It would appear that these opponents of brick kiln migration are at some level aware of the motivations for migrating and seek to draw a veil over them.

Jharkhandi activists demanded a separate state of Jharkhand on the basis that the adivasi-dominated communities of greater Jharkhand had historically been a majority in the region, that *adivasi* livelihoods and ways of life were under threat from dikus (outsiders), and that the territory should thus be reclaimed in the name of the true 'sons of the soil' (Weiner 1988).[19] Jharkhand finally gained statehood in November 2000, but activists were disappointed in the way in which it happened and the scant regard that was paid to the *adivasi* communities in the process, as undermining the idea of Jharkhand as a state in which *adivasis* would be protected. Activists are now more than ever driven to 'protect' *adivasi* livelihood and cultures.

One aspect of this protectionism is the campaign against seasonal labour migration from Jharkhand to the brick kilns of other Indian states. In the rhetoric of the Jharkhandi activists, *adivasis* are the true 'sons of the soil', historically wrenched from their land by rapacious outsiders, *dikus*, who transport them to far away places. This chimes with Spencer's insightful analysis of political modernity in which a central image of the nation-state is that it consists of people 'living in the same place'.[20] An obsession with controlling migration is a symptom of the quest to maintain this illusion. Seeing migration as the exception rather than the norm of human experience, the ideology of the nation-state attempts to maintain the purity of its citizenry by controlling the movement of people.

In fact, Jharkhand has for centuries seen movements of people (cf. Roy 1995), and even in earlier periods there is evidence that migrants had, in many cases, actually run away from home. In the face of such historical mobility, the anti-migration campaign serves to recreate and reinforce the image of Jharkhand as an *adivasi* state. The control of migration enables both an opportunity for a better and clearer display of the ideal vision of the state[21] as well as well as space for the manipulation and recreation of that image. The anti-migration campaign thus allows the Jharkhandi political elite to manipulate and recreate the image of the ideal *adivasi* citizen of the state—an embodied image of a socially and sexually transformed Jharkhandi. The campaign contests the old high-caste representations of tribals as morally impure, drunken, and sexually promiscuous to produce an image of purer *adivasi* bodies—the aboriginal citizen not only of Jharkhand but also of the Indian state.

In seeking to recreate Jharkhand's 'authentic *adivasi* tradition', institutions like the *dhumkuria* (better known in Muria areas as the *ghotul*), a village dormitory where post-pubescent unmarried youth would sleep and participate in erotic song and dance, are being revived as learning institutions, rather than as spaces for pre-marital sexual relations (cf. Elwin 1947 and Gell 1992). In similar fashion, the akhra is being revived as a village meeting place, emphasizing the so-called communitarian nature of *adivasi* villages, rather than a village dancing circle where girls and boys dance together to sexually charged songs and rhythms. In Tapu increasing Brahminical and Christian influence had led to the disappearance of the *dhumkuria* and the decline of the akhra in some areas.

Stories from the Tapu area seem to suggest that the brick kilns have become a 'functional surrogate' for the space of freedom once provided by the akhra, the village dancing circle, or the older *dhumkhuria*, the village dormitory for youth. As a space of freedom, the brick kilns represent an obvious threat to the image of adivasi society, and more specifically *adivasi* womanhood, that the elite would like to have accepted. A survey conducted by a university professor in four districts of Jharkhand, investigating the reasons why people migrate to the kilns confirmed that the majority of those who left went in order to escape from a fight at home, to explore a new country, or to live out amorous relationships. Since this result was at striking odds with the arguments of his colleagues and friends who were vehemently protesting against brick kiln migration, the professor decided not to publish his results.

Whereas Jharkhandi activists are able to talk about migration to the brick kilns in terms of a human rights discourse—as a movement to be stopped on grounds that it furthered *adivasi* exploitation, brick kiln migration enables many migrants to reject Jharkhandi *adivasi* elite notions of an authentic, 'morally pure', *adivasi* citizen of the state.

Ironically, the spaces of 'freedom' provided by the brick kilns serve to maintain older notions of the tribal self. Thus, rather than being a phenomenon dictated by mere economic necessity, migration to the brick kilns may also be seen as part of a distinctive Tapu politics of challenging the moralizing purifying discourse of the adivasi state.

POLICTICAL AND POLICY IMPLICATIONS

In the indigenous activist's anti-migration stance, the material issues, which really should be at stake in improving the lives of poor *adivasi* migrants, get buried deep in the ground. Rather than closing borders, policies need to be focused on addressing the conditions of migration (see also David Mosse 2002, 2005 and Rogaly *et al.* 2001, 2002). This means guaranteeing that workers have better living conditions with better houses, clean, piped water, and proper sanitation facilities. It also means ensuring decent health facilities—access to good doctors with subsidized health care and medicines. Attention to better and guaranteed wages and safe working conditions is crucial. And most of all, brick kiln labour needs support in becoming unionized so that labourers have the political space to ensure that these minimum conditions for their betterment are met.

NOTES

1. A version of this chapter first appeared as a journal article in *Contributions to Indian Sociology* (n.s)., 40 (1), pp. 91–119. The author wishes to thank Sage Publications for allowing the article to be adapted for this volume.
2. According to the 2001 Census there are 30 tribes in Jharkhand including the Munda, Santhal, Oraon, Gond, Kol, Kanwar, Savar, Asur, Baiga, Banjara, Bathudi, Bedia, Binjhia, Birhor, Birjia, Chero, Chick-Baraik, Gorait, Ho, Karmali, Kharwar, Khond, Kisan, Kora, Korwa, Lohra, Mahli, Mal-Paharia, Parhaiya, Sauria-Paharia, and Bhumij.
3. Pseudonyms are used for most place and people names.
4. P. Willis, *Learning to Labour: How Working Class Kids Get Working Class Jobs*, Westmead, Hants, England: Saxon House, 1978, p. 120.
5. Government of India, *Emigration to Assam: Commission of Enquiry*, Calcutta: Office of the Superintendent of Government Printing, 1861, p. 2.
6. S.D. Badgaiyan, 'Tribal Worker in the Industry', in D. Thakur and D. Thakur (eds), *Tribal Labour and Employment*, New Delhi: Deep and Deep Publications, 1994, p. 177.
7. M. Weiner, *Sons of the Soil: Migration and Ethnic Conflict in India*, Oxford: Oxford University Press, 1988, p. 161,

8. Rogaly *et al.* (2001) highlight the problems of quantifying the scale of seasonal migrant labour in an interesting attempt to estimate the number of seasonal migrants entering Bardhaman District, West Bengal, in the rice harvesting season.

9. In this part of India, a dhangar was a person who, in return for their availability at any time for a multitude of tasks ranging from farm work to general cleaning and building work, was provided meals, clothes, housing, and a nominal annual wage by his employer. Most dhangars in Tapu and the surrounding village were children between the age of 5 to 13.

10. J. P. Parry, 'Ankalu's Errant Wife: Sex, Marriage and Industry in Contemporary Chattisgarh', *Modern Asian Studies*, 35(2), 2001, p. 808.

11. Parry, 'Ankalu's Errant Wife', p. 808.

12. Radhika Chopra, 'Maps of Experience: Narratives of Migration in an Indian Village', *Economic and Political Weekly*, 30(49), 1995, p. 159.

13. *Sardars*, labour contractors, no longer force people to migrate in the way they are alleged to have in earlier periods (especially to the tea gardens). They are, however, important in determining where people migrate to and sometimes who they go with.

14. The data this table draws on was obtained from stories of people's departure and open-ended interviews with every single household in Tapu. Hence, the classifications are the author's own.

15. Parry (1999) also draws attention to this contradiction in Wolf's (1992) data on factory women in Java.

16. Dupont (2000, p. 109) says that 24 per cent of houseless migrants surveyed cited familial tensions as the primary reason for migrating. People are of course often reluctant to admit in brief questionnaires that familial tensions resulted in their migration. This is perhaps evidenced by the fact that of the 36 respondents Dupont selected for in-depth interviews, about one-third mentioned familial tensions as important in their migration trajectory only when pressed (Dupont 2000, p. 123, fn. 35).

17. A. De Haan and B. Rogaly, 'Introduction: Migrant Workers And Their Role In Rural Change', *Journal of Development Studies*, 38(5), 2002, p. 4.

18. Baviskar (1997, p. 217) also reports tribal activists in Gujarat hiding upper caste surnames.

19. Although the demand for a separate state of Jharkhand initially focused on the idea that the culturally autonomous tribal people of the area should have the right to govern themselves, in later years the movement did become more inclusive. The new rhetoric also asserted that Jharkhand had become an internal colony of the state of Bihar.

20. J. Spencer, 'A Nation "Living in Different Places": Notes on the Impossible Work of Purification in Post-colonial Sri Lanka', *Contributions to Indian Sociology*, 37(1 & 2), 2003, p. 44.

21. Ibid., p. 21.

REFERENCES

Appadurai, A., *Modernity At Large: Cultural Dimensions Of Globalisation.* Minneapolis: University of Minnesota Press, 1996.

Badgaiyan, S. D., 'Tribal Worker In The Industry', in D. Thakur and D. Thakur, (eds), *Tribal Labour And Employment*, New Delhi: Deep And Deep Publications, 1994, pp. 175–89.

Baviskar, A., 'Tribal Politics And Discourses Of Environmentalism', *Contributions To Indian Sociology* (N.S.), 31 (2), 1997, pp. 195–223.

Breman, J., *Of Peasants, Migrants And Paupers: Rural Labour Circulation And Capitalist Production In West India*, Delhi: Oxford University Press, 1985.

———, *Wage Hunters And Gatherers: Search For Work In The Urban And Rural Economy Of South Gujarat.* Delhi: Oxford University Press, 1994.

———, *Footloose Labour: Working In India's Internal Economy*, Cambridge: Cambridge University Press, 1996.

———, 'The Study Of Industrial Labour In Post-Colonial India—The Formal Sector: An Introductory Review', *Contributions To Indian Sociology* (N.S.), 33(1&2), 1999, pp. 1–43.

Chopra, R., 'Maps Of Experience: Narratives Of Migration In An Indian Village', *Economic And Political Weekly*, 30(49), 1995, pp. 3156–62.

Corbridge, S., 'The Continuing Struggle For India's Jharkhand: Democracy, Decentralisation And The Politics Of Names And Numbers', *Commonwealth And Comparative Politics*, 40(3), 2002, pp. 55–71.

De Haan, A., *Unsettled Settlers: Migrant Workers And Industrial Capitalism In Calcutta*, Hilversum: Verloren, 1994.

———, 'Migration And Livelihoods In Historical Perspective: A Case Study Of Bihar, India', *Journal Of Development Studies*, 38(5), 2002, pp. 115–42.

———, A. and B. Rogaly, 'Introduction: Migrant Workers And Their Role In Rural Change', *Journal Of Development Studies*, 38(5), 2002, pp. 1–14.

De Neve, G., 'Expectations And Rewards Of Modernity: Commitment And Mobility Among Rural Migrants In Tirupur, Tamil Nadu', *Contributions To Indian Sociology* (N.S.), 37(1&2), pp. 251–80.

Devalle, S., *Discourses Of Ethnicity: Culture And Protest In Jharkhand*, New Delhi: Sage Publications, 1992.

Dupont, V., 'Mobility Patterns And Economic Strategies Of Houseless People In Old Delhi, in V. Dupont, E. Tarlo, D. Vidal (eds), *Delhi: Urban Space And Human Destinies*, Delhi: Manohar/ Centre De Sciences Humaines, 2000, pp. 99–124.

Elwin, V., *The Muria And Their Ghotul*, Bombay: Oxford University Press, 1947.

Gardner, K., *Global Migrants, Local Lives: Travel And Transformation In Rural Bangladesh*, Oxford: Oxford University Press, 1995.

Gell, S., *The Ghotul In Muria Society*, Switzerland: Harwood Academic Publishers, 1992.

Government Of India, *Emigration To Assam: Commission Of Enquiry*, Calcutta: Office Of The Superintendent Of Government Printing, 1861.

Lal, D., *The Hindu Equilibrium, Volume 2: Aspects Of Indian Labour,* Oxford: Clarendon Press, 1989.

Meillassoux, C., *Maidens, Meal And Money: Capitalism And The Domestic Community,* Cambridge: Cambridge University Press, 1981.

Mosse, D., S. Gupta, M. Mehta, V. Shah, and J. Rees, 'Brokered Livelihoods: Debt, Labour Migration And Development In Tribal Western India', *Journal Of Development Studies,* 38(5), 2002, pp 59–88.

———, S. Gupta, And V. Shah, 'On The Margins In The City: Adivasi Seasonal Labour Migration In Western India', *Economic And Political Weekly,* 29 July 2005, pp. 3025–38.

Munda, R. D., 'Autonomy Movements In Tribal India: With Particular Reference To The Jharkhand Movement: A View From Inside', presented at The Workshop On Indigenous Peoples: The Trajectory Of A Contemporary Concept In India at Upsala (Seminar For Development Studies, Kursgarden).

Mukherji, S., 'The Process Of Wage Labour Circulation In Northern India', in G. Standing, (ed.), *Labour Circulation And The Labour Process,* London: Croom Helm, 1985, pp. 252–89.

Osella, F., and C. Osella, 'Migration, Money And Masculinity In Kerala', *Journal Of The Royal Anthropological Institute,* 6(1), 2000, pp. 117–33.

———, 'Migration and Commoditisation Of Ritual: Sacrifice, Spectacle And Contestations In Kerala, India', *Contributions To Indian Sociology* (N.S.), 37(1&2), 2003, pp 109–39.

———, and K. Gardner, (eds), *Migration, Modernity And Social Transformation In South Asia,* New Delhi: Sage Publications, 2004.

Parry, J. P., 'Ankalu's Errant Wife: Sex, Marriage And Industry In Contemporary Chhattisgarh', *Modern Asian Studies,* 35(2), 2001, pp. 783–820.

———, 'Nehru's Dream And The Village "Waiting Room": Long Distance Labour Migrants To A Central Indian Steel Town', *Contributions To Indian Sociology* (N.S.), 37(1 & 2), 2003, pp 217–49.

Prakash, A., *Jharkhand: Politics Of Development And Identity,* Hyderabad: Orient Longman, 2001.

———, J. Biswas, D. Coppard, A. Rafique, K. Rana, and A. Sengupta, 'Seasonal Migration, Social Change And Migrants' Rights: Lessons From West Bengal', *Economic And Political Weekly* 36(49), 2001, pp 4547–59.

———, D. Coppard, A. Rafique, R. Kumar, A. Sengupta, and J. Biswas, 'Seasonal Migration And Welfare/Illfare In Eastern India: A Social Analysis', *Journal Of Development Studies* 38 (5), 2002, pp. 89–114.

———, and D. Coppard, '"They Used To Go To Eat, Now They Go To Earn": The Changing Meanings Of Seasonal Migration From Puruliya District In West Bengal, India', *Journal Of Agrarian Change* 3(3), 2003, pp. 395–439.

Roy, S. C., *The Mundas And Their Country,* Ranchi: The Catholic Press, 1995 (1912).

Shah, G., P. Bose, G. Hargopal, and K. Kannan, *Migrant Labour In India*. Gujarat: Centre For Social Studies, 1990.

Spencer, J., 'A Nation "Living In Different Places": Notes On The Impossible Work Of Purification In Postcolonial Sri Lanka', *Contributions To Indian Sociology* (N.S.), 37( 1&2), 2003, p. 1–23.

Standing, G., (ed.), *Labour Circulation And The Labour Process*, London: Croom Helm, 1985.

Unnithan–Kumar, M., *Identity, Gender And Poverty: New Perspectives On Caste And Tribe In Rajasthan*, Oxford, Providence: Berghan Books, 1997.

————, 'Spirits Of The Womb: Migration, Reproductive Choice And Healing In Rajasthan', *Contributions To Indian Sociology* (N.S.), 37(1&2), 2003, pp. 163–88.

Weiner, M, *Sons Of The Soil: Migration And Ethnic Conflict In India*, Oxford: Oxford University Press, 1988, (1978).

Willis, P, *Learning To Labour: How Working Class Kids Get Working Class Jobs*, Westmead, Hants, England: Saxon House, 1978.

Wolf, D., *Factory Daughters: Gender, Household Dynamics And Rural Industrialisation In Java*, Berkeley: University Of California Press, 1992.

# 8

# 'When You Go to Other Places, You Have to be Smart'

## Seasonal Migration in Southern Madhya Pradesh

*Sophie Llewelyn*

## INTRODUCTION

This chapter shares findings from an ethnographic study of seasonal labour migration from Chandpur,[1] a village of 312 households located in southern Betul district, Madhya Pradesh (MP). Livelihood strategies in Chandpur—as elsewhere in this region—are pursued within a context of agricultural scarcity and hierarchical social relations, which circumscribe the range of possibilities available to the village's largely tribal poor. Caste, class, and gender relations mediate access to agricultural land and extension services, political representation and social protection, employment opportunities, and sources of credit. Interlocked credit and employment markets render land-poor tribal households vulnerable to debt bondage. Partly in response to these circumstances, seasonal migration has emerged as an increasingly popular livelihood strategy for poor tribal households.

Migration from Chandpur is not a new phenomenon. In the past, however, migration was an annual affair—an *en masse* trip to harvest wheat at an operation 70 km from the village. This journey was facilitated by a local landholding elite, to whom tribal workers were tied as bonded labourers. Twenty years since the last of these yearly trips, bondage relations have loosened, and Chandpur has become integrated into a regional market for migrant labour. Tribal workers now draw from their own extensive social networks and from new relationships with contractors to actively solicit extra-local work, and to recruit friends and kin. Compared with previous generations of workers in Chandpur, contemporary migrants enjoy far greater freedom to exercise their personal agency in determining where, how, and for whom they will work, for at least part of the agricultural year.

Nonetheless, important continuities persist between the regional market for migrant labour that has evolved over the last decade and the semi-feudal local economy of generations past. Extra-local employers reinforce structural constraints on migrants' agency through their exploitative recruitment and payment practices, including the use of debt to control the workforce. Migrant workers endure dangerous working conditions, extended separation from loved ones, and heightened vulnerability and dependency at distant worksites. Each of the migrants who participated in this study lives in chronic debt, and none reported migrant earnings sufficient to graduate from poverty. But even though migration rarely presents a means out of insecurity, many migrants are nonetheless able to draw from extra-local work to increase household income and to construct more empowering social identities.

This chapter is divided into five sections. The section one provides information about the regional and local context and the methodology of the study. Section two describes contemporary migration patterns from Chandpur. Section three draws from interviews with migrants to explore in greater detail the ways in which men and women migrants negotiate the institutions that mediate their access to multilocational livelihoods. The chapter concludes with policy recommendations for migrant support.

REGIONAL CONTEXT

Chandpur straddles a highway in Bhainsdehi, a southern tehsil of Betul district, just north of the Maharashtra (MH) border. Betul is situated among a cluster of districts in southern MP described by Dasgupta *et al.* as 'spatial poverty traps' for their hilly topography, poor infrastructure, and limited access to natural resources, information, and markets. An estimated 51 per cent of the district's population lives below the government poverty line (Debroy and Bhandari 2003). Agriculture in Betul is predominantly rain-fed; in Bhainsdehi tehsil, only 14 per cent of the net sown area is irrigated (UNDP 2002). Despite the region's poor agricultural infrastructure, however, rural livelihoods remain heavily dependent on agriculture: only 12 per cent of Betul's workers were employed in the rural non-farm sector in 2001 (UNDP, 2002). In Bhainsdehi, 41.9 per cent of workers are employed as agricultural labourers. The majority of these workers are men and women from the Gond and Korku tribes, who together comprise 62 per cent of the tehsil's population (Bhatt and Bhargava 2005).

Given the seasonal vulnerability associated with mixed rainfed farming, it is not surprising that labour migration from Betul is substantial and growing in importance (Som, Kleih, Kumar, and Jena 2002). While labour mobility has increased in recent years, migration from the region is not a new phenomenon: seasonal migration from the district can be dated to the end of the nineteenth century. Baker's (1993) historical study of the Central Provinces—present day southern Madhya Pradesh—links the advent of worker migration in the 1880s both to heightened agricultural scarcity under British rule, and to the development of railways and roads at this time. The *Betul District Gazetteer* of 1907 records an early instance of migration for the kharif harvest, noting that 'a large temporary exodus takes place from the south of the District to Berar[2] for harvesting the *juar* crop, and from the north labourers go to the Nerbudda Valley to cut the wheat' (cited in the *Betul District Gazetteer* 1971). Long distance migration also emerged towards the end of the nineteenth century, when thousands of tribal workers began migrating from the region to work as indentured labourers in the tea plantations of Assam (Baker 1993; Omvedt 1980). Today, migrants from Betul tend to choose temporary destinations much closer to home.

METHODOLOGY

Research for this study was conducted under the auspices of Shastri Applied Research Project, 'Globalization and the Poor: Sustaining Rural Livelihoods in India'. The project, a collaborative effort between researchers from Jawaharlal Nehru University, the Council for Social Development, and the University of Guelph, included both quantitative and qualitative components. As one of three junior researchers hired by the University of Guelph qualitative research team, I spent 14 weeks living and working in Chandpur with a research assistant, Neha Shouche. Methods included focus group interviews, social mapping and seasonal calendar group exercises, intensive participant observation, and semi-structured interviews with migrants, elders, teachers, shopkeepers, self-help group leaders, local and extra-local employers, and politicians. Fieldwork began in September and was concluded in December 2004, following a visit to the village's most important migrant destination—a brick kiln in Amravati district, Maharashtra.

Local Context

Chandpur was selected as a study site in part because of the high rates of seasonal out-migration reported among tribal workers. Like many villages of its size, it is a composite of several caste/tribe-based hamlets, or *dhanas*. Slightly more than half the village's households are tribal, with Korkus numerically dominant but more socially and economical marginalized than Gonds. The village is surrounded by agricultural land: low lying, irrigated plots belong to caste Hindu farmers; Gond and Korku farmers work peripheral, hillside, rain-fed plots, many of them cleared from forest land under a land distribution programme in the 1980s. Beyond these farms, a complex network of footpaths and bullock-cart tracks connect Chandpur to the innumerable tribal villages that dot this hilly landscape.

A generation ago, the village economy was essentially semi-feudal: Gond and Korku people worked as bonded labourers for Brahmin and Thakur landowners. Today, most Gond and Korku households are land-poor farmers, who supplement their farm income with agricultural labour or sharecropping[3] on larger farms, and increasingly, with migrant work. A social map of Gondi dhana shows that 80 per cent of Gond households draw an income from agricultural wage labour, either exclusively or in addition to income derived from their own farms and seasonal non-timber forest product (NTFP) collection. The Korku community is also heavily engaged in off-farm work: data collected by The Shastri Applied Research Project (SHARP) quantitative researchers indicates that 90 per cent of households in Korku dhana practice agricultural labour as either their primary or secondary source of livelihood. About 40 per cent of tribal households are landless.

Because agricultural employment follows seasonal patterns, the village's labour force is only periodically fully employed. Large-scale farmers recruit labourers on a daily basis, going door-to-door the evening before a major harvest or weeding job is scheduled. Periods of high demand are short, however: one respondent reported that the longest stretch of solid employment she can expect is eight days' weeding during the rainy season. Slack season under-employment represents a chronic form of insecurity.

Table 8.1 presents a calendar of agricultural employment available at different times in the year, and lists the wages associated with each task. Daily wages vary according to demand for labour: the base rate for agricultural workers is Rs 20 for women, Rs 25-30 for men; during periods of peak demand wages may rise to Rs 25–30 for women, Rs 40 for men. These wages are low for the region, and workers reported that they had not been raised in ten years. The local labour market is highly segmented: workers may be paid different rates for performing the same job, depending on their gender, perceived efficiency, and bargaining power.

Non-agricultural work in the village is more remunerative, but difficult to come by, and self-employment in the tertiary sector is rarely a sustainable option. Gond and Korku entrepreneurs do sometimes open shops in their respective hamlets, but these small businesses have a high rate of bankruptcy: landless and land-poor customers tend to buy on credit, which often goes unpaid.

Given the seasonal scarcity associated with rain-fed agriculture in this region, and the limited local employment opportunities available to workers, it is not surprising that poor households' living expenses routinely exceed their earnings. However, access to credit is highly constrained. While nearby commercial banking facilities do exist, banks do not extend the annual consumption loans on which most households rely. Moreover, many respondents expressed suspicion of formal financial institutions, which have humiliated local borrowers in the past: 'If you fail to return the money you borrow from them, they will just come to your house and take things from you'. For regular borrowing, poor people turn to moneylenders.

The majority of Chandpur's poor tribal households are chronically indebted to local moneylenders, taking yearly loans of Rs 1,500 – Rs 3,000, on which they are charged a 50 per cent interest rate, with the principal and interest due after six months. Most poor people have long-standing relationships with a particular money lending family, and are obliged, by their annual need to borrow, to make good on

## Table 8.1: Calendar of Agricultural Work in Chandpur

| Month | Type of work | Wages |
|---|---|---|
| June | Ploughing and Sowing This takes place during the season of *Mrg Nakshatra*—a period of about 18 days immediately before the rainy season begins. Crops sown include: soy, *toowar dal* (pigeon pea), sunflowers, peanuts, *jowar* (sorghum), *barboti* (green beans), *bajra* (millets), sesame, *urad dal* (black lentils). Cotton and chillies are sown in nurseries, then transplanted once they reach the appropriate size. | Ploughing and Sowing: man guides bullocks, woman follows with seeds Men: Rs 80–100 if he owns bullocks and implements, Rs 35–40 if bullocks belong to employer. Women: Rs 20. Transplanting: Women: Rs 20/day Children: Rs 15/day |
| July | Weeding (cultivation) The first round of weeding, for farmers who have the means, is done with a team of bullocks and a man. It is performed with a small implement so as not to harm the plants. Skilled, delicate work with a high social value. Spray Towards the end of the month, pesticides are applied to soy, toowar, barboti, chiliies... Sowing (on irrigated farms) cabbage , white radish, pumpkin, cauliflower, fenugreek. | Weeding: Men: Rs 35–40 if they use the farmer's bullocks; Rs 80–100 if bullocks are their own. Spraying: Men: Rs 40/day for the sprayer; Rs 20/day for the person who carries water to him. |
| August | Sowing Traditional grains, *kangli, jagni,* and *kutki* are sown primarily on tribal farms. Hand-weeding Hand weeding commences. Workers use a sickle to remove little weeds from around the plants. | Weeding is paid by the row. Men, women and children earn: Rs 20/day for 2 rowsRs 30/day for 3 rows |
| September and October | Harvest By the 20th of September, the kharif (rain-fed) harvest has begun. In order of appearance: Mung beans, barboti beans, soy, sunflowers, peanuts, *urad dal, jowar* and bajra, chilies. Spraying | Harvest: - Soy: Women cut the soy: Rs 25; men load: Rs 40 - Peanuts: Paid in-kind on piece-rate basis: 1/8 of harvest. - Jowar: Paid in-kind: 3kg/day - Other: m: Rs 30; w: Rs 20 |

Contd...

Table 8.1 (Contd.)

| Month | Type of work | Wages |
|-------|-------------|-------|
| | Cotton.<br>Threshing<br>Kangli, jagni, and kutki (minor millets) are harvested then threshed using bullocks. Soy and jowar is threshed by machine, the thresher's owner is paid 3% of the threshed crop for the use of his machine. | Some local workers migrate at this time to Itarsi, Hoshangabad, Harda in M.P.; Amravati district in MH for soy and jowar harvest. Pay rates are generally the same.<br><br>Threshing:<br>Men may be hired to help with bullock or machine threshing: Rs 30/day |
| November | Ploughing and Sowing (on irrigated land) Wheat, chana (chick pea), batana (similar to chana), muttar (peas) Spraying Cabbage and cauliflower Harvest Fresh toowar is harvested for home consumption. Cotton harvest begins Cabbage and cauliflower harvest starts Orange harvest begins in Chandpur and in MH. Chandpur harvest provides little work for locals: orange contractors from MH generally bring their own workers.<br><br>End of the month: Weeding Chana is thinned. Workers can bring home thinnings for their own consumption. | Men guide bullocks; women sow. Men: Rs 80–100 if he owns bullocks and implements, Rs 35–40 if bullocks belong to farmer. Women: Rs 20. Cotton harvest: primarily women: Rs 20/day some Men: Rs 25–30/day<br><br>MH Orange harvest: some local workers migrate to work for Maharati contractors, moving between plantations. Men climb trees and pick, women load oranges: Men: Rs 70/day; Women: Rs 30/day Weeding: Women: Rs 20/day Children: Rs 15/day |
| December | Harvest Dried toowar: wood is saved for kindling, making brooms and thatching. Toowar is crushed and dried. | Women cut the toowar; men load. w: Rs 25; m: Rs 35 Some local workers migrate to Sirasgao/Karasgao, MH for this harvest. |
| February | Harvesting wheat, chana, batana. Threshing wheat, chana. | Harvesting Wheat: Paid in-kind: Men: 6kg/day* Women: 4kg/day* |

| | | |
|---|---|---|
| | | (*Rate is uncertain. Could be as high as 8 kg for men, 6 kg for women) People from Korku *dhana* and Banjara *dhana* migrate primarily to Itarsi for the wheat harvest and are paid in-kind, but rates are higher there. Chana: Men: Rs 35 Women: Rs 20-25 Some local workers migrate to MH, where a team of up to 9 is paid Rs 250–300/acre. |
| March to April | *Mauwa* harvesting *Chironji* harvesting | For mauwa and chironji, big farmers' trees may be sharecropped or labourers hired: M: Rs 40 to climb the tree W: Rs 20 to collect fruit from the ground Some Korku workers now migrate to MH for chironji harvest. |
| May | Ploughing/farm preparation Rock picking: on big people's farms that have good soil, minimal rocks | Rock picking: Women: Rs 20 Children: Rs 15 |

*Source*: Author.

promises of repayment. Seed loans are also common in Chandpur. The same 50 per cent interest rate applies: after harvest, the borrower must repay the principal plus one half by weight.

Borrowing sums of money larger than Rs 3,000 from local lenders entails entering into an agreement whereby the debtor is obliged to work for the lender as a *naukar*, or attached labourer, for a year's duration. It is not uncommon for landless or land-poor villagers to enter into debt bondage of this sort in response to a livelihood shock, or to a predictable stress such as a wedding or other social expenditure: key informants estimated that up to one-third of Korku households include at least one person who works as a naukar. But even though the practice is widespread, it remains a source of shame for tribal households.

In the past, patron-client relations in the village were lifelong, and routinely enforced through violence and humiliation: 'Our fathers and grandfathers weren't educated. They had to sit in those people's houses and couldn't move unless they were told. Their bosses used to beat them'. Debt bondage relations have since taken on a more contractual character, and while an element of coercion endures, it is primarily economic in nature. People enter into bondage on a year-long contract, which essentially converts wages into debt, by paying workers upfront, so that their labour is represented as repaying a loan. Going rates for naukars in the village are Rs 5,000/year in exchange for a man's labour, Rs 2,500 – 3,000/year for a woman's, and Rs 1,500 for a child's. In addition to this sum, *naukars* are provided one meal a day. Debt relations are often far more prolonged than the annual contract system might suggest, however. Rates of pay are set so low that many households that enter into debt bondage as a temporary coping strategy are forced to borrow additional amounts from the lender, thereby forcing them to renew the relationship once their debt has come to term.

Workers strongly dislike the loss of freedom that accompanies naukar work. Most offensive to respondents are the beck-and-call relationships in which naukars must participate and the lack of limitations regarding the type of work a lender can order them to perform. Working hours are set according to the whim of the lender, and naukars' duties can involve dirty and ritually degrading jobs. For Gond and Korku women who perform domestic work in the homes of caste Hindu lenders, debt bondage is associated with a heightened risk of sexual assault.

MIGRATION FROM CHANDPUR

This study's qualitative methodology was not well suited to describing in precise terms the numbers of people who currently migrate. Numbers derived from social mapping exercises, key informant interviews and observation suggest that the Korku community in the village is most heavily engaged in labour migration: social maps show that up to 85 per cent of Korku households include at least one migrant. About 40 per cent of Gond households were reported to include a migrant. Far fewer caste Hindu households migrate, although some poor OBC households do include migrant workers. Respondents reported that the number of households choosing to migrate is increasing every year.

Participants in the study dated the emergence of contemporary migration patterns to the mid-1990s, when news of extra-local opportunities first arrived in Chandpur via kinship connections with nearby tribal communities. As more households began to migrate with work groups from neighbouring villages, local confidence in the process grew. Contractors started arriving in Chandpur in 1999/2000; they were a visible presence in the village's tribal dhanas during September and October of 2004.

Brick kiln contractors first arrive in June, a time of seasonal scarcity when small-scale farmers seek loans for agricultural inputs. The recruitment process is as follows: on his first visit to the community, a contractor approaches villagers at the market or near the bus stand and asks for people who know how to make bricks. The contractor offers a cash advance, usually Rs 2,000–3,000, and in some cases as much as Rs 10,000. Advances are interest-free, providing that the money is repaid after the first season's work. If migrants are unable to work off their advance in its entirety during one season, they could find their rate of payment docked in the following year, although this is a fact unlikely to be mentioned during initial negotiations. The kiln contractors make a second visit in November, to confirm arrangements for migrants' departure. When the time comes to migrate, either a truck is sent from the factory or the migrants take the bus. Workers remain at the kiln from December to June, with a week's break in March, for Holi.

Agricultural work pays less than brick-making and contracts are short-term, so recruiters rarely offer sizeable advances. Field crop contractors arrive with news of work only a week or two before the harvest is to begin. Recruitment occurs during the morning. A contractor will generally make arrangements with a single man, who then recruits others to accompany him. Migrants may request an advance on their wages of up to Rs 500, although Rs 200–300 is a more common amount. This money is spent on provisions for the workers' two- to three-week trips: migrants cannot expect to visit a market during the harvest, and must carry with them all the food that they will need.

The majority of migrants from Chandpur travel to agricultural work in groups of 10–20 men, women, and young children. The social networks that facilitate contemporary migration extend throughout the vicinity, and it is not unusual for either individual migrants or small groups from Chandpur to migrate with larger groups of friends and relatives from neighbouring hamlets.

In the five years that have passed since contractors first arrived in Chandpur, migrant-contractor relations have strengthened and their roles have in some ways blurred. Certain migrants have become active agents in recruitment networks, allowing established contractors to take a more passive approach to their work. Local harvest leaders tend to work with the same contractors year after year, recruiting neighbours to their gangs, negotiating advances and organizing group travel at a pre-arranged date.

Bhanu Markom, a landless Gond who has migrated seasonally to brick kilns since 1996, provides an example of the way in which workers use their social networks to recruit friends and relatives to migrant work. Bhanu and his wife, Ramrati, were working at a kiln in Karasgaon, Maharashtra, in 1997, when they heard from a fellow worker about a better opportunity at a kiln that had recently opened in Daryapur, Maharashtra. Bhanu, a big man with a confident, charismatic personality, visited the Daryapur kiln in the spring, and negotiated a cash advance from the manager. He and Ramrati returned to Daryapur the following year, and worked there through the winter. On returning to the village in the spring, the couple shared their good experience with relatives and neighbours from their *dhana*, many of whom liked the idea of a cash advance. As the years passed, Bhanu recruited significant numbers of workers to the kiln. This does not necessarily entail knocking on relatives' doors, but rather acting as a source of information for prospective migrants, and linking friends in need of credit with the brick kiln manager. As a result of Bhanu's efforts, the Daryapur operation was Chandpur's single largest source of external employment in 2004. In December of that year, 80 people from Chandpur and its surrounds migrated to Daryapur.

The knowledge-sharing networks that facilitate seasonal migration also include stakeholders other than contractors and migrants. Several of the Gond women who participated in the study learned about migration opportunities via the *dahiwalli*, a Gond woman who sells yoghurt and buttermilk throughout the vicinity. The dahi walli lives in a nearby tribal village, but visits Chandpur's Gondi dhana on a weekly basis, where she sells yoghurt door-to-door. She is not herself a migrant, but as a person with strong connections to migrant households throughout the immediate region, the *dahiwalli* is an important source of information for prospective women migrants—

particularly women who have been widowed, or abandoned by their husbands, and who therefore face barriers to accessing extra-local work through the male contractors who visit the village.

Participants in the study identified 27 different migrant streams originating in Chandpur. These are depicted in Figure 8.1. Rates of pay, duration of migration, and living and working conditions at migrant destinations are detailed in Tables 8.2a and 8.2b. The majority of migrant streams have as their destination short-term agricultural harvesting work, although as mentioned, the largest source of extra-local employment is the Daryapur brick kiln, about a three-hour journey from Chandpur. Migrants may participate in several two- to three-week harvesting trips over a given season, or they may combine agricultural work with longer-term (three to six month) construction or brick kiln work over the winter. Interviews with migrants at the brick kiln suggested that workers who once migrated to multiple harvests are increasingly replacing that work with longer-term migration to the kiln.

MIGRANT STORIES AND ANALYSIS

Seasonal migration presents a means for poor households in Chandpur to diversify their livelihoods by gaining access to more regular, in some cases more remunerative employment than that is available locally. By enabling poor households to access sizeable, zero-interest cash advances, contractors provide migrants with an important alternative to the high-interest seasonal loans that they would otherwise have to pursue through village patrons. Migration should not be perceived as a means out of insecurity, however.

Payment for migrant work is generally low, having been agreed to months in advance by people under pressure to meet immediate needs even at the expense of future income generation. Working conditions at migrant work sites are poor, worker housing is inadequate, and sanitary provisions are non-existent. Migrant workers tolerate these conditions in part because of the vulnerability induced by accepting work in distant, unfamiliar communities. But, employers take additional measures to create conditions that are inimical to collective action for change. As detailed in Table 8.2b, management at the Daryapur brick kiln maintains a captive, docile workforce by withholding wage payments until the kiln's final day of operation.[4]

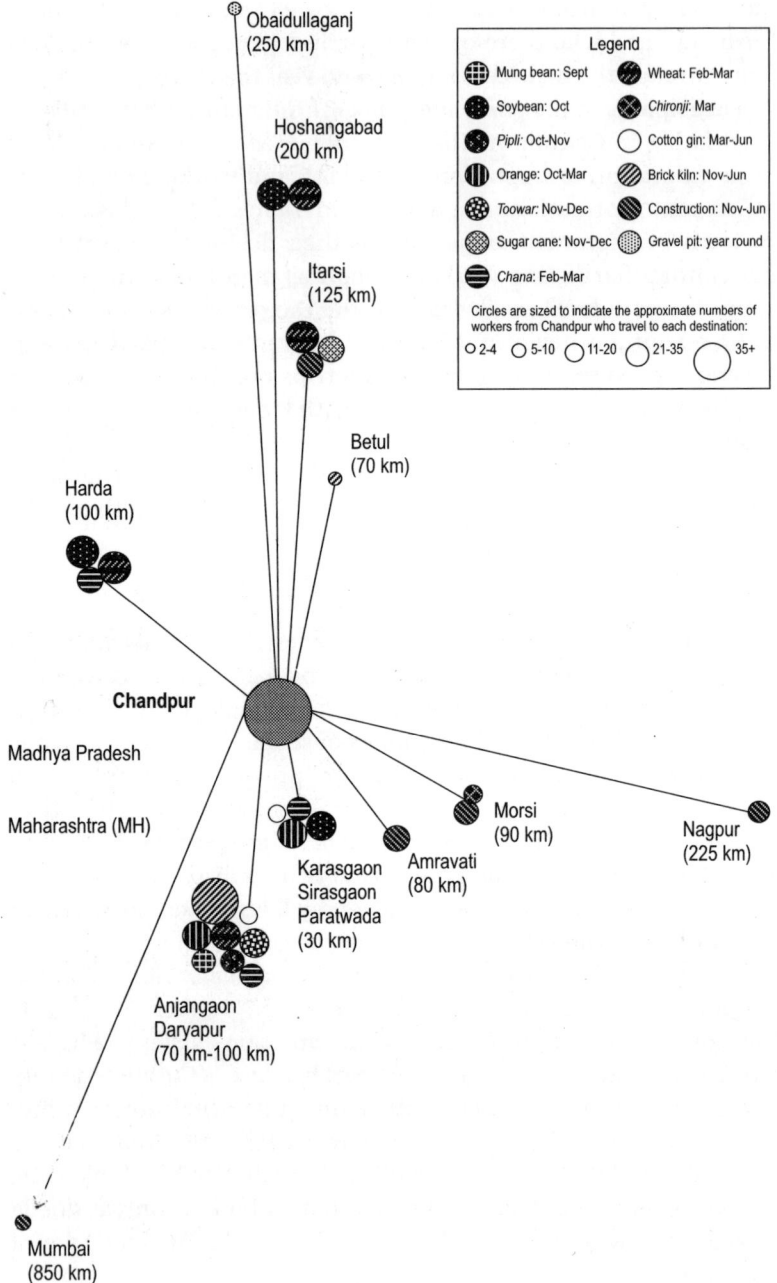

Figure 8.1: Labour Migration from Chandpur: Destination and Activity

Table 8.2 a: Description of Migrant Work

| Harvest | Destination | Timing and Duration | Description of working/living conditions | Payment | Travel | Size of Stream* |
|---|---|---|---|---|---|---|
| Mung Bean | Anjangaon, MH | Sept: About 3 weeks. | Migrants work in pairs, usually husband-wife teams. Accommodation by the side of the field, in cloth tents provided by farm owner. | Piece rate: Rs 2/Kg | Bus to nearest village. | Small |
| Soybean | Hoshangabad, MP Harda, MP Sirasgaon, MH | Oct: 3–4 weeks, depending on yields. | Migrants work for contractors who provide labour to large soy farmers. For daily wages: women cut soybean with a sickle, men carry and stack the harvest. Where harvest is contracted by the acre: men and women migrants both cut soybean, local workers load harvest onto a tractor. Accommodation by the side of the field, in cloth tents provided by farm owner. Water generally provided by farmer, from a purchased barrel. Firewood from nearby forest. Health: Soybean plants irritate migrants' hands. Cuts from the sickle are not uncommon. | Daily wages are paid by contractor: W: Rs 25 M: Rs 40 Or, harvest is contracted by the acre, payment (approx. Rs 300) paid by contractor to team leader, divided among team members. Payment is not usually higher than Chandpur wages, but daily work is guaranteed. | Bus/train to nearest village. Migrants move between fields/farms on foot: time consuming, tiring. | Large |

Contd...

Table 8.2 a (Contd.)

| Harvest | Destination | Timing and Duration | Description of working/living conditions | Payment | Travel | Size of Stream* |
|---|---|---|---|---|---|---|
| *Pipli* (long pepper) | Anjangaon, MH | Oct–Nov: About 2 months | Migrants work directly for plantation owner, who solicits labour via a contractor.<br><br>Migrants work individually, harvesting trellised pipli plants from the bottom up, working along the row. Fruit is dropped in a small basket, emptied into a larger sack. Sack is weighed at the end of the day, weight recorded and added weekly to arrive at payment. Work also involves weeding banana plants with a sickle.<br><br>Workers build their own kaccha houses with material collected on the plantation. Water available from on-site well, firewood collected on plantation. | Piece rate: Rs 2/kg.<br><br>Workers generally pick 15–25kg/day = Rs 30–50/day on average.<br><br>Payment is weekly, on market day. Paid by farm owner/ manager. | Bus to nearest village. | Small |
| Orange | Paratwada, MH Assegaon, MH | End of Oct – Mar: 4–5 months | Migrants work for contractors, who purchase orange harvest from plantation owners.<br><br>Men climb the orange trees, pick fruit into cloth bags tied around their waists, empty below the tree. Women load oranges beneath the tree into crates, carry crates to central pile. Both men and women load contractors' truck. | W: Rs 30/day<br>M: Rs 70/day<br><br>Paid by contractor, weekly. | Contractors send trucks to collect migrants in the village.<br><br>Migrants move between plantations in truck. | Medium |

| Crop | Location | Season/Duration | Work, payment details | Payment | Transport | Farm size |
|---|---|---|---|---|---|---|
| | | | Migrants move between plantations as they complete the harvest. Workers sleep in the plantations. Sometimes the plantation owner will provide basic housing; sometimes workers sleep beneath the trees. | | | |
| *Toowar* (pigeon pea) | Anjangaon, MH | Nov–Dec: About 3 weeks | Women cut the harvest; men load. | W: Rs 25/day M: Rs 40/day | Bus to nearest village. | Small |
| Sugar cane | Itarsi, MP | Nov–Dec | *Work, payment details are unclear* | | Bus/train to nearest village. | Small |
| *Chana* (gram) | Harda, MP Siragaon, MH Anjangaon, MH | Feb–Mar: About 3 weeks Feb–Mar: About 3 weeks | Trips are organized by a leader, who makes arrangements with a contractor. Accommodation by the side of the field, in cloth tents provided by farm owner. Water generally provided by farmer, from a purchased barrel. Firewood from nearby forest. | Contracted by the acre: Rs 250–300/ acre. Contractor pays leader, who distributes wages. Earnings depend on number of workers, their speed. | Bus /train to nearest village. Migrants move between fields/farms on foot: time-consuming, tiring. | Medium |
| Wheat | Hoshangabad, MP Harda, MP Anjangaon, MH | | Migrants work in pairs to cut and bundle the wheat. Accommodation by the side of the field. Migrants either make their own temporary shelters or sleep in cloth | Payment is in-kind, piece rate: Migrants receive 5% of their harvest (one 8kg bundle for every twenty bundles cut). | Bus/train to nearest village. | Large |

Contd...

Table 8.2 a (Contd.)

| Harvest | Destination | Timing and Duration | Description of working/living conditions | Payment | Travel | Size of Stream* |
|---------|-------------|---------------------|------------------------------------------|---------|--------|-----------------|
| | | | tents provided by farm owner. Water generally provided by farmer, from a purchased barrel. Firewood from nearby forest. | People work in pairs. Each member of a pair can expect to make up to 10kg/day, worth Rs 60 cash. Local system is a fixed, in-kind wage: W: 4kg/day M: 6kg/day In some cases, harvest in the village is contracted by the acre – unsure of rate. | | |

Source: Author.

Note: * This is a rough estimate of the number of groups that migrate for each harvest A small stream might include just one or two groups (10–20 people) from the village and its immediate surroundings, a medium stream three groups (20–40 people), a large stream many groups: up to a hundred migrants.

Table 8.2 b: Description of Non-agricultural Work

| Work | Destination | Timing and Duration | Description of working/living conditions | Payment | Travel | Size of Stream |
|---|---|---|---|---|---|---|
| Construction | Itarsi, MP<br>Morsi, MH<br>Amravati, MH<br>Nagpur, MH<br>*Mumbai, MH (only one interviewee has taken construction work in Mumbai) | Nov–Mar: 3–5 months.<br><br>*Semi-permanent (again, in the Mumbai case) | Migrants work for a building contractor, moving between sites as they finish the job. Women carry cement and bricks in steel head pans, passing up the building materials to men, who lay bricks. Men also mix cement.<br><br>Migrants live in tents of cloth and plastic in empty lots in the city. Water facilities are provided – drinking water comes either from tanks or taps on the grounds.<br><br>In some cases, employers supply rudimentary housing, as well as drinking water, bathing facilities and toilets on the site itself. A large site might house and employ up to 100 workers. | M: Rs 70/day<br>W: Rs 42/day<br><br>*These wages are for Mumbai; they may be lower elsewhere. | Bus/train to site. | Medium |
| Brick kiln | Daryapur, MH<br>Betul, MP | Early Dec– Jun: About 6 months | Daryapur kiln: Migrants work in pairs of men and women. Men attend to the machine that prepares the clay mixture, carry the mixture to the women. Women make bricks by packing heavy iron molds with the clay, then turning out the shaped clay onto the ground | Piece rate: Rs 100/1000 bricks. Couples can earn about Rs 100/day. Each Sunday, couples are paid Rs 200 for groceries at | Daryapur: Transport provided: Migrants cram into a little yellow van. | Darya-pur kiln: Large<br><br>Betul kiln: one couple<br><br>Contd... |

Table 8.2 b: (Contd.)

| Work | Destination | Timing and Duration | Description of working/living conditions | Payment | Travel | Size of Stream |
|---|---|---|---|---|---|---|
| | | | for drying. Dry bricks are stacked by the women, then taken for baking by labourers from Gujarat, who use a donkey with panniers to transport them the 100m to the kiln itself. Labourers from Uttar Pradesh fire the kiln. Workers spend their first week at the kiln building kaccha row houses on site, using bricks and mud. Owner provides plastic for roofing. Although migrants may return year after year, housing decays during rainy season and must be rebuilt. About 140 people live and work at the kiln; housing is clustered according to migrants' place of origin. Migrants' quarters are about 6' x 8'. Migrants typically sleep outside. Drinking water is provided from a tank; a nearby river is used for bathing and washing clothes. Women collect firewood from a forested area nearby. Betul kiln (a smaller operation): Men dig the clay; couples prepare the mixture together; women form the bricks, using a mold, then stack the | the Sunday market and other small expenses. Full payment occurs in June, when expenses are totaled and subtracted from the value assigned to the total number of bricks made. This system prevents migrants from leaving prematurely, and leaves some room for employers to cheat illiterate workers. All brick kiln migrants take advances, usually of Rs 2000 – 3000. These are given in June. They are interest-free, so long | Betul: bus to site. | |

| | | | | | | |
|---|---|---|---|---|---|---|
| | | | dry bricks, which are taken by other workers for baking. Workers live in homemade tents of cloth and plastic, stretched over a wooden frame. Firewood is collected from a nearby forest. Only about 12 people live and work here. *All migrants complain about working conditions in brick kilns. They have to stand in/work with cold, wet clay beneath a scorching sun. Each of the five women brick kiln migrants I spoke with told me that they had become ill as a result – one still experiences joint pain, which first appeared when she worked at the kiln one year prior to our interview. | as the advance is worked off within a year's time. After this for bricks may be imposed. | | |
| Cotton gin | Anjangaon, MH Karasgaon, MH | Oct–Nov: 1–2 months | Women load unprocessed cotton into machine, remove processed cotton. Men sew processed cotton in sacks, load sacks. Shifts are 8 hours long. Migrants live in a dormitory. In the summer, they may sleep outside the dormitory to stay cool. *Accidents in the ginning factory occur with some regularity: one woman told me that the machines occasionally | Rs 50 – Rs 70/day. Payment is monthly. Workers can take up to Rs 500 from their wages over the month, for groceries, etc. | Bus to factory. | Small |
| | | Mar–May: 1–2 months | | | | |

Contd...

Table 8.2 b: (Contd.)

| Work | Destination | Timing and Duration | Description of working/living conditions | Payment | Travel | Size of Stream |
|---|---|---|---|---|---|---|
| | | | catch fire; workers can injure themselves in the machines. | | | |
| Gravel pit | Obaidullaganj, MP | Mar–Jun: 3 months | Workers carry boulders to a rock-crushing machine; operate the machine, loading in rocks and removing gravel; load trucks with gravel. Housing is on-site, in huts. Firewood is collected nearby. *Juhi Bai, who worked at a gravel pit, complained about the dust and smoke from the machine, and the exposure she suffered working under the *karak dhoob* (hot sun): 'my colour changed there.' | Rs 50 – Rs 90/day  Weekly payment, distributed by group leader. | Bus to site. | V. Small: I met only two people who had worked at the gravel pit. |

*Source:* Author.

Intentional fragmentation of the workforce, a phenomenon identified elsewhere in India by Breman (1996) and Harriss–White (2003) further reduces the potential for worker organization. At the Daryapur kiln, Chandpur migrants find themselves part of a highly heterogeneous group of workers, recruited from different areas of origin and paid different rates for performing specialized duties. Gond and Korku migrants from Chandpur, Muslim migrants from Uttar Pradesh, and tribal migrants from Gujarat each perform different tasks at the kiln, so social interaction is kept to a minimum. In the evening, workers from each of the groups retire to separate camps on opposite sides of the vast open-air brick factory. Many migrant respondents expressed a sense of alienation from other workers, which is wholly unfavourable to worker organization.

Clearly, tribal households do not leave oppressive social relations behind them when they set off for migrant work. Instead, migrants' access to resources is tightly constrained by caste, class, and gender hierarchies that operate beyond the village, at a regional level. Evidence for this assertion is best provided by the persistence of tied labour in brick kiln work. Many of the kiln migrants who contributed to this study are chronically indebted to contractors, caught up in a borrowing cycle that compels them to spend half of each year performing arduous work at an open-air brick factory 100 km from their homes. Ramrati Markom, who with her husband, Bhanu, has helped many friends and relatives to migrate, nonetheless expressed regret about her obligation to return to the kiln:

Ramrati explains that she feels reluctant to work at the brick kiln this year. She knows she'll miss her children. Her household took an advance of Rs. 2000 in the rainy season, so she has no choice but to return to the kiln. She and Bhanu asked for the advance because it rained too much this year— there wasn't enough work and they had nothing to eat. All of the money from the previous year had been spent, mostly on consumption. They had no choice but to borrow money. Every year it is the same: they run out of money and ask for an advance from the manager. Then they have to work at the brick kiln the next year to pay it off.

Migrants seek employment at the kiln at their own initiative, but they make this decision in response to severe economic compulsion, and with little expectation of the ongoing annual obligation that taking an initial advance tends to entail. Mosse *et al.* (2002) refer to migration of this sort as a forced livelihood option.

## Migration as an Alternative to Local Forms of Bonded Labour

Despite the element of bondage that debt relations between migrants and their extra-local patrons hold, the decision to migrate is nonetheless for many migrants a move towards less exploitative labour relations than those faced at home. Daru *et al.* (2005) 'worst forms' approach to bonded labour provides a helpful means of conceptualizing this difference. Daru *et al.* depict debt bondage as a continuum, along which various forms of bondage may be positioned according to their severity. The authors distinguish milder forms of bondage from more severe forms by the length of contract, working conditions, limitations on freedom of movement, and feasibility of loan repayment. These factors are consistent with the criteria used by labourers in Chandpur to differentiate between more or less favourable arrangements. However, in evaluating their own working arrangements, Chandpur migrants placed most emphasis on a job's perceived impact on their personal dignity and the social status of their household. Ideologies of work are gendered, so men and women perceive the work that they do in different ways. But laying aside the crucial issue of gender for a moment, by Daru *et al.*'s criteria, as well as those of the migrants I spoke with, work at the Daryapur kiln entails a far milder form of bondage than does naukar work in the village.

Many of the migrants who participated in this study originally pursued long-term extra-local work as a means of accessing credit towards a lump sum expenditure without having to mortgage their labour to a local lender. When I asked a group of migrants at the kiln how many of them had been naukars in the past, they laughed among themselves, embarrassed, 'We've all been naukars...' but one man spoke up:

I was a naukar! I herded cattle for Rs 4,000 a year. When you're a naukar, you have to work for the whole year for Rs 4,000, Rs 6,000. The boss can call you to work at any time, to do anything. Here we know when we're working. We just work in the day, and we make more money doing this work than we did as naukars, in just half a year.

Findings from this study support Breman's assertion (1996) that workers generally experience what he calls neobondage— contractual arrangements of the type extended to workers at the kiln—in ways that are substantially different from their experience of 'traditional' forms of bondage in agriculture or domestic service. While long-term migrant work is physically onerous, low paying, and emotionally taxing both for migrants and their relatives, poor households choose this work in part because it may be performed with dignity. Where the humiliation that surrounds beck-and-call bondage relations in Chandpur meant that the topic was difficult to broach with respondents, male workers at the kiln registered pride in their employment. Migration can thus be seen as a route by which Chandpur's tribal people may negotiate more remunerative employment and a more empowering social identity, if not a means out of poverty.

### Who Gets Left Out? Social Exclusion and Chronic Poverty

But if migration, for all its challenges, presents poor people with a viable means of moving into milder bondage, then why do more severe forms of bondage persist? The answer to this question rests partly in recognizing that the poor are a heterogeneous group whose access to resources can be highly uneven. As established in the section 'Regional Context' earlier seasonal migration from Chandpur is facilitated by complex, kin-based social networks. These networks allow migrants to compare experiences with specific contractors, organize work gangs, gain access to new and better employment opportunities, and support one another at extra-local worksites. Given the risk that migrants incur when they accept work from a stranger, at a distant locality and in an unregulated industry, access to these knowledge-sharing networks represents a critical safeguard against abuse, and a crucial step in moving towards accumulative migration.

However, Chandpur's poorest include households that are prevented, by a combination of vulnerabilities, from participating in these networks. Two of the households that contributed to this study are victims of social exclusion; both have experienced heightened insecurity as a result of their migration decisions.

Mohit and Sunita Khumbre are a Gond couple, who migrated several years ago, through a contractor, to harvest field crops in Maharashtra. Mohit suffers from chronic alcoholism, and the two have few friends and relatives in the village. The couple was motivated to migrate as a means of escaping the village's segmented labour market: because of their evident poverty and lack of bargaining power, local employers pay them below-average wages for agricultural work. However, owing to their exclusion from informal sources of social support, they had no choice but to bring both their daughter, Anita, and Mohit's elderly father with them. At the worksite, the labour contractor mistreated them, and dishonoured the household by forcing the old man to work, despite his visible fragility. Mohit and Sunita felt vulnerable sleeping outside by themselves, in a makeshift shelter by the side of the fields. They worried that animals might enter their house in the village.

Neither Mohit nor Sunita have since pursued migrant work. Although they are acutely aware of their poverty and unhappy with their situation, the Khumbres now choose the security of bonded labour at home over the dangers they associate with working outside of the village. Mohit removes cow and buffalo manure from a patron's courtyard for an annual wage of Rs 2,000; their daughter, Arathi performs domestic work before and after school, for Rs 1,000/ year. Although I had seen Sunita performing domestic labour for a caste Hindu family, the Khumbres refused to discuss her work. Each of the family members continues to pursue wage labour on the side, at rates that are locally sealed at Rs 20/day.

Entering into local bondage ensures that immediate needs are met, but it places heavy limits on people's freedom to pursue alternative opportunities in the future. Wood (2003) has called patron–client relations a 'Faustian bargain', whereby 'preparation for the future is continuously postponed for survival and security in the present'.[5] As a household that lives in an area of high out-migration, but whose members are themselves immobilized by bondage, the Khumbres may see their vulnerability and exclusion reinforced by their inability to take part in the social and economic changes that follow from migration (Kothari 2002).

Meena bai and Manik Vishwakarma, an OBC household who are newcomers to Chandpur, face exclusion both from the village's largely tribal migrant networks and from Chandpur's informal credit market. They have migrated to the soy harvest in Itarsi with a gang from Manik's natal village for the last 12 years. Since accepting an advance of Rs 10,000 from a Betul-area kiln manager in 2002, the couple now migrates in the winter as well. Because they do not want to remove their three children, aged 7–12, from school, they must leave them to care for themselves in the village. Meena worries about the children constantly, but she and Manik have no other option: they are forced by their continued indebtedness to return to the kiln on a yearly basis. When we spoke in 2004, the Vishwarmas still owed

Rs 7, 000 to the kiln manager and were preparing to migrate again. They listed inadequate facilities, poor working conditions, and ill health among the hardships they have endured at the kiln. Although working and living conditions are far better at the Daryapur kiln, Meena and Manik do not have access to the social networks through which such information is shared.

The kiln is in a hilly jungle area, on the outskirts of the district headquarters. The couple lives in a homemade tent—a wooden frame covered in cloth. The other workers live in the same area, also in tents. There are 10–12 workers altogether, all from a different village. The same group of people returns each year. Meena tells me, 'We get on well with those people; they are poor just like us. Working as we do, no one has enough time to fight. Poor people have to live within their limits.' Everybody stays in their tents in the evenings; they don't take their meals together. Meena says they only speak to one another during the day, while at work.

At work, Manik digs the clay; Meena fetches the water. They make the brick mixture together. She puts the mixture into the mold, then removes the mold to dry the bricks, while he continues to dig. When the bricks are dry, Meena takes four on her left arm, one in her right hand, and carries them to the stacking area. Other labourers come and pick up the bricks for baking.

'It is not a good way to live'. Last year, they had unseasonal rain in January: it ruined the bricks they had made, made it impossible for them to work. Their tent provided little protection against the elements, and both became sick in the cold, damp conditions. 'There was mud everywhere! It was very messy!' The children, at home by themselves, also became sick. Because they could not make bricks in the wet weather, Meena bai and Manik were not able to earn money. They asked to borrow more money from the contractor, but were denied the loan.

Each of these households lacks the social capital necessary to locate more remunerative, safer migrant work, and at the time of my fieldwork, both were becoming increasingly indebted, and indeed more and more socially marginalized, as a result of the relatively severe forms of debt bondage into which they had fallen. While the Khumbres' bondage can be seen as resulting from their decision to stay put, and the Vishwakarmas' linked to their decision to migrate, both families' examples lend evidence to Kothari's assertion that 'migration is best understood as both a *cause* and *consequence* of chronic poverty for those who stay put and for those who move' (emphasis in the original).[6] Migrants with greater access to social capital may migrate with or through friends and relatives, and thereby supplement their farm income, move into milder forms of bondage, and negotiate a more autonomous social identity. But poverty, exclusion, and exploitation that households like the Khumbres and Vishwakarmas experience tend to be reinforced by their migration decisions.

## Gender Relations

In examining migration as it is shaped by, and is in turn brought to bear on gender identities and ideologies of work and mobility, our focus shifts to gender relations as they are negotiated at the micro, intra-household level. Migration decisions are always influenced by social rules about the way men and women should behave and what kind of work is appropriate to each. However, respondents' analyses suggest that necessity tends to intervene in migrants' interpretations of gender roles. Women's involvement in extra-local work contravenes common conceptions of gender-appropriate behaviour, by compromising a woman's ability to care for children and other dependents. But the extent to which women experience migration as a source of dissonance depends partly on their situation. A small proportion of women migrants conceptualized their decisions to migrate in terms of a response to a loss of male support, a situation they saw as freeing them to defy certain gender norms and make an independent living. This was true of Juhi bai Khumbre, who drew on kinship connections to migrate to Mumbai, thereby escaping a violent situation in her home.

The first job Juhi bai took in Mumbai was working in people's houses. 'It was servant work' – washing clothes, washing dishes. The work was not profitable, and she didn't like it at all! So her brother helped her to get a new job, selling vegetables at a market. He helped her to get a train pass so she could travel from market to market, and a weighing machine, and vegetable stock. She had observed sellers in the past, so learning the business and counting out change wasn't a problem. 'I'm not educated but when you go to other places you have to be smart, and you get smart. Many people can't do this but I can; I've gone many places – Bombay, Bhopal, Indore... When you live alone you have to be smart.'

Juhi bai's market was held daily. She sold spinach, fenugreek, potatoes, cabbage, chillies, garlic... (laughing) 'The people there use different words for vegetables... I started calling out '*Methi! Palak!*' ('Fenugreek! Spinach!'), but nobody could understand what I meant. They just kept walking because they didn't understand! I had to learn new words for everything!' The other sellers and customers helped her with the new language. People there were very nice and she got along well with everybody at the market. Some people from her natal village even came to see her there.

After the interview, we reflect on her migration experiences and discuss what it's like to travel a lot. 'You have to be smart,' she says, 'and it makes you smart'. She developed independence and self-reliance through working outside the village. She's not afraid of anything now, and she's proud of herself for that.

Since returning from Mumbai to care for her children ten years ago, Juhi Bai has taken migrant work at a gravel pit and a cotton gin, pursuing these opportunities through kin relations. She is actively involved in one of Chandpur's self-help groups, through which she has learned to raise goats: she now has a herd of eleven. As the primary earner in her household, she sometimes finds her responsibilities overwhelming, but Juhi is determined and resourceful, qualities she claims to have honed during her time in Mumbai.

Juhi Bai described migrant work as a means around local under-employment and discriminatory payment practices, which reinforce unequal gender relations by undervaluing women's work. Even though her earnings did not improve her position in the household, migration proved to be an empowering strategy. Returning to the village to take up familial responsibilities, her perspective on women's mobility and the kind of work that women can do had changed.

However, where Juhi migrated independently, many more women migrate as members of household units. In these cases, it is usually the male head of the household who takes a lead in accessing employment opportunities and who exercises the greatest influence over intra-household decision-making. Men's livelihood decisions are informed, just as women's are, both by their positions in hierarchies of class, caste, and age, and by their relationships to gender ideals, in this case to dominant forms of masculinity. As Jackson (1999) has noted, central to notions of manliness in the Indian context is a man's responsibility to provide for and protect his family; Vera-Sanso's research (2001) adds to this understanding an emphasis on maintaining self-reliance and domestic authority. For Chandpur men, meeting gendered expectations entails avoiding becoming a naukar, at any cost.

The strong, politicized dislike for local debt-bondage observed among male workers has been widely noted by researchers (Breman

1996; Da Corta and Venkateshwarlu 1997; De Neve 1999). *Naukar* work, with its beck-and-call demands, proscriptions on personal mobility and autonomy, economic exploitation and strong dimension of personal dependence, undermines men's self esteem in multiple ways. Perhaps most significant among the challenges that bondage presents to a man's sense of masculinity is its erosion of his capacity to support a family and to protect women relatives from sexual threat, especially should they be driven into naukar work too.

There is a growing awareness in the literature on bonded labour that women required to service a household debt by performing domestic labour are vulnerable to physical and sexual assault (ILO 2005). Yet this dimension of bondage has received inadequate attention. Vera–Sanso's (2001) discussion of the social concerns that shape female labour force participation in Chennai represents an important contribution, however. Her observations regarding the central place of female chastity among the concerns of poor households are highly applicable to the politics of bondage and gender relations in Chandpur. Vera–Sanso highlights the tendency for community members to represent women who work for particular hours or in specific jobs as 'needlessly exposing themselves to unwanted sexual encounters, if not actually seeking them',[7] and examines the implications that a woman's sullied reputation can have for her husband's perceived masculinity, and indeed her entire family's social and economic position. Her analysis emphasizes men's heavily felt responsibility to maintain their place in local masculine hierarchies by providing for their families, so that the women in their households do not have to perform risky domestic work and their families may be kept 'on the right path'.[8] Men's strong desire to maintain an acceptable position in local masculine hierarchies, by protecting their female family members from inappropriate work, is also an influence on male-dominated decision-making on migration from Chandpur.

If given the opportunity, workers will tend to choose the most materially, socially, and symbolically beneficial employment available to them. For the male workers who participated in the study, this best-case scenario increasingly involves extra-local work. Where local bondage compromises a man's ability to provide for his family, protect his wife, and maintain his household's reputation, brick kiln work is far more compatible with local masculine ideals.

Migration to the Daryapur kiln is collectively organized by men, and represents an important and enjoyable instance of male collectivity. The sense of male camaraderie on the morning of the brick kiln migrants' departure was very strong: men talked and laughed together before their houses, celebrating the start of their long trip with country liquor, while women took care of the packing. At the Daryapur kiln, male migrants work together to operate the clay-mixing machine, and also perform the heavy work of transporting the clay. This work, while physically demanding, is socially valued as mechanized, manly, modern work. While both male and female migrants to the Daryapur kiln emphasized the physical exhaustion brought on by their difficult labour, the enthusiasm and pride with which men infused their commentaries was generally absent from women workers' testimonies.

Women interviewees were more reserved in their descriptions of brick kiln work, less likely to draw a strong distinction between borrowing from village lenders and taking an advance from contractors, and more likely to express regret over their household's decision to migrate. Each of the women interviewed about the kiln shared incidents of sickness, which they associated with the kiln's impossible working conditions. Women workers pack the clay brought to them by their male partners into heavy iron molds, turn out the molds to dry, then stack the dry bricks. This labour is performed while squatting on the cold, wet, muddy ground, and is accorded a lower social value than is their male partners' work.

Living conditions at the kiln are difficult for everyone, but especially for women, as living at the kiln complicates women's performance of domestic responsibilities. Women interviewees pointed to the limited availability of good firewood as a significant challenge. However, a greater challenge is that of meeting gendered expectations while separated from dependents at home. If men express their care for family members primarily through performing a role of provider and protector, women are more likely to express care through attention to reproductive responsibilities—washing the family laundry, preparing food for husband and children, heating water for family members' morning baths (Vera–Sanso 2001). Women migrants to all destinations highlighted their sadness at leaving children behind, or in those cases where children accompanied their parents to worksites, at having to neglect their children during their long workdays. Because women's mobility is limited in relation to men's, it is always their male partners who return periodically to the village to share wages with dependents. Women migrants to the kiln might spend months at a time without communicating with loved ones at home.

Attention to gendered discourses of work and mobility thus reveal important differences between men and women's experiences of extra-local work. Migration to the Daryapur kiln represents a way for male workers to eschew humiliating, emasculating local bondage arrangements in favour of more dignified, remunerative, and gender-appropriate work. It is therefore an important way for low-income tribal men to negotiate empowering gender identities as providers and protectors. Women who migrate to the kiln benefit from their households' access to lower interest rates on loans and more regular, more highly paid work than is locally available. However, many women were unhappy with their households' decision to migrate, and indicated that, were their contributions to household decision-making less constrained by intra-household gender hierarchies, they would choose to remain in the village. In contrast to their male relatives, women migrants face significant challenges in negotiating more empowering gender identities, as their gendered responsibilities entail a more intimate form of care, impossible to perform when separated from dependents. Women like Juhi, who migrate of their own initiative, are in many cases able to draw from their experiences to question local gender norms. For a larger number of women, however, migration cannot be described in such empowering tones.

CONCLUSIONS AND RECOMMENDATIONS

Seasonal migration plays an increasingly important role in the livelihood strategies pursued by poor tribal households in Chandpur. Although migration from the community is not without historical antecedent, contemporary labour mobility is perceived by many migrants as a break from—rather than an extension of—local structures of inequality. With the community's growing integration into a regional market for migrant labour, tribal households have begun to address their discrimination, deprivation, and intense seasonal vulnerability by negotiating multilocational livelihoods.

Most migrants from Chandpur travel in groups to perform agricultural work on commercial farms in Maharashtra and MP. Although short-term migration to harvest chana or soy is not without its risks, short-term migrant work provides more reliable employment than that available locally, while minimizing time spent away from dependents. This chapter has focused, however, on longer-term migration to brick kiln work, an increasingly popular form of extra-local employment, which, in 2004, drew larger numbers of workers than any other migrant stream. The interest-free cash advances associated with work at brick kilns are an attractive option for workers who would otherwise have to pay exorbitant interest on annual loans, or mortgage their labour locally. However, in pursuing brick kiln work, tribal households do not escape the chronic debt that had previously tied them to local lenders, but merely transfer their debt relations to extra-local employers. Nonetheless, given the constraints on poor tribal workers' access to equitable credit and employment, longer-term seasonal migration appears to be the most remunerative, socially empowering option available. For this reason, support for seasonal migrants must become a key priority for development programming in areas of high out-migration such as southern MP.

This chapter has highlighted two populations that require particular attention on the part of policy makers. The first includes households that are excluded from the social networks through which migrants share knowledge of employment opportunities, connections to reputable contractors, and various forms of social support. A key determinant of seasonal migration's impact on rural livelihoods can be located in households' access to these networks. Exclusion from migrant networks does not entirely prohibit migration, as even the very poor may find work through contractors who visit the village. However, households who migrate to distant worksites without benefit of peer advice and support are highly vulnerable to abuse by exploitative employers, and therefore subject to the increased social marginalization associated with severe forms of bondage.

Policy makers can support safer, more remunerative employment by developing initiatives to increase access to information about extra-local work opportunities. Towards this goal, the Western India Rainfed Farming Project has established migrant information centres at panchayat offices in source areas and at points of convergence on migration routes (Mosse et al., 2005). Out-migrants register with these centres, post information about upcoming opportunities, and use the centres to share their experiences with extra-local employers. An alternative approach to facilitating information exchange might make use of self-help group (SHG) meetings to promote informal dialogue between past migrants and potential migrants, and to generate lists of blacklisted employers; SHG facilitators could maintain these lists and share them with their colleagues.

SHGs also present an important means of diminishing poor tribal households' reliance on exploitative employers/lenders, by providing equitable access to credit. In Chandpur, where seven SHGs were operating in 2004, members were able to use SHG funds to curb their borrowing from local moneylenders, a benefit that they talked about with pride. However, these groups are not designed to respond to the needs of a seasonally mobile population, and they tend to exclude the very poorest, whose risk of falling into severe bondage is high. The ILO's South Asian Project against Debt Bondage (SAPDB) organizes microfinance institutions (MFIs) to extend services to households who are at risk of bondage, engaged in mild forms of bondage, or recently released from severe bondage (Daru *et al.*, 2005). Recognizing that households vulnerable to bonded labour have specific financial needs, the SAPDB encourages MFIs to take a two-tiered approach, by providing a menu of special services to this group while maintaining their regular work in the community at large, with the goal of facilitating vulnerable families' eventual transition to standard financial services. A similar approach could be taken in designing credit services appropriate to the needs of vulnerable migrant labourers. A flexible attitude to repayment would be essential to ensuring the success of initiatives of this sort.

The second priority group highlighted in this chapter is that of women workers, who have trouble reconciling their work as migrants with their responsibilities towards dependents. In Chandpur, the Satpura Integrated Development Institution (SIRDI), a locally active NGO, has developed numerous programmes to support poor, tribal women in their efforts to reshape local gender relations. SIRDI's work on women's empowerment has included consciousness-raising events and capacity building workshops; its initiatives have helped to increase female participation in public meetings, as well as boosting women's confidence to contribute to decision-making at the household level. While it is essential to include both men and women workers in any initiative to support seasonal migrants, organizations like SIRDI can use their expertise in gender and development to involve women migrants in participatory programming to address their specific needs.

Findings from this study suggest that chief among women migrants' concerns is the well-being of children and other dependents left behind when couples migrate. Arrangements for community-based support for migrants' dependents will differ between communities; effective interventions will include local stakeholders in creating strategies to meet dependents' needs. In Chandpur, primary school teachers have introduced flexible classroom hours to accommodate students' increased responsibility for household chores while their parents are away. Lunchtime meal programmes have contributed to a rise in attendance by children from poor families, and could be extended to provide after-school meals to the children of migrants, thereby lightening the burden on their caregivers. However, meal programmes need adequate administrative support if they are to succeed, as rural teachers are already overburdened with teaching and administrative responsibilities.

NOTES

1. All names have been changed, in order to preserve the anonymity of the people who contributed to the study.
2. A British Raj province whose borders correspond to those of present day Amravati, Maharashtra.
3. Sharecroppers in Chandpur either rent land for a set fee—given to the landlord upfront—or make an in-kind payment at the end of the year, consisting of 50 per cent of the harvest. While villagers prefer the former arrangement, households that cannot afford to pay for land in advance must accept the latter.
4. This practice was defended in paternalistic tones: the kiln's manager suggested that Korku workers would spend all their money on drink were it not withheld during the season. The weekly allowance paid to couples is too low to cover their bus fare home.
5. G. Wood, 'Staying Secure, Staying Poor: The 'Faustian Bargain', *World Development*, 31, 2003, p. 468.
6. U. Kothari, 'Migration and Chronic Poverty', Manchester Institute for Development Policy and Management, University of Manchester, 2002, p. 7.
7. P. Vera–Sanso, 'Masculinity, Male Domestic Authority and Female Labour Participation in South India' in C. Jackson (ed.), *Men at Work: Men, Masculinities, and Development*, Portland, OR : Frank Cass, 2001, p. 186.
8. Ibid., p. 187.

# REFERENCES

Baker, D.E.U., *Colonialism in an Indian Hinterland: The Central Provinces, 1820–1920*, Delhi: Oxford University Press, 1993.

*Betul District Gazetteer*, P.N. Shrivastav, District Gazetteers Department, Bhopal, Madhya Pradesh, India, 1971.

Bhatt, S.C., and G.K. Bhargava, *Land and People of Indian States and Union Territories: Madhya Pradesh*, New Delhi: Kalpaz Publications, 2005.

Breman, J., *Footloose Labour: Working in India's Informal Economy*, Cambridge, UK: Cambridge University Press, 1996.

Da Corta, L., and D. Venkateshwarlu, 'Unfree Relations and the Feminisation of Agricultural Labour in Andhra Pradesh, 1970–95', *The Journal of Peasant Studies* 26, 1997, pp. 71–123.

Daru, P., C. Churchill, and E. Beemsterboer, 'The Prevention of Debt Bondage with Microfinance-led Services', *The European Journal of Development Research* 17, 2005, pp. 132–154.

Debroy, B., and L. Bhandari, *District Level Deprivation in the New Millennium*, New Delhi: Konark Publishers, 2003.

De Neve, G., 'Asking for and Giving *baki*: Neo-bondage, or the Interplay of Bondage and Resistance in the Tamil Nadu Power-loom Industry', in J. Parry, J. Breman, and K. Kapadia (eds), *The Worlds of Indian Industrial Labour*, Thousand Oaks, CA: Sage Publication, 1999, pp. 379–406.

Harriss–White, B., *India Working: Essays on Society and Economy*, Cambridge, UK: Cambridge University Press, 2003.

Jackson, C., 'Men's Work, Masculinities, and Gender Divisions of Labour', *The Journal of Development Studies* 36, 1999, pp. 89–108.

Kothari, U., 'Migration and Chronic Poverty', Manchester Institute for Development Policy and Management, University of Manchester, Chronic Poverty Resource Centre, Manchester, UK, 2002.

International Labour Organization, 'A Global Alliance against Forced Labour: Global Report under the Follow-up to the ILO Declaration of Fundamental Principles and Rights at Work', International Labour Office, Geneva, Switzerland, Retrieved 26 Feb 2006, from: http://www.ilo.org/dyn/declaris/DECLARATIONWEB.DOWNLOAD_BLOB?Var_DocumentID=5059

Mosse, D., S. Gupta, M. Mehta, V. Shah, J. Rees, and the KRIBP Project Team, 'Brokered Livelihoods: Debt, Labour Migration and Development in Tribal Western India', *Journal of Development Studies* 39, 2002, pp. 59–88.

———, S. Gupta, amd V. Shah, 'On the Margins in the City: Adivasi Seasonal Labour Migration in Western India', *Political and Economic Weekly* 40, 2005, pp. 3025–38.

Omvedt, G., 'Migration in Colonial India: The Articulation of Feudalism and Capitalism by the Colonial State', *The Journal of Peasant Studies* 7, 1980, pp. 185–212.

Som, R., U. Kleih, Y. Kumar, and S.K. Jena, 'Rural Non-farm Employment in Madhya Pradesh: Findings of a Participatory Rural Appraisal in 8

Villages', NRI Report no. 2694, Natural Resources Institute, University of Greenwich, UK, Retrieved 2 April 2006 from: http://www.nri.org/rnfe/pub/papers/2694.pdf

United Nations Development Programme, 'The Madhya Pradesh Human Development Report 2002: Using the Power of Democracy for Development', New Delhi, India, Retrieved 2 April 2005 from: http://www.undp.org.in/hdrc/shdr/mphdr/dwnld_chap_MP02.htm

Vera–Sanso, P., 'Masculinity, Male Domestic Authority and Female Labour Participation in South India', in C. Jackson (ed.), *Men at Work: Men, Masculinities, and Development*, Portland, OR: Frank Cass, 2001, pp. 179–98.

Wood, G., 'Staying Secure, Staying Poor: The 'Faustian Bargain'', *World Development* 31, 2003, pp. 455–71.

# 9

# The National Employment Guarantee Act and Migration Policy

## Lessons from Andhra Pradesh and Madhya Pradesh

*S. Laxman Rao*

## INTRODUCTION

Based on primary data collected from eight villages across Madhya Pradesh and Andhra Pradesh during early 2007, this chapter addresses the question of whether the National Rural Employment Guarantee Act (NREGA) is measuring up to expectations regarding its ability to reduce labour migration from rural areas. Large-scale seasonal or circular migration is a regular feature of most of the districts where the NREGA is being implemented. 'Reducing rural-urban migration' is one of the basic objectives of the Act (GoI 2005). Reviewing wider evidence, the chapter also examines how the NREGA is delivering on its core promises such as employment generation, payment of statutory minimum wages, equal wages for men and women, unemployment allowance, a reliable system of wage payments, decentralization, transparency, and accountability.

## EMPLOYMENT GUARANTEE: CORE COMMITMENTS

The NREGA states that its basic objective is to enhance livelihood security in rural areas; work guarantee can also serve such other objectives as creating productive assets, protecting the environment, empowering women, and fostering social equity. 'It empowers ordinary people to play an active part in the implementation through *gram sabha*s, social audits, and participatory planning. The NREGA is an Act of the people, by the people and for the people' (GoI 2005). The core features of the Act are:

- Adult members of every household who are willing to do unskilled manual work can register themselves and receive a job card.
- Every adult member whose name appears in the job card is entitled to apply for unskilled manual work.
- Every registered household shall be provided not less than 100 days of wage employment in a financial year.
- At least one-third of the wage seekers shall be women.
- Applicants shall be provided work within the village; if work is provided outside a radius of five kilometres they should be paid an extra 10 per cent of the wage rate.
- Payment of 'the statutory minimum wage applicable to agricultural workers; wages shall be paid at least once in a fortnight.
- Equal wages to men and women.
- Contractors and machinery shall not be engaged.
- Only works approved by the *gram panchayat*, the intermediate panchayat, and the zilla parishad shall be taken up.
- The gram panchayat will accept applications for work and issue a dated receipt to the applicant.
- If an applicant is not provided with work within fifteen days, he/she shall be entitled to a daily unemployment allowance.
- If wages are not paid within a fortnight, the workers shall be entitled to a compensation.
- Workers are entitled to work site facilities such as safe drinking water, child care, shelter, and first aid.

CONCEPTS, POLITICS, AND IMPLEMENTATION PATTERNS ACROSS DIFFERENT STATES

The appeal of the employment guarantee to policymakers is that it contains a strong element of social protection, by providing work where and when it is needed, and at the same time creating productive assets. The fact that benefits go to the 'deserving poor', who are prepared to work for these benefits, helps to make resource transfers politically acceptable. Wages can be set at a level which targets the resources towards the poor, but not so high that middle-income workers are attracted. Public works schemes of this kind have been termed 'self-targeting'. However, many of these advantages cut both ways. To select only the able-bodied poor means that those unable to engage fully in the productive economy such as orphans and other vulnerable children, the elderly or the disabled, are excluded. The emphasis on 'shared assets' begs questions over how such assets will be shared, and whether elites will attempt to capture them. Employment guarantee provides no more than temporary alleviation of the worst manifestations of poverty — it does not equip workers to engage in more productive employment by providing them with necessary skills.

Much of the literature on the NREGA tends to assume that wage employment schemes are implemented in a political vacuum. The effectiveness of the centrally sponsored programmes such as the NREGA is influenced, among other factors, by how the state leadership receives the policy, interprets it, and adapts it. The initial trends of the performance of the Employment Guarantee Schemes over the last one year or so can be seen from the available field evidence and the official statistics. The implementation of the NREGA presents a highly complex picture with each state taking its own trajectory despite a Central Act and clear Operational Guidelines.

In the first year of implementation, the four best performers were Rajasthan, Madhya Pradesh, Assam, and Chhattisgarh (Dreze and Oldiges 2007). On the other hand, the scheme floundered badly in Bihar, Maharashtra, Orissa, and Andhra Pradesh for various reasons, including a lack of political commitment and a lack of demand by workers for unskilled work. In Bihar, the NREGA is being implemented in all 38 districts of the state although the Centre notified only 28 districts. Bihar added more districts and used the official BPL list to select the 'beneficiaries' which contravened NREGA specifications (Development Alternatives 2006). The average days of employment provided to a household in the state during the financial year 2006–7 was only 35. Even after a year of implementation Bihar had not put in place the required field level functionaries. Dated receipts are not given to the applicants demanding work. Officials are not forthcoming in sharing the NREGA records during social audits. In some locations the registered persons did not work under the scheme because they had alternative opportunities that fetched higher wages (Rural

Development Ministry, GoI 2007). Andhra Pradesh has diluted the Employment Guarantee Scheme by diverting NREGA funds to its favoured housing programme (*The Hindu*, 1 July 2007) (see Box 9.1).

A survey conducted in Orissa found that around 70 per cent of the NREGA funds have been siphoned off by officials and implementing agencies. The survey could not find a single household that received 100 days of wage employment (Rai 2007). In Kerala, a lack of demand for unskilled manual work is a major factor for the poor performance of the NREGA (Jacob and Richard 2006). The poor performance of the scheme in Maharashtra — a state that implemented the Employment Guarantee Scheme for three decades — is attributable in large

---

BOX 9.1: DILUTING THE NREGA IN ANDHRA PRADESH

The AP government has dovetailed the Employment Guarantee Scheme with a housing scheme named after Indira Gandhi. Under this scheme, part of the subsidy given to the beneficiaries is paid from the NREGA funds. Each beneficiary is paid Rs 3,200. But official records show that the beneficiary has worked under the NREGS for 40 days at Rs 80 a day. The beneficiaries under this scheme are selected by local political leaders and officials. The employment needs of the household may or may not be taken into account. When the author visited MD village of Medak district nearly half of the households were building new houses. Many of these beneficiaries already owned a house. Most of them were either extending the existing houses or building new structures. Most of them were not aware of the NREGA. A majority of the beneficiaries applied for job cards after they had built the foundation of the house because without job cards the subsidy amount would not be transferred to them. The Congress government has a target of six million houses by 2009, the year in which the Assembly elections are due. Moreover, the Chief Minister Rajasekhara Reddy announced that 'drainage works which were so far barred under the NREGA would be permitted shortly.' (*The Hindu*, 14 September 2007). Drainage works would inevitably involve a high material component and use of machinery and skilled workers. AP utilized only a half of the NREGA funds in the first year. Despite all this, the NREGA was extended to four more districts in the state.

measure to the absence of political commitment (Datar 2007). Uttar Pradesh and West Bengal have also not shown political commitment towards the scheme.

Official figures show that no state government had fully utilized NREGA funds during the first financial year 2006–7. The utilization of funds at the national level was 71.5 per cent. Surprisingly, Andhra Pradesh ranks 22nd among 27 states as it utilized only 52 per cent of the available funds. The levels of utilization in poorer states hover around the national average: Madhya Pradesh (82 per cent), Bihar (71 per cent), Orissa (78 per cent), Uttar Pradesh (72 per cent), Jharkhand (79 per cent), Uttaranchal (72 per cent), and Chhattisgarh (84 per cent).[1]

The average number of employment days delivered per beneficiary household in 2006–7 varied from as low as 14 (in West Bengal) to a high of 72 (in Assam). The national average was 43, while 20 out of 27 states reported an average of less than 50 days. As many as eleven states failed to deliver a minimum of one-third of all employment days to women. Only 53 per cent of NREGA funds were spent on high-priority areas of water conservation and drought proofing in 2006–7 (Banerjee 2007). In many states, the panchayats have not been empowered to implement the scheme. Social audits and representations made by people's representatives and civil society organizations are not taken seriously by most states; nor is follow-up action taken on the feedback from social audits.

A more recent evaluation of the NREGA in Madhya Pradesh finds that demand-driven and participatory ways of implementation are not adhered to as the panchayats followed conventional top-down approaches such as the registration of households and issuance of job cards using an official survey of 2003. Apart from the under-performance of the programme with respect to its core commitments, such as 100 days of work at the statutory minimum wages and unemployment allowance, the study discovered instances of misappropriation of funds at the panchayat level. However, the performance levels of MP are higher when compared with national averages. On the positive side, MP is doing better with respect to the utilization of funds, the proportion of labour-intensive works and decentralization. Yet the panchayats are overburdened with workloads and they lack capacity to effectively implement the scheme. Although awareness levels have improved, aggrieved workers do not have a clue as to whom to approach as there is no grievance redressal mechanism in place (Samarthan 2007).

A performance audit of the NREGA conducted by the Comptroller and Auditor General of India has also found that state governments have fallen short of the provisions of the Act. The audit found widespread anomalies such as: undue delay in formulating state employment guarantee schemes and issuing job cards; diversion of funds to unauthorized works or works with high material component; non-payment of minimum wages and unemployment allowance; delay in payment of wages; absence of records on job applications; and manipulation of muster rolls. Under-utilization of funds and reluctance on the part of the states to release their share of the funding were also found by the audit. Social audits were not held by the states. 'Non-conduct of social audit strikes at the root of the demand-driven bottom-up approach of the NREGA' (Principal Director of Audit 2007).

The new evidence shows that the weaknesses of the NREGA that were found by social audits conducted, for instance, in the districts of Dungarpur and Jhalwar (Rajasthan), Anantapur (Andhra Pradesh), and Villupuram (Tamil Nadu) remain largely unaddressed (Gopal 2007; Sowmya 2006; Dreze and Sowmya 2007; *Outlook* 2008). The Samarthan study also finds that: 'Social audits have not been taken up. There is a lack of awareness at the Panchayat level about the process and relevance of social audits. The government had taken some initiatives in this regard but a significant impact is yet to be seen.'

Two years on, the NREGA in Andhra Pradesh has produced mixed results. Two important factors, *inter alia*, have contributed to the lower number of days—as against the promised 100 days—in the second year: first, the Indiramma housing scheme (see Box 9.1), people were building their houses instead of doing the NREGA work; second, they had alternative work. In some poor and dry villages of the Rayalaseema region farmers are unhappy with the NREGA because it has pushed up local wage rates and they fear that this could make agriculture unviable. As for migration, it appears that the NREGA has made a visible impact in some drought-prone and backward villages of Anantapur and Medak districts. Workers of these villages said that migration was no longer necessary. In Anantapur district, the NREGA work is now more dependable. To avoid delays in wage payment, the AP government implemented a pilot initiative where wage payment was entrusted to women's self help groups; this experiment has proved successful. Overall social audit are yet to make a difference but they have had positive impacts in some locations (Elliott 2008, personal communication).[2]

Rather than reviewing the poor performance of the NREGA in the first year to make it more effective, the Centre has extended the scheme to 130 additional districts. This was done despite the gross under-utilization of funds by several state governments when 90 per cent of the funding is contributed by the Centre.

This brings out the dynamics of electoral and coalition compulsions and its influence on the course of the NREGA. If the initial trends are any indication, it is highly likely that the scheme will continue until the next general elections which are due in 2009 irrespective of its performance. The emerging pattern also shows that the trajectories that the states have taken are not related to mere administrative matters but have serious implications for the delivery of the core commitments.

METHODOLOGY AND STUDY LOCATIONS

The primary data were collected through sample surveys conducted in 2006–7 in the states of Andhra Pradesh and Madhya Pradesh. The reference period for this survey was March 2006 to February 2007 coinciding with the first year of the NREGA implementation. Quantitative data were collected on migration and the NREGS from 500 sample households spread across eight villages of four districts in MP and AP. Qualitative information was collected through participatory methods.

The AP districts are Chittoor and Medak representing Rayalaseema and Telangana regions of the state respectively. Mandla and Tikamgarh are the MP districts selected from the Mahakoshal and Bundelkhand regions of the state respectively. Two villages were chosen from each district: one village is relatively remote and backward, and the other is relatively more developed and better connected to markets and urban centres. The Madhya Pradesh villages are: PT and GG of Mandla, and SM and MB of Tikamgarh. The Andhra Pradesh villages are: VP and OP of Chittoor, and MD and GU of Medak. Sample households were selected through a multi-stage stratified random sampling method.

This study also draws on a number of secondary sources. The scheme that had completed one year at the time of this survey, was being implemented in a diverse and complex context. It was a relatively new scheme and was still evolving. However, the implementation of the scheme produced certain clear trends, and policy lessons can already be drawn. Due to the absence of empirical basis most of the assessments of the NREGA tend to reflect the predispositions of the author(s) by discussing only success stories or the worst performing locations. This empirical study is an attempt to give an objective account of the interface between the NREGA and migration.

EMPLOYMENT GUARANTEE AND THE AWARENESS LEVELS

The NREGA states that the Employment Guarantee Scheme is a self-targeting scheme. The Act emphasizes the participation of workers in its planning and implementation. Its success therefore depends a great deal on whether poor workers are aware of their rights, roles, and responsibilities. Even after a year of implementation, awareness levels are low. Table 9.1 presents the findings on village-wise awareness levels about the NREGA. Although the vast majority of the sample households have heard of the Employment Guarantee Scheme, their awareness levels are poor on basic entitlements such as minimum wages, equal wages for men and women, right to demand work, and unemployment allowance. Most of the respondents who are familiar with at least one feature of the Act are aware only of the '100 days of work' entitlement. Awareness levels decrease as we move up to higher levels of entitlements.

Awareness levels in general are higher in MP, particularly in the tribal villages of GG and PT where demand for the NREGA work was very high. The MP government has shown better political will in reaching out to the poor and involvement of civil society has also made a difference. Local caste/class dynamics in the non-tribal villages of MP is a major factor responsible for lower awareness levels. In AP, awareness levels are much lower in the backward village MD where literacy levels are very low. The government publicity through mass media and wall signs could not reach the poor and illiterate people.

If the data are analyzed by household income quintiles (Table 9.2) it is seen that poorer households are the least aware of their rights, especially where illiterate people depend on local officials and elected representatives for information on schedule of works, payment of wages, wage rates, etc. The lack of information suggests that village panchayats are not engaged as fully as intended in the Act. Some

Table 9.1: Awareness Levels of the NREGA by Village

| | | AP Villages | | | | MP Villages | | | | AP | MP | All (AP and MP) |
|---|---|---|---|---|---|---|---|---|---|---|---|---|
| | | OP | VP | GU | MD | GG | PT | SM | MB | | | |
| Aware of the | Yes | 89 | 97 | 8 | 50 | 95 | 97 | 58 | 76 | 54 | 77 | 65 |
| scheme | No | 11 | 3 | 92 | 50 | 5 | 3 | 42 | 24 | 46 | 23 | 35 |
| Aware of at | Yes | 83 | 97 | 5 | 36 | 83 | 73 | 54 | 61 | 49 | 65 | 57 |
| least one entitlement | No | 17 | 3 | 95 | 64 | 17 | 27 | 46 | 39 | 51 | 35 | 43 |
| 100 days of work | Yes | 75 | 97 | 55 | 37 | 83 | 73 | 54 | 58 | 47 | 65 | 56 |
| | No | 25 | 3 | 45 | 63 | 17 | 27 | 46 | 42 | 53 | 35 | 44 |
| Minimum wages | Yes | 40 | 27 | 4 | 5 | 82 | 34 | 51 | 61 | 17 | 56 | 36 |
| | No | 60 | 73 | 96 | 95 | 18 | 66 | 49 | 39 | 83 | 44 | 64 |
| Equal wages for | Yes | 57 | 68 | 1 | 23 | 0 | 10 | 9 | 0 | 32 | 5 | 19 |
| men and women | No | 43 | 32 | 99 | 77 | 100 | 90 | 91 | 100 | 68 | 95 | 81 |
| Unemployment | Yes | 0 | 0 | 1 | 3 | 80 | 31 | 29 | 3 | 1 | 35 | 18 |
| allowance | No | 100 | 100 | 99 | 97 | 20 | 69 | 71 | 97 | 99 | 65 | 82 |
| Wage payment | Yes | 0 | 0 | 0 | 0 | 0 | 0 | 10 | 0 | 0 | 4 | 2 |
| in two weeks | No | 100 | 100 | 100 | 100 | 100 | 100 | 90 | 100 | 100 | 96 | 98 |
| Entitlement to | Yes | 0 | 0 | 0 | 0 | 7 | 0 | 15 | 23 | 0 | 12 | 6 |
| demand work | No | 100 | 100 | 100 | 100 | 93 | 100 | 85 | 77 | 100 | 88 | 94 |

*Source*: Author.
*Notes*: * All figures are percentages.

might go so far as to suggest that this privatizing of public information by officials for personal gain provides yet another example of the difficulty of breaking old habits.

Most of the card holders have not formally applied for work. Less than 2 per cent of the households are aware of the work site facilities. As for the unregistered households, 66 per cent of them reported that they had not applied for the job card because they were not aware of the scheme. Government functionaries and the elected representatives are reluctant to educate the poor about their entitlements.

The lack of knowledge among the registered workers about what is legally due to them has resulted in poor demand for employment. Instead of being a demand-driven people's programme, the general perception among people is that the NREGS is yet another *rozgar yojana* employment scheme. This disconnect at the village level is one of the major factors contributing to low participation in the scheme by poor households.

However, officials made greater efforts to improve awareness towards the end of the first year as they tried to achieve the targets in terms of the number of days of work and utilization of funds. Some crucial aspects such as the formal application for work and the payment of unemployment allowance were not implemented in our study locations.

Table 9.2: Awareness Levels of the NREGA by Income Quintiles*

| | | Q1 | | Q2 | | Q3 | | Q4 | | Q5 | | AP all | MP all | AP and MP |
|---|---|---|---|---|---|---|---|---|---|---|---|---|---|---|
| | | AP | MP | AP | MP | AP | MP | AP | MP | AP | MP | | | |
| Aware of NREGS | Yes | 44 | 80 | 53 | 82 | 61 | 73 | 64 | 80 | 57 | 71 | 53 | 77 | 65 |
| | No | 56 | 20 | 47 | 18 | 39 | 27 | 36 | 20 | 43 | 29 | 47 | 23 | 35 |
| Aware of at least | Yes | 40 | 61 | 45 | 71 | 59 | 66 | 64 | 66 | 47 | 60 | 49 | 66 | 57 |
| one entitlement | No | 60 | 39 | 55 | 29 | 41 | 34 | 36 | 34 | 53 | 40 | 51 | 34 | 43 |
| 100 days of work | Yes | 38 | 61 | 41 | 71 | 59 | 64 | 64 | 66 | 47 | 60 | 47 | 65 | 56 |
| | No | 62 | 39 | 59 | 29 | 41 | 36 | 36 | 34 | 53 | 40 | 53 | 35 | 44 |
| Minimum wages | Yes | 21 | 54 | 9 | 63 | 20 | 59 | 18 | 47 | 24 | 57 | 17 | 56 | 37 |
| | No | 79 | 46 | 91 | 37 | 80 | 41 | 82 | 53 | 76 | 43 | 83 | 44 | 63 |
| Equal wages for | Yes | 25 | 3 | 27 | 2 | 44 | 5 | 39 | 0 | 38 | 20 | 32 | 6 | 19 |
| men and women | No | 75 | 97 | 73 | 98 | 56 | 95 | 61 | 100 | 62 | 80 | 68 | 94 | 81 |
| Unemployment | Yes | 2 | 38 | 0 | 32 | 3 | 31 | 0 | 33 | 0 | 42 | 1 | 35 | 18 |
| allowance | No | 98 | 62 | 100 | 68 | 97 | 69 | 100 | 67 | 100 | 58 | 99 | 65 | 82 |
| Wage payment in | Yes | 0 | 0 | 0 | 2 | 0 | 0 | 0 | 0 | 0 | 17 | 0 | 4 | 2 |
| two weeks | No | 100 | 100 | 100 | 98 | 100 | 100 | 100 | 100 | 100 | 83 | 100 | 96 | 98 |
| Entitlement to | Yes | 0 | 6 | 0 | 17 | 0 | 10 | 0 | 6 | 0 | 20 | 0 | 12 | 6 |
| demand work | No | 100 | 97 | 100 | 83 | 100 | 90 | 100 | 94 | 100 | 80 | 100 | 88 | 94 |

Source: Author.
Notes: *Each quintile denotes 20%. Q1 is the bottom quintile and Q5 is the top quintile. All figures are percentages.

Madhya Pradesh villages had higher levels of awareness. This partly reflects the way in which the state has adapted the scheme. The government has enlisted the support of NGOs to ensure that people are aware of their entitlements and it has succeeded in making the programme more attractive to the poor. MP had launched a major awareness campaign to reach the rural poor. The poor have perceived the scheme as having certain distinct advantages. MP has been more pro-active as it has demonstrated its commitment through timely utilization of funds, number of works completed and person days of work provided. Official data also show that MP has fared better than most other states.

By contrast, Andhra Pradesh has adopted a kind of 'business as usual' approach and has failed to implement it as a rights-based transfer programme. AP has not made serious attempts to make the poor aware of their entitlements. So, there is a perception among the poor that the scheme is yet another government scheme with all the attendant irregularities. The only difference, however, is some awareness about 100 days of work and higher wages.

---

BOX 9.2: A RIGHTS-BASED APPROACH:
CONSPICUOUS BY ITS ABSENCE

'We have job cards and we are waiting for the government to provide us work,' was the common refrain of poor households during focus group discussions. The legal guarantees that the NREGA offers have not reached the poor even after one year of its implementation. The NREGA envisages a rights-based approach through people's participation, decentralization, accountability, and transparency. This approach departs radically from the traditional top-down process. But the local officials and elected representatives seem to have other priorities and are reluctant to act on those lines because this would make them accountable to the poor besides adding to their work load. Works are being identified in a centralized fashion without the participation of the gram panchayats. The poor are clueless about the commencement and duration of works.

The process of demand-driven employment is largely non-existent and work is provided by the officials when it is available. The awareness building programmes do not focus on the substantive rights such as the right to demand work and claim unemployment allowance. The widespread perception is that the Employment Guarantee is yet another *rozgar yojana* (employment scheme) albeit with small improvements such as job cards and the promise of 100 days of work. The poor performance of the NREGA in Maharashtra, a state with three decades of experience with the Employment Guarantee Scheme, sends out a clear message (Datar 2007; Patil 2006; Jadhav 2006). Therefore the failures of the Act in the first year cannot be brushed aside as mere problems of a learning phase.

---

Several other studies have also brought out the low levels of awareness (PRIA 2006; Samarthan 2006; Louis 2006; Development Alternatives 2006). Most state governments have no awareness building strategy. The idea that the NREGA is a demand-driven scheme has not yet reached the local officials in several states. Workers were mostly unaware of their rights and the processes that are required to claim the rights. Transparency guidelines were not seen to be compulsory (CBGA 2006). An evaluation of the NREGA in AP and Karnataka finds that panchayats are not being encouraged to be in charge of the scheme. (Thakur 2006).

FROM PAPER TO PRACTICE: NREGA ON THE GROUND

Nearly two-thirds of the sample households in both states have job cards and this proportion is higher in MP where 90 per cent of households have job cards. However, only 25 per cent of the registered households actually worked under the scheme in the first year. The participation rates are higher in MP as 40 per cent of card-holding households worked under the scheme.

Higher awareness levels and a higher proportion of households willing to do manual work are among major factors accounting for the better response in MP. But in AP, half of the households without job cards said that they did not have the members willing to depend on the job guarantee scheme; the rest of the households reported that they were not aware of the scheme. This is due to the lack of demand in AP for hard manual labour from better-off households. These households often have such members as full-time farmers, educated youth, and non-farm workers including the self-employed who normally do not do the kind of work provided under the scheme. Only 2 per cent of households without job cards in MP said that they had no members to work under the scheme.

Due to the lack of awareness of the requirement to formally apply for work, none of the sample households had formally applied for work. Therefore none of the card holders could claim unemployment allowance. But a quarter of registered households informally approached either the village officials or the panchayat representatives for work.

In the first year the NREGA provided, on an average, only 25 days of employment per household. This is only a quarter of 100 days of work that the Act promises. Moreover, two-thirds of the participating households worked in instalments indicating that they worked in short spans of one week or ten days. This violates the Act's entitlement that says that the employment shall be for a continuous period of at least fourteen days. The vast majority of participating households expressed dissatisfaction about the short spells of work. The unpredictability of employment was another drawback reported by the workers. They were expecting more work during the lean seasons but the work was provided by the officials according to their requirements and decisions.

---

BOX 9.3: FROM ELITE CAPTURE TO ELITE BACKLASH

The indifference of the local elite and officials to the NREGA was noticeable in all the study villages. In some locations this indifference bordered on resistance and opposition, and even sabotage. The provisions of the Act relating to workers' entitlements, accountability, and transparency offer very little scope for manipulation and collusive association between the village elite and the local bureaucracy. The opposition of the elite was more evident in the AP villages. Take the case of DL of Medak district which is a peri-urban village just 40 km from the state capital. This village has a large labour force. At the end of the first year, DL had issued only 60 job cards. Although the gram sabha had identified 56 works, only one work had been executed where just 10 persons worked receiving wages lower than state minimum rate. The elite in this village feel that there is nothing for them in the scheme because it bans machines and contractors and wages would be paid directly to the workers through post office accounts. And it is very difficult to siphon off money and distribute patronage. Rich farmers of the village fear that if the scheme is implemented effectively it would push up the local wage rates and they would face labour shortages during peak seasons.

Officials and Panchayat representatives say that there is no demand for manual work in the village as there are easier opportunities in the industries around the village. However, focus group discussions with the poor Dalits and OBCs revealed that they did not apply for job cards as they were not aware of the scheme.

---

The NREGA promises that the wages would be paid within two weeks of the completion of work. But this survey found that only 45 per cent of the households received wages within the promised time. AP performed better in this regard while the time lag in MP was longer with 40 per cent of the households reporting that they received wages after three months. Paradoxically, the shorter time lag in AP is due to the corrupt practices resorted to by the field assistant, village elders, and the influential caste leaders. They mostly underpaid the workers after the completion of works on the pretext of avoiding delays in the transfer of wages. In violation of the guidelines, they later withdrew the full wages from the post office. This was a result of a collusive association between these influential people and the local post office functionary. In addition, in both AP and MP, women workers received lower wages and the wage differential was higher in AP. While men received a mean wage of Rs 72 in AP, women received Rs 65; the corresponding figures for MP are Rs 55 and 53.

More important, 60 per cent of the NREGA workers across AP and MP reported that the scheme was not dependable as a source of livelihood. While this proportion is slightly higher in MP, where two-thirds of workers felt that the NREGS work was not reliable, almost a half of the workers in AP opined that it was difficult to say because the scheme was new. Most of the participating households liked the type of work provided because they were used to the work and it was provided in their habitation. The short duration of work and delays in wage payment were the main reasons cited by those who were not happy with the scheme.

NREGA AND MIGRATION

Migration from rural India is a complex process characterized by a variety of drivers and varied outcomes. The movement of workers follows different streams covering a wide range of occupations. Daily commuting to nearby villages and urban locations is on the rise and this has emerged as an important stream of mobility (see Chapters 3 and 4 in this book). The range of activities pursued at the destination is also steadily expanding. The type of work ranges from highly skilled white collar jobs to unskilled manual work. Using the same reference period as that of the NREGA, the current survey collected data on migration and commuting from the eight study villages. The three streams of mobility covered are: circular or seasonal migration, permanent migration, and commuting. For the purpose of this study, circular migration is defined as a temporary move from, followed by return to, normal place of residence, for purposes of employment. A permanent migrant is one who lives at the place(s) of work for more than a year although they may visit their native village on occasions.

Table 9.3 presents the village-wise profile of migrants and commuters that worked under the scheme during the first year. It shows that in AP the NREGA attracted only a couple of circular migrants and commuters in each village, the highest number being four in MD. None of the commuters and migrants of GU worked under the scheme. The performance of the NREGA has been very poor in GU. A majority of the workers in AP are from the poorer quintiles, that is from the bottom three quintiles; and there are no workers from the top quintile. Participation rates are higher in drought-prone and relatively remote villages of MD and OP in Medak and Chittoor districts.

Table 9.3: Migrants and Commuters that Worked under the NREGA by Village and Income Quintiles

| Village/State | Q1 | | Q2 | | Q3 | | Q4 | | Q5 | | All | |
|---|---|---|---|---|---|---|---|---|---|---|---|---|
| | No | % | No | % | No | % | No | % | No | % | No | % |
| OP | 0 | 0 | 1 | 7.1 | 1 | 14.3 | 1 | 12.5 | 0 | 0 | 3 | 6.4 |
| VP | 0 | 0 | 0 | 0 | 0 | 0 | 2 | 25.0 | 0 | 0 | 2 | 4.3 |
| MD | 2 | 14.3 | 2 | 14.3 | 0 | 0 | 0 | 0 | 0 | 0 | 4 | 8.5 |
| Andhra Pradesh | 2 | 14.3 | 3 | 21.4 | 1 | 14.3 | 3 | 37.5 | 0 | 0 | 9 | 19.1 |
| GG | 1 | 7.1 | 3 | 21.4 | 2 | 28.6 | 2 | 25.0 | 1 | 25 | 9 | 19.1 |
| PT | 9 | 64.3 | 4 | 28.6 | 2 | 28.6 | 2 | 25.0 | 3 | 75 | 20 | 42.6 |
| MB | 2 | 14.3 | 4 | 28.6 | 2 | 28.6 | 1 | 12.5 | 0 | 0 | 9 | 19.1 |
| Madhya Pradesh | 12 | 85.7 | 11 | 78.6 | 6 | 85.7 | 5 | 62.5 | 4 | 100 | 38 | 80.9 |
| All (AP and MP) | 14 | | 14 | | 7 | | 8 | | 4 | | 47 | |
| | (29.8%) | 100 | (29.8%) | 100 | (14.9%) | 100 | (17%) | 100 | (8.5%) | 100 | (100) | 100 |

*Source*: Author.

*Note*: Figures in brackets denote the proportion of commuting and migrant NREGS workers in each quintile. No such workers in GD and SM.

A similar trend can be seen in MP but the overall participation rates are considerably higher. Relatively far tribal villages of MP had a much higher level of participation because of the lack of alternative opportunities. The tribal village of PT accounted for the highest number of workers. In PT almost 60 per cent of migrant NREGS workers are from the bottom two quintiles indicating higher representation of poorer migrants in NREGS works. In SM there are no mobile workers among the NREGA participants.

None of the permanent migrants, including the unskilled ones, worked under the scheme although there are permanent migrants from all the study villages except PT. This is understandable because the NREGA is a new scheme and permanent migrants live at the destination. Most of the mobile workers who participated in the programme worked as unskilled manual workers when they migrated or commuted. Nearly 80 per cent of mobile NREGA workers reported the following unskilled activities that they pursued at the place of work: agriculture labour, construction work, porter, rickshaw pulling, stone quarry work, forest labour, and non-farm work.

Table 9.4 gives the village-wise details of the total number of circular migrants, permanent migrants, and commuters, and the proportion of the workers from these streams that worked under the NREGA. In AP 5.4 per cent of commuters and 5 per cent of circular migrants worked under the NREGA. The corresponding proportions in MP are 22 per cent and almost 30 per cent and across the states the proportions are 9.2 per cent and 20 per cent respectively.

The higher participation rate of migrants and commuters in MP is explained by a lack of alternative wage labour opportunities when the migrants are at home, higher wages paid under the NREGA and better implementation of the scheme by the government. It seems that the NREGA has proved more attractive in MP owing to subsistence agriculture, poor infrastructure, low farm wage rates, and the lack of non-farm opportunities. For instance, in MB of Tikamgarh district, elderly members of a couple of migrant households had found the scheme very helpful as they find the conditions of work at destinations very tough.

Distribution of migrant and commuting NREGA workers by household income quintiles shows that in AP these mobile workers come essentially from the poorer households, that is from the bottom three quintiles, and there are no mobile workers from the top quintile. The results for MP show a different pattern: there is participation in the NREGA work from all quintiles. But the participation rates steadily decline as we go up the income hierarchy. This is partly explained by

Table 9.4: Village-wise Participation Under the NREGA by Mobility Stream

| Village/State | Commuter | | | Circular Migrant | | | Permanent Migrant | | | All | | |
|---|---|---|---|---|---|---|---|---|---|---|---|---|
| | Total | Worked under NREGA | % | Total | Worked under NREGA | % | Total | Worked under NREGA | % | Total | Worked under NREGA | % |
| OP | 21 | 2 | 9.5 | 11 | 1 | 9.1 | 9 | 0 | 0 | 41 | 3 | 7.3 |
| VP | 20 | 2 | 10.0 | 41 | 0 | 0 | 5 | 0 | 0 | 66 | 2 | 3.0 |
| GU | 45 | 0 | 0 | 3 | 0 | 0 | 5 | 0 | 0 | 53 | 0 | 0 |
| MD | 7 | 1 | 14.3 | 25 | 3 | 12 | 21 | 0 | 0 | 53 | 4 | 7.5 |
| AndhraPradesh | 93 | 5 | 5.4 | 80 | 4 | 5.0 | 40 | 0 | 0 | 213 | 9 | 4.2 |
| GG | 24 | 6 | 25 | 22 | 3 | 13.6 | 1 | 0 | 0 | 47 | 9 | 19.1 |
| PT | 0 | 0 | 0 | 37 | 20 | 54.1 | 0 | 0 | 0 | 37 | 20 | 54.1 |
| SM | 3 | 0 | 0 | 24 | 0 | 0 | 1 | 0 | 0 | 28 | 0 | 0 |
| MB | 0 | 0 | 0 | 28 | 9 | 32.1 | 0 | 0 | 0 | 28 | 9 | 32.1 |
| Madhya Pradesh | 27 | 6 | 22.2 | 111 | 32 | 28.8 | 2 | 0 | 0 | 140 | 38 | 27.1 |
| All (AP & MP) | 120 | 11 | 9.2 | 191 | 38 | 19.9 | 42 | 0 | 0 | 353 | 47 | 13.3 |

*Source*: Author.

two factors: the generally lower incomes of households there leading to greater demand for manual work; and the lack of alternative opportunities especially in the non-farm sector.

DAYS OF WORK, WAGES, AND RETURNS

The number of person-days, wage rates, and returns for migrating and commuting households as well as all households are presented in Table 9.5. The figures demonstrate that in the first year of implementation, the NREGA has failed to deliver on its key promises. Across the study villages in the two states, each participating household was provided, on an average, 23 days of work. The corresponding figures for AP and MP are 34 and 20 respectively. Only one household, out of 500 sample households, had worked for 100 days.

In both AP and MP the daily wages received by the workers are lower than their respective statutory minimum wages. The mean daily wages received are Rs 70 in AP and Rs 54 in MP which are lower than Rs 82 and Rs 64 — the official minimum wages. By contrast, circular migrants and commuters received Rs 100 and Rs 69 a day in AP and MP respectively, representing wages that are higher than their respective statutory minimum wages. But the differential between the two wage rates is higher in AP suggesting that migration/commuting is more attractive in AP.

In terms of the total earnings from the scheme, each household received an average amount of Rs 2,580 and Rs 1,061 in AP and MP respectively. Interestingly, this amount is less than 10 per cent of the average amount earned by migrating and commuting households in both states. The incomes derived from migration and commuting are Rs 27,697 and Rs 14,911 in AP and MP respectively.

Even after the completion of the first year, the scheme has not attracted even one permanent migrant from the study villages. Moreover, 'unskilled manual work' would appeal to only a half of circular and permanent migrants because the findings of this study show that 52 per cent of migrants reported unskilled occupations. The results on commuting and migrant workers who participated in the Employment Guarantee Scheme show that these mobile workers did not stop migrating or commuting but they worked under the scheme when they were at home. The NREGA work served as a supplementary

## Table 9.5: Number of Days and Wage Income Under the NREGA and from Migration/Commuting by Income Quintiles

| Days/Pay | Q1 AP | Q1 MP | Q2 AP | Q2 MP | Q3 AP | Q3 MP | Q4 AP | Q4 MP | Q5 AP | Q5 MP | All AP | All MP | AP and MP |
|---|---|---|---|---|---|---|---|---|---|---|---|---|---|
| Number of days/hh under NREGS | 29 | 24 | 36 | 14 | 29 | 23 | 37 | 21 | 80 | 15 | 34* | 20 | 23 |
| Number of days per migrant & commuting hh | 256 | 232 | 239 | 188 | 213 | 211 | 277 | 253 | 253 | 176 | 246 | 219 | 240 |
| Number of days per person under NREGS | 22 | 14 | 24 | 10 | 17 | 14 | 22 | 14 | 40 | 13 | 22* | 13 | 15 |
| Number of days per person from migration & commuting | 260 | 218 | 244 | 188 | 212 | 200 | 274 | 271 | 258 | 177 | 246 | 215 | 239 |
| Daily wage per worker under NREGS | 80 | 53 | 71 | 57 | 62 | 54 | 63 | 53 | 80 | 54 | 70# | 54 | 59 |
| Daily wage per person from migration & commuting | 79 | 62 | 79 | 57 | 97 | 70 | 114 | 75 | 185 | 77 | 100 | 69 | 93 |
| Total earnings per hh under NREGS | 2,341 | 1,248 | 2,717 | 820 | 2,029 | 1,270 | 2,617 | 1,123 | 6,400 | 794 | 2,580 | 1,061 | 1,421 |
| Total earnings per hh from migration & commuting | 22,289 | 13,609 | 17,979 | 9,963 | 20,998 | 12,707 | 36,239 | 18,705 | 57,760 | 14,688 | 27,697 | 14,911 | 24,708 |

*Source:* Author.

*Notes:* All figures are means; wages and incomes are in Rs.

*The number of days per worker and per household in AP are higher due to the dovetailing of the APREGS with the housing scheme. AP data include some cases of 40 days of work per household @ Rs 80 a day, i.e., the housing scheme beneficiaries. Without the housing scheme transfers the figures will be much lower.

# Wage rate in AP is higher because it includes the housing scheme subsidy. The wage rate is Rs 65 without the housing scheme beneficiaries.

option. Therefore circular migrants can combine different activities depending on the availability of work.

The NREGA has not had any visible impact on circular migration due to a combination of factors: the scheme is relatively new and the vast majority of the poor do not know their entitlements; and the uncertainty stemming from the migrants' experience with the public works schemes relating to the concerns such as the work availability, wage payment, and linkages. By contrast, migration is seen as a more dependable option with regard to work availability, wage rate, and frequency of wage payment. As the following exposition illustrates, migration from the study villages has been a way of life for most of the migrant households for the past couple of decades.

In the words of Kalua Singh Baiga (50) of PT village in Mandla district of MP: 'Government employment schemes come and go; each new government introduces new schemes; I have seen a number of such schemes but no scheme has proved reliable so far; migration has been the main source of livelihood for us for more than two decades; we can always eke out a living by migrating to Jabalpur regardless of the party in power and the scheme under operation in the village.'

There are certain streams of migration in the study villages that are not only the most important sources of household income but over the years they have also become accumulative options. These streams are: sugarcane cutting through seasonal migration from Medak district and construction work in Bangalore through circular migration from Chittoor district of AP; and seasonal migration to Haveli areas for agricultural work from Mandla district of MP. As Table 9.6 shows the dependability of migration stems from higher returns and predictability and dependability of work. Ramappa of VP in Chittoor district of AP says: 'Each experienced migrant earns around Rs 200 a day working in Bangalore. The real estate activity in Bangalore is booming and the demand for workers is growing. I have heard of employment guarantee scheme. In fact, most of my friends have taken job cards. But there no one is prepared to work under the scheme. They will not work in the village as long as the Bangalore work is attractive. But we had better keep these identity cards (job cards) because you never know the government may link these cards to some other schemes.'

## CONCLUSION: THE LONG ROAD AHEAD

The findings of this study, and those of other evaluations of the scheme, show that the NREGA fell short of its core commitments in its first year. The isolated success stories have been the exception rather than the rule. In several states, the Employment Guarantee Scheme appears to be degenerating into a top-down target-oriented programme. The political will is lacking to reach out to the poor regarding the core rights that the Act confers on them.

Despite the poor performance of the scheme in the first one and a half years, the Central Government has not made any serious efforts to make the scheme more effective. The Centre has instead extended the NREGA to another 130 districts. This once again, proves that in India funding is not a constraint for pro-poor programmes and the outlays do not translate into outcomes. Implementation experience of the previous job schemes suggests that the poor performance in the initial years, in terms of the failure to meet 'targets' such as the number of person-days and funds utilization, leads to a target-oriented approach in subsequent years. The scheme is largely being implemented with a top-down approach. Diluting the scheme is one of the convenient ways chosen by the state governments to meet the targets.

### Employment Guarantee and Migration

The NREGA in general has not had any noticeable impact on migration. The scheme completed its first year when the survey was conducted. The awareness levels of the poor about their entitlements were low leading to poor registration, low demand for work, and the inability on the part of workers to claim other entitlements. This has resulted in a great deal of uncertainty about work availability and the delays in wage payment.

The Act promises only unskilled manual work and in doing so excludes the skilled migrant workers. The current survey finds that almost a half of the migrants of the study villages reported skilled occupations. Only 20 per cent of circular migrants worked under the NREGA. It provided, on an average, only 25 days of work per household and 15 days of work per worker in the first year. At this rate, the scheme is unlikely to influence the circular migration in a significant way. The wage rates of circular migrants in general are higher than those of the NREGA workers and thus migrating is a more attractive option in terms of financial returns.

The levels of participation vary: in MP persons from all quintiles participated in the scheme whereas in AP most of the workers were from poorer households. Official data also show that poorer states have seen greater demand for manual work. Relatively developed states have experienced lower demand for manual work. This trend broadly applies to migration as well. In relatively developed states there is likely to be higher demand for skilled work from migrants. As the case of Kerala illustrates, a large proportion of educated youth registered themselves under the scheme expecting white collar or skilled jobs.

In the AP villages, none of the regular migrants had worked exclusively under the NREGA. In MB village of Tikamgarh district in MP, however, young circular migrants of a couple households migrated to Delhi leaving behind elderly members who found the scheme very helpful as they are more vulnerable to the tough working and living conditions at the destination. These elderly migrants are basically unskilled and are used to the work provided under the scheme. And in the tribal village PT of Mandla district in MP, a large proportion of seasonal migrants worked under the NREGA before and after their migration but none of them had given up migration. In GG village of the same district, some circular migrants postponed their migration and left the village after completing the NREGA work.

Table 9.6: The NREGA and Migration: A Comparative Perspective

|  | NREGA | Migration |
| --- | --- | --- |
| Wages or returns | Lower | Higher |
| Number of days per year | Lower | Higher |
| Work availability | Unpredictable; inadequate | Predictable and more dependable |
| Wage payment | Delayed or unpredictable | No delays or predictable |
| Advances | Not paid | Advances are paid in some migration streams. |
| Dependability | New scheme; uncertainty | Familiar with the process; more dependable |
| Nature of work | Only unskilled manual/ earth work | Wide choice and scope for mobility |
| Prospects | No or limited scope for learning and/or skill upgradation | Opportunities for learning and/or skill upgradation |

*Source*: Author.

The evidence presented here supports the view that it is too early to evaluate the NREGA in terms of its ability to reduce migration from rural areas in that the scheme is yet to deliver on its key promises. The findings suggest that the NREGA has a long way to go before it can make a visible impact on migration from rural India. But this is unlikely to happen as governments refuse to learn lessons from the failures of the scheme. The Centre has already announced the extension of the scheme to the entire country in preparation for the general elections. Numerous suggestions for the improved implementation of NREGA have been made by civil society organizations, social activists, and independent researchers, and state governments would do well to heed these.

NOTES

1. *The Hindu*, 16 June 2007 (Hyderabad).
2. Professor Carolyn Elliott is a Senior Fulbright Research Scholar and Visiting fellow, CESS, Hyderabad. She conducted field research in 26 AP villages during January–March 2008.

REFERENCES

Banerjee, A., *The Promise of Work: Milestones and Pitfalls*, New Delhi: Praxis India, 2007, available at: *www.praxisindia.org*

Centre for Budget and Governance Accountability, 'Survey to Monitor Implementation of NREGA in Andhra Pradesh, Chhattisgarh, Jharkhand, Madhya Pradesh', New Delhi, 2006.

Datar, C., 'Failure of National Rural Employment Guarantee Scheme in Maharashtra', *Economic and Political Weekly*, 25 August 2007.

Development Alternatives—Pricewaterhouse Coopers, *National Rural Employment Guarantee Scheme in Bihar*, 2006.

Dreze, Jean and Sowmya Kidambi, 'Long Road to Employment Guarantee', *The Hindu*, 10 August 2007.

———, and Christian Oldiges, 'Commendable Act', *Frontline*, 20 July 2007.

Gopal, K. S., *Capturing Imagination of Stakeholders: National Rural Employment Guarantee Act*, Hyderabad: Centre for Environmental Concerns, 2007.

Govt of Andhra Pradesh, *AP Rural Employment Guarantee Scheme*, Status Report issued in November 2006.

Jacob, A. and V. Richard, 'NREGA: A Reasonable Beginning in Palakkad, Kerala', *Economic & Political Weekly* , 2 December 2006.

Jadhav, V., 'Elite Politics and Maharashtra's Employment Guarantee Scheme', *Economic & Political Weekly*, 16 December 2006.

Louis, P., 'NREGA: Birth Pangs in Bihar', *Economic & Political Weekly*, 2 December 2006.

Ministry of Rural Development, Government of India, *NREGA 2005: Operational Guidelines*, New Delhi, 2005, available at: www.rural.nic.in

Participatory Research in Asia, *Role of Panchayati Raj Institutions in Implementation of NREGA*, (National Study, Phase I), New Delhi, 2006.

Patil, S., 'Empowerment, Co-option and Domination: Politics of Maha-rashtra's Employment Guarantee Scheme', *Economic & Political Weekly*, 16 December 2006.

Principal Director of Audit, Economic and Service Ministries, *Draft Performance Audit of Implementation of NREGA*, New Delhi, 2007.

Rai, P., *Rural Job Scam: Survey Report on Implementation of NREGA in Orissa*, New Delhi: Centre for Environment and Food Security, 2007.

Samarthan Centre for Development Support, *National Rural Employment Guarantee Act Monitoring Report on Status in Madhya Pradesh*, Bhopal, 2007.

——, *Madhya Pradesh Rural Employment Guarantee Scheme: Voices from the Grassroots*, Bhopal, 2006.

Samarthan and Poorest Area Civil Society Programme, *Status of NREGA Implementation: Grassroots Learning and Ways Forward*, Bhopal, 2006.

Sivakumar, S., 'Walking with a Purpose', *Frontline*, 6–19 May 2006.

# 10

# Serving Migrants

## Reflections on the Aajeevika Bureau Experience

*Rajiv Khandelwal, Elon Gilbert, and Whitney Gantt*

## INTRODUCTION

This chapter addresses the question of how to enhance the contributions of migration to reducing poverty in areas that have little prospect in the medium-term of providing even minimal livelihoods for their overwhelmingly poor rural populations. The authors examine this question through a narrative on the formative years of the Aajeevika Bureau, an innovative programme dedicated to improving livelihood opportunities for poor, migrant labourers from largely tribal communities in southern Rajasthan.

The chapter critically examines the assumptions underlying the Bureau's strategy and programmes and outlines its plans for testing them via impact monitoring and studies. Skill training aimed at enhancing productivity assumes a connection between skill levels and prospects for getting a better job. However, the Bureau's research and experiences have shown that skills are just the starting point, in moving towards improved and sustainable livelihood systems for migration-dependent families. These findings have led to the development and piloting of a range of complementary services that precede, accompany, and follow the actual migration, both for the migrants and their families.

The challenges to livelihood improvement are particularly daunting for circular migrants where the prospects for advancement are often limited. Many of the Bureau's current and prospective clients fall into this category. Although circular migrants comprise the migrant population with the greatest needs, the Bureau has limited capacities and needs to target those individuals that can benefit most from the services they provide. The chapter examines the ways in which the Bureau is addressing the dilemma posed by this situation.

The Bureau acknowledges from the onset that there is a need to empirically validate what are essentially a set of logical premises that are based on observation and experience. The purpose is not simply to account to its stakeholders, but as importantly to identify more effective and efficient ways of achieving its objectives. Beyond modifying existing services and possibly adding additional ones, the Bureau is considering if and how to massively scale up services. Without reaching significantly greater numbers of migrants, the aggregate effects on poverty will be very limited. In the broader national context, the Bureau is piloting a set of services that might be selectively scaled up by other organizations, public and private, with the capacity to deliver those services to large numbers of people. As that happens, the Bureau's role may evolve to focus more on action research aimed at assessing performance and devising/field testing improvements in services.

The remainder of this section provides an overview of the difficulties faced in the job market by migrants from southern Rajasthan. The next section describes the programmes and experiences of the Bureau from its establishment in 2004 upto the present. The section 'Aajeevika Bureau' covers a range of lessons and challenges that the Bureau has experienced in its early years. The synergies and tensions the Bureau faces in trying to concurrently improve livelihoods and address social equity are examined in the section 'Lessons, Challenges, and Change'. The final section looks at future directions and ways to improve the effectiveness of services for migrants, as well as the Bureau's roles vis-a-vis other agencies and migration dependent communities themselves.

## DIFFICULTIES FACED BY TRIBAL MIGRANTS FROM RAJASTHAN IN THE JOB MARKET

The majority of rural, tribal poor who enter the labour market as migrants do so with few skills, little information, and virtually no support services. The outcome is that they are paid poorly, find themselves trapped in punishing manual labour with few prospects for advancement, and have no protection from exploitation. Wages tend to be especially poor in the cases of casual factory or farm labour.

Lack of skills and education mean that employment opportunities in urban services such as driving, equipment repair, data entry operation, and secretarial services are largely unavailable to these migrants. The jobs that are accessible are usually short term, irregular, unstable, and highly prone to fluctuations in the market (labour supply, raw material procurement, seasonality, etc.).

The absence of services for seasonal migrants aggravates their vulnerability. Inadequate shelter, unavailability of food at reasonable prices, and poor health facilities make migrant life one of high costs and multiple risks. Most migrants fall completely outside the network of formal financial services—which makes it difficult to save, obtain loans, and make transfers.

The fact that Rajasthani migrants find employment in other states renders them even more vulnerable to exploitation. Out-of-state migrant labourers must work harder and longer than in-state migrants and they have few support networks. It is also easier for local authorities to ignore and even harass inter-state migrants. Because policy makers and government officials view the presence of migrants as a burden on stretched urban resources and infrastructure, there are few government services for migrants despite their immense contribution to the economy. Discrimination by caste and social status are further impediments to advancement, though less so in urban than rural environments.

Nevertheless, on balance, migration does alter behaviour and creates progressive mindsets among people and communities. It gives rise to new aspirations among those who have known little other than poverty in their home areas. In its work with migrants, the Bureau often encounters successful cases of rural to urban mobility—from absolute poverty to a life of a certain economic dignity. Migration does offer promise, but for this potential to be realized by significantly greater numbers of migrants requires that migrants obtain services, skills, and support. It is in the context of this challenge that Aajeevika Bureau came into being.

## Aajeevika Bureau—An Initiative to Support Migration and Migrant Workers

### Genesis and Goals

Aajeevika Bureau arose as an action initiative from a 2003 study sponsored by the United Nations Development Programme (UNDP) to understand rural livelihoods across Rajasthan (ARAVALI 2003). The major finding of the study was that short-term migration is rapidly replacing agriculture as the primary source of income for many families, particularly those in poor, predominately tribal areas. The study confirmed that migration is no longer primarily a response in times of drought and distress, but a regular livelihood strategy for the rural poor.

As a direct outgrowth of this study, one of the organizations involved in conducting the study initiated a programme to provide services for rural migrants. This organization became known as the Aajeevika Bureau and was registered as a separate legal entity in 2005. It is now established as a full-fledged initiative for migrants from southern Rajasthan.

The goal of Aajeevika Bureau is the achievement of significant improvement in livelihood opportunities of poor, migrant labourers from southern Rajasthan. The Bureau's objectives include:

- To provide new opportunities to upgrade skills and find employment, and to contribute to a skilled and confident migrant labour force which is able to negotiate higher returns in the labour market;
- To work towards reducing the hardship associated with migration and create a more positive and protected environment for migrant labour;
- To garner greater social and legal legitimacy for migrants;
- To generate new knowledge and facilitate its application in programmes and policy associated with migration.

Aajeevika Bureau works both at source areas in south Rajasthan as well as in selected, high-intensity migration destinations. Currently the Bureau works in four blocks of Udaipur and Rajsamand districts and in two destination centres, namely Idar and Ahmedabad.

## Programmes and Services

The Bureau's work encompasses knowledge generation and dissemination; policy advocacy; and a range of facilitation services for migrants at both source and destination locations. These services are delivered directly through the Bureau and/or in partnership with other organizations.

Registration is the entry point into the Bureau's set of support services and it is fully established at the block levels. By the end of 2006, the Bureau had registered nearly 3,000 migrants. Registration creates a valid labour record and establishes the person as a bonafide migrant who may cycle through multiple locations and employers looking for work.

The photo ID service, which had issued 1,800 cards by the end of 2006, is a highly visible and popular service of the Bureau. The cards are being used as an introduction to the individual's bonafide for employers, peers, and even the police!

The Bureau offers rigorous skills training for migrants to improve their employment opportunities and enhance their confidence to negotiate a place in the labour market. The Bureau has conducted regular training rounds in the construction sector—masonry, plumbing, electricity work, welding, fabrication, and carpentry. Hotel and restaurant services comprise the other major areas of training. The Bureau has also conducted training programmes for other high earning potential occupations such as driving, equipment repair, and domestic services.

Since the Bureau began its training, nearly 350 migrants have been trained. While technical skills form the bulk of the training content, participants are also equipped with knowledge that enables them to gain confidence in urban settings. Typically the training modules have included literacy and numeracy skills, health and hygiene, labour laws and workers' rights, market information, work ethics, financial management, and building self-confidence.

The Bureau offers a placement and exchange service for any registered migrants coming through its offices. Rural youth trained by the Bureau are offered placements with construction companies, contractors, and hotel and restaurant establishments. The Bureau's placement services are operating briskly with about 400 placements at the end of 2006. Several contractors and establishments seeking labourers with specialized skills call upon the Bureau for new recruits.

Recently, the Bureau has begun to focus on providing support services to migrants' families including communication assistance, linkage with government schemes, and provision of emergency assistance to dependents during the migrants' absence. These services enable migrant workers to have greater job stability as they are less likely to have to rush home to deal with family crises.

Aajeevika Bureau also provides legal aid and counselling services in response to a steady inflow of migrants' complaints and cases involving employer fraudulence and malpractice. Typically the Bureau team records complaints and offers the complainant preliminary advice. Often, the Bureau asks the party against whom a complaint is being lodged to come to the centre for discussions, and, on occasion, the Bureau team mediates a settlement. In some cases, the team has sought legal advice or has referred the case to the labour court or police. Workshops that focus on legal and labour rights have become a regular feature at the Bureau's block level centres.

In addition to the services described above, the Bureau is launching financial services for migrants, including savings, credit, and remittance components aimed at reducing the debt and expenditure associated with migration. The Bureau also engages continuously in knowledge generation on migrant issues to inform and advocate for broader policy and programme support from government, donors, and other organizations. Through its policy advocacy and networking activities, the Bureau is addressing migrants' pressing need for legal aid, arbitration, and unionization.

## LESSONS, CHALLENGES, AND CHANGE

### Reducing Poverty

One of the Bureau's main objectives is to enhance the contributions of migration to poverty reduction and widespread research has shown that migration fuels economic growth and has led to poverty reduction in certain contexts. A number of studies, including the case studies presented in this book, show that migration earnings can reduce poverty at the household level and over time, in the sending area.

When migration leads to asset accumulation, it is likely that it will contribute not only to poverty reduction but also raise the health, child welfare, and social status of migrants. The Bureau's efforts to improve the conditions in which migrants live, have the capacity to augment the percentage of pay that migrant labourers retain. For example, ensuring that migrants receive basic entitlements through public programmes, especially education and healthcare, can improve job prospects and reduce the number of days of work missed due to illness, contributing to labour productivity. Food and credit programmes support migrants' right to a livelihood, improve the health and child welfare of migrants, and improve returns to their labour. Rights-based social justice initiatives that advocate for migrant entitlements improve living conditions and reduce expenditure on food. Safeguarding migrants' health decreases the probability that labourers will have to return home without completing a work cycle. Furthermore, healthcare debt accounts for a large percentage of overall household debt and reducing this debt helps enable migrants to retain more of their earnings.

## Increasing Productivity

The Bureau's experiences clearly illustrate that increasing productivity through acquiring professional and coping skills is central to successful migration and its potential to contribute to poverty reduction. The skills gained through the Bureau's training programmes are enabling migrants to differentiate themselves from other job applicants and enhance their chances of finding employment in the first place. This in turn, further sensitizes employers to the fact that not all migrant workers are the same. The expanding economy and rising wage rates are creating opportunities for migrants from disadvantaged communities to acquire jobs that historically were not open to them – however, they must have the necessary skills to get their foot in the door.

Once a migrant has a job, the lessons from training programmes can help ensure that workers stay healthy and perform well. Financial and communication services reduce the need for workers to make expensive and time consuming visits to their home communities that may result in job loss. Stability in turn can enhance prospects for advancement. The scope for migrants to benefit from increased skills and productivity is clearly much greater with longer term employment than with the occupations where circular patterns are the rule.

## THE REAL COSTS OF TRAINING

In its efforts to offer migrants more secure and sustainable returns for their labour, the Bureau faced several early challenges. The majority of its clients are poor, mainly tribal youth who have recently become or are about to become migrants. They have typically dropped out of school; they have almost no ability to take risks and are normally dependant on what they can earn for themselves. Calculations of the costs of training that take account of income forgone by trainees are especially relevant for this group. Providing training for migrants who have extremely limited resources to invest in training necessitates approaches that reduce the time required for training without compromising quality and rigour. Currently, most training is residential and carried out in urban areas at costs that are beyond the means of nearly all potential participants. Thus, for the moment the training must be subsidized.

The Bureau is exploring ways to concurrently reduce costs per trainee/training session and improve cost recovery. Recognizing the urgent need of the migrants for income, no training programmes exceed a month. These fast-track training programmes are oriented to give trainees good site practice and experience since that is what employers consider when making hiring decisions.

### Training is Not Enough: Complementary Services

Perhaps the most important lesson has been that although training is certainly necessary, it is not sufficient for a more stable and remunerative migration experience. Placement services and employment counselling are essential. In the absence of this support, the trainees have little chance of finding a suitable position and are likely to lapse back into unskilled modes of employment.

Poverty and indebtedness create situations of chronic instability and unfavourable conditions for long-term employment. Job attrition rates are high and trained youth have a high risk of dropping out altogether from the skilled job market. A significant component of attrition is related to the circular or seasonal character of the employment, but it is also a function of difficulties that migrants (especially those from disadvantaged groups) have in adjusting to new situations; and, quite critically, of being disconnected from their home communities. In its initial days, the Bureau teams were surprised to witness the wilful drop-out of trainees from what appeared to be excellent job opportunities. We learned that this category of migrants needs to retain the ability to respond to household crises, access social networks, and maintain a degree of dignity at their workplaces, even at the expense of higher incomes and future employment prospects.

Migrant labour, particularly from tribal groups, may shirk from the regimentation of more formal employment because of the restrictions it imposes on their mobility.

There is clearly a formidable range of migration related issues that the Bureau and others might address. The challenge for the Bureau is to identify those issues and services which are both high priority and consistent with the organization's capacities at this stage of its development. The soon-to-be-launched set of financial services was an obvious choice from the perspective of need, but represents a serious leap for the organization requiring careful preparation and extensive interaction with organizations with vast micro-finance experience.

ADVOCACY

Employment in the unorganized, informal sector is expanding more rapidly than in formal/organized sectors. Informal labour markets commonly exploit migrant labour. The Bureau is frequently called upon to assist victimized migrants through arbitration, legal aid, or even police intervention. There is little doubt that most migrant workers will become more politically aware and want to organize. Although the training provided by the Bureau may well provide migrants with skills that will enable them to organize to protect their rights, the primary focus of training is concerned with teaching professional and basic survival skills.

An area where the Bureau is more directly involved in advocacy work is in policy advocacy. The Bureau is guided in this by the negative attitude of governments and officialdom in India towards migration, and, as evidence discussed in Chapter 1 shows, this is typical of more widely negative attitudes.

Rather than maximizing the potential for migration to contribute to rural poverty reduction, many policies either place direct controls on population movement or indirectly create obstacles to labour movement. Again, these are reviewed in Chapter 1, and are as abundant in India as anywhere.

Finally, most policies fail to account for the cross-sectoral livelihood strategies of migrants and fail to protect their rights. Governments do little, if anything, to reduce the discrimination that migrants face and they rarely enforce labour laws or persecute public officials who harass, abuse, or exploit migrants.

For an organization whose effectiveness is related to being able to serve as an intermediary between the labourer and the employer, advocacy poses a real dilemma for the Bureau that it must resolve on a case-by-case basis. The easy answer is to consider leaving the advocacy and political roles to other organizations and continue to feature the improvement of migrants' basic competencies, but it is obviously not so clear-cut. Improvements in working conditions, conditions of service, income and productivity are all interlinked. Efforts to promote social justice can reduce discrimination and diminish social obstacles to employment. Greater enforcement of labour laws and an improved bargaining position for migrant labourers also promote social justice objectives, giving a voice to disadvantaged and politically under-represented groups while simultaneously improving labour outcomes. At a minimum, the Bureau must continue to foster connections with government, commercial associations, and worker organizations and selectively collaborate with them as guided by the Bureau's goals and objectives.

SOCIAL EQUITY AND IMPROVED LIVELIHOODS:
SYNERGIES AND TENSIONS

While synergies exist between efforts to improve social equity and to reduce poverty, these objectives can also contradict one another, as discussed in Chapter 1. Even where migration outcomes reduce poverty, they may undermine social equity.

In addition to an inimical policy environment, migrants face numerous social obstacles. There are cultural and religious prohibitions that prevent certain social groups from working in occupations or living in certain areas. Furthermore, migrants face discrimination because of their temporary residency status and as a result they pay more than the residents for basic necessities like food and water, diminishing their disposable income. Migrants also tend to earn significantly lower wages than residents; in China, rural migrant labourers typically earn half of what urban workers with similar skills earn (World Bank 2006).

Social constraints also affect the educational attainment of different migrant groups, as well as their access to social networks, and dictate where migrants work and for how much. The most disadvantaged migrants face further discrimination when they move, enter the lowest paying jobs, and often reinforce their poverty in a cycle of consuming whatever they earn. Thus, those with more social capital climb the social ladder; on occasion they do so by exploiting the work of the most disadvantaged. Even those poorer migrants who make the leap from survival to accumulative status seem to do so by exploiting the work of other migrant labourers who have fewer initial resources to draw on (Khandelwal and Joshi 2007). Finally, in order to migrate one must possess resources; thus, the very poorest members of a community have less probability of accessing the potential gains of migration.

Yet, despite the adverse conditions that migrants often face, they may actually be improving their economic position at the same time that they are threatening their health and well-being.

FUTURE DIRECTIONS IN SERVICES FOR MIGRANTS

As the Bureau faces the future, the range of opportunities and challenges described in the previous sections translate into an agenda that exceeds prospective organizational capacity to a major degree. Services such as ID cards, communications, and financial services have been added to the core set of trainings to enhance the prospects for sustainable improvements in the livelihoods of migrants. There is major scope for such complementary services and more generally to make qualitative improvements in the Bureau's programmes. These should be explored, but there is also the issue of scaling up. The current and prospective capacities of the Bureau seem unlikely to have more than modest impact on poverty reduction in the area, at least directly. With limited resources what balance should the Bureau aim for, between getting better and getting bigger? Among a growing field of organizations and programmes concerned with services to migrants, where is the comparative advantage of the Bureau and what type of player does it seek to be in the future? What is the scope for partnering with other organizations, public and private, so as to be able to make quantum improvements in scope and scale required to seriously affect livelihoods throughout the area and beyond? Trade-offs must be considered and hard choices made in refining strategy and developing programmes for the next decade. This final section is more of a sharing of the thinking of the Bureau's leadership on these matters to stimulate debate than a blueprint ready for implementation. As such, there are far more questions than answers.

## TARGETING

The Bureau's experiences to date illustrate both, the considerable potential for services to migrants to reduce poverty and the complexity of this task. Skills acquired through training can improve a migrant's chances of securing and holding employment with better conditions of service than he or she might otherwise find. However, the scope for this happening is relatively limited in occupations that are basically seasonal or circular in character. Many, if not most of the migrants from predominately tribal areas in southern Rajasthan practice and depend on circular migration. This reality can work at cross purposes for those, who due to necessity or choice, have to maintain active connections with their home areas, including participation in agricultural activities. Further, this situation presents the Bureau and other providers of services to migrants with potentially difficult choices.

Within the tribal communities which the Bureau remains committed to work for, should the focus be on the groups and individuals that are most able and willing to make the transition to longer term stays in destinations? To a fair degree, willingness is reflected in the selection of occupations and the associated training/preparation that is required. Migrants may select brick making or agricultural work, mainly because it allows them to spend significant periods of time in their home communities, not because they necessarily see it as the only possibility or particularly like the work. The Bureau's training programmes may have little to offer to migrants in these occupations. Several of the complementary services (ID, communications, financial) might offer some benefits, but the potential to improve entry level potential through the acquisition of productivity enhancing skills is largely missing. From a poverty reduction perspective, a compelling argument can be made to focus on occupations/groups where differences in skills and productivity levels are recognized and rewarded accordingly.

Willingness to try (train) for jobs requiring skills is related to levels of self-confidence and basic abilities. This is evident among the Bureau's trainees in hotel and restaurant services, professions that feature a degree of skill differentiation and scope for advancement. The Bureau's programmes can help migrants acquire skills and gain self-confidence in the process, but basic abilities and attitudes must be present. Social exclusion has reinforced feelings of inferiority that are often difficult to overcome and can seriously inhibit an individual's ability to function effectively in the work environments commonly found in the destination areas. The Bureau is gaining in its ability to recognize the essential qualities required for success in a number of occupations where migrants are prominent and is improving screening and selection processes for its training programmes. This does leave many out. Registration and preliminary livelihood counselling can be offered to a large numbers of migrants. Even though only a minority are likely to go on into the Bureau's training programmes, most can be at least steered in directions that might better connect their aspirations and abilities than might otherwise be the case.

At the other end of the spectrum, there are those with well above average abilities who possess the potential to acquire the skills required to secure better jobs. These individuals can qualify for existing training programmes and positions in the private and public sectors and the role of the Bureau may be limited to making the necessary connections as a direct outgrowth of the initial counselling and screening processes.

Scaling Up

The Bureau's services currently reach several hundred migrants and their families directly and this number has been growing rapidly. There is clearly a significant need and demand for the services that are presently confined largely to the southern districts in Rajasthan and a few major destinations, mainly in Gujarat.

The Bureau could make a significantly larger contribution to poverty reduction by dramatically scaling up, but this would require a much larger organization, or more likely a different organizational model entirely. However, within its present configuration, the Bureau can provide guidance to others in scaling up, even if the direct coverage of its own activities remains limited. Major scaling up is most likely to come from other organizations. Concurrently, the core set of services, notably registration, counselling, and training could be linked to sets of complementary services provided by partner organizations in both source and destination areas. The Bureau's role might be more as a broker of information within a network of clusters of service providers, rather than the hub of a wheel. In that way, the services could have a cumulative effect, both in terms of the range/depth of functions and the numbers participating. Partnering with other organizations could enable the Bureau to scale up services to migrants without actually providing them itself. Partnering is very attractive in theory, but requires substantial skill and effort in practice. Experiences with collaboration involving both NGO and government agencies in Rajasthan examined by Alsop *et al.*, (2000) suggest much higher incidence of cautionary tales than success. The transaction costs associated with partnering are major, even when like-minded organizations are involved. The Bureau's own experience with partnering has been mixed, but definitely positive on balance, most notably with block and community level organizations that provide more comprehensive sets of services to cover limited geographic areas; and partnering seems likely to feature prominently in the future. More generally, the Bureau's comparative advantage seems to lie in building the institutional capacity within the public and private sectors to provide services to migrants as well as sharpening the focus of policy makers on how such services can further policy objectives at the state and national levels.

## A Balancing Act

The Bureau is most likely to remain small and geographically focused on southern Rajasthan. However, its core capacities may evolve mainly in the direction of action research and impact monitoring of services for migrants, rather than trying to have its basic set of services reach significantly larger numbers of communities and migrants, either directly or via franchising arrangements through other organizations. At the same time, the Bureau might continue to provide advisory services and train the trainers working for other organizations at the block and community levels and facilitate the scaling up of services to migrants within Rajasthan and beyond in the process.

The Bureau may further its organizational goals more as a think-tank for migration and services to migrants, but with a grass roots orientation, rather than academic in character. The Bureau plans to retain its presence in communities in source areas and in the major destinations. Direct engagement with migrants through the provision of services as well as studies, both guide the development of the Bureau's programmes and lends credibility to its efforts in various fora. However, the focus at community level might shift to designing/ implementing pilots in collaboration with partners; M&E/impact assessments of services provided by others; and research at both source and destinations. For the latter two topics, the Bureau might progressively focus on topics, methodology, and surveying/digesting results of more formal research carried out largely by others.

A major question is the extent to which the Bureau should try to improve conditions in the home areas, not with a view to reducing migration, but enhancing prospects for sustainable livelihoods in migration-dependent communities. In this regard, the ability of family members to survive and hopefully thrive in the home areas is a key element affecting the success of the migration experience. Health and financial difficulties at home often compel migrants to abandon their jobs prematurely and with personal financial loss. Communication, financial, and insurance services can all help. But, basic improvements in conditions and opportunities in the home communities are also required for migration to become a more remunerative and positive experience. This may seem ironic since poor conditions and limited opportunities at home usually contribute to migration. This challenge is especially evident for circular migrants who retain strong links with their home areas.

In this context what is the relationship between migration and sustainable development in the home areas and how can they positively reinforce one another? This is not simply a challenge for the Bureau, but for all government and private organizations engaged in efforts to develop the rural districts of southern Rajasthan as well as the communities themselves. A better understanding of this relationship is central to devising strategies that will work, as well as to identifying the roles of various players, including the Bureau. This topic lies beyond the scope of this chapter, but is the focus of a recent article by the authors (Kandelwal and Gilbert 2007). It would be ironic indeed if the Bureau's efforts on behalf of migrants became part of the path to sustainable development in the source areas.

REFERENCES

Aravali, 'Aajeevika—Livelihoods in Rajasthan: Status, Constraints and Strategies for Sustainable Change', Discussion Paper Series 6, Human Development Resource Centre, UNDP, India, 2003.

Alsop, R., E. Gilbert, J. Farrington, and R. Khandelwal, *Coalitions of Interest: Partnerships for Processes of Agricultural Change*, International Food Policy Research Institute and the Overseas Development Institute, New Delhi: Sage Publications, 2000.

Khandelwal, R., and E. Gilbert, 'Getting Set to Go: Upgrading Migration through an Innovative Education Programme', *Journal of Education for Sustainable Development*, 1(1), 2007.

The World Bank, '*World Development Report 2007*: Development and the Next Generation', Washington DC, 2006.

# 11

# Seeking Informal Social Protection

## Migrant Households in Rural West Bengal

*Deeptima Massey*

### INTRODUCTION

A young woman in rural West Bengal, India approaches her mother-in-law to borrow some rice and salt as she stays behind with her two infants while her husband migrates for three months to work as a construction worker; in Orissa a mother of three children with appendicitis is rushed to hospital by her neighbour because her husband is away working in rice fields for a fortnight; a sixty year old widow seeks employment in her brother's chilli fields to earn money as her son migrates for brick kiln work. These are examples of how family members left behind by migrants have to cope. The migration literature often underplays the experience of those who are left behind and focuses exclusively on the migrant and the migration process in isolation. There are two key issues concerning people who are left behind: first, that the departure of a migrant member is also the onset of financial, health, and food struggles for those staying behind in the source area, and second, to overcome these difficulties, people staying behind may draw on various social relations outside their immediate family for support.

In this chapter, based on research in Murshidabad, West Bengal, the issue of informal 'social protection' for those staying behind in poor migrant households is discussed. Staying behind brings economic and physical hardships and insecurities for women and it is during this time that they seek informal social protection from friends, relatives, and other people with whom they have some kind of social relationship (this may include the local school teacher, employer, or political leaders). The chapter begins with a systematic overview of people staying behind in the study area and then goes on to describe the various hardships and insecurities faced by such people and the social protection they need. This chapter will firstly establish the fact that although most migration patterns and streams do have members staying behind in the source area, these people have been omitted from discussions or any research inquiry. The chapter also shows the broad spectrum under which members staying behind have been examined.

This chapter is based primarily on a project funded by the DFID—funded Development Research Centre on Migration, Globalisation, and Poverty at the University of Sussex. The project involved an eight-month long ethnographic field study of Jalpara village in Murshidabad district, West Bengal.[1] In-depth interviews were conducted with members staying behind, which in this case were women, from June 2005 to January 2006. The project focused on understanding the formal and informal social protection that migrants as well as members staying behind have access to.[2] The aim was to explore and identify the various ways in which migrants overcome hardship while travelling to their work destinations, and to discover how those staying behind cope with arranging food, ill health, and general day-to-day living. However, this chapter focuses only on informal social protection that family members who stay behind seek while the migrant is away for work.

SOCIAL PROTECTION BY MEMBERS STAYING BEHIND:
A REVIEW OF THE LITERATURE

Often, when a male member migrates from a household, he leaves behind his wife and children in the source area. For poor families, it often becomes difficult to obtain enough to eat even when the migrant is away for short trips of one week to two months (depending on the type of work). There is usually very little cash left with the family in the village and any unanticipated expenditure on health care or emergencies can push the family into a financial crisis. In such situations, women often approach relatives (natal kin or in-laws), friends, and neighbours to borrow food or cash.

So far within the social protection literature, such relations and the support they provide have been called 'informal protective mechanisms'[3] or 'informal safety nets' (Devereux, 1999). Some scholars have also called such informal relationships 'social capital' (Narayan 1997; Ellis 2000). Social capital can be understood as 'social networks' through which people interact with each other to seek economic opportunities. Within the livelihoods framework (Carney 1998), social capital has been recognized as an asset if and when it generates employment or other income generating activity. But, apart from considering social capital exclusively as an asset for economic outcomes, it also needs to be studied in relation to its necessity for non-economic benefits.

There have been several studies, which examine the role of social capital in assisting an individual or all household members to migrate. These studies have examined the role of various networks during the different stages of migration: the onset, journey, at destination, and during the return journey. In a study of migrants from Orissa, men were able to gain employment in Surat's textile industry with much ease because of their social contacts in the destination area. 'Newcomers are accompanied on their first journey or are met when they reach the city by relatives or fellow villagers who give them shelter, food and help in finding work.'[4] Another example of work facilitated by social relations at the destination is among migrants in Vietnam's Red River delta region, where they adopt new farming skills by contacts with friends and family who are settled in the destination in the Central Highland region (Winkels and Adger 2002).

Other than social relations at the destination, migration can also be initiated through favourable contacts within the source area itself. This was so in Gaocheng, rural China, where it was stated that 'pioneer migrants establish chain migration connections; as migration from a village takes off, these networks become available to households throughout the village.'[5] Repeated movement of migrants to similar work areas may become helpful in building ties with the employer at the workplace. It gives the migrant recognition at the destination. This was found in Deshingkar and Start's study (2003) among tribals from Mandla migrating to Havelli (Madhya Pradesh). Here, the green revolution resulted in increasing the labour demand substantially and 'now, after several years stable relations with employers have been established and these offer much security. The labourers just go to the destination at a certain time of the year even without waiting for a call from the employer.[6] Over the years, this has proved helpful because now the migrant does not have to start afresh in order to find work, negotiate wages, or look for an employer. In West Bengal, among the Santals, it was found that 'long-term relations with individual employers' in Barddhaman district, West Bengal, made migration and wage negotiation easier.[7]

So far, the preceding discussion in this section reflects the role of social relations in facilitating the migration process at various stages of movement for the migrant. But these relationships may also exist or be required by those staying behind when the migrant has departed. Most of the studies do not mention explicitly the role of social relations as an essential form of support to members staying behind in the source area. This chapter examines this missing link between members staying behind and the social relations they engage in to seek various kinds of support.

Some studies on remittances and migration have argued that the returns from migratory work ensure a regular flow of income to the household and this helps the members at home with their needs, ensures economic security, and gradually increases the well-being of the entire household (Afsar 2003; Koc and Onan 2004). However, there are instances where remittances are very irregular and the amount of money sent home is too little to meet all their day-to-day needs.

Studies of people left behind explore the relationship between poverty and staying behind or staying put, who is excluded from undertaking migration as a livelihood strategy and why (Kothari 2002, 2003), and how migrants make efforts to stay put or stop migrating (Rogaly 2003). The term 'staying put' includes not only members staying behind in migrant households but also includes households remaining in the source area without any experience of migration, or those who had stopped migrating. This broad categorization of 'staying put' members makes it difficult to highlight the specific insecurities and hardships that members staying behind face when the migrant leaves home from those that may be ongoing in the source area and are being faced by all households irrespective of migration.

A recent collection of papers in the journal *Population, Space and Place* (May/June 2007) has also focused on people staying behind.

The papers highlight the role of social relations and social protection mechanisms. For example, Knodel and Saengtienchai (2007) studied parents left behind in rural Thailand, showing how the migration of some members has led to a new social support system between the source area and destination and how migration expands social networks over a wider geographical distance.

Other studies have covered different contexts: in a study of Londoni village, in Biswanath, Bangladesh, Gardner and Ahmed (2006) studied social protection as help that British resident migrants offer to their extended kin left behind in Bangladesh. Social protection in this study included giving loans for education and setting up of businesses, sending money for weddings, and helping build or repair houses. In Murshidabad, 'help in kind from kin is crucial' for women when their husbands migrate for agricultural work.[8] Similarly, in eastern Uttar Pradesh during the absence of the male members, although the family remained a 'separate residential unit', it remains a part of wider kin networks with the usual obligations and rights. This is best observed during marriages, festivals, and situations of crises (Jetley 1987). But social relations and kin networks may not always be supportive. In the same study in eastern Uttar Pradesh, it was also found that 'a migrant who is better off than others may be a cause of jealousy, and his family may then face hostility in the neighbourhood'.[9] In another study in rural Bangladesh, 'those who were left behind also faced a range of problems while the migrant was away'...'in some cases the villagers or kin occupied their land in the absence of the migrants'.[10]

JALPARA: DESCRIPTION OF THE STUDY LOCALITY

Murshidabad, the district in which the study was located, has one of the perennial migration streams from where every year, tens of thousands of labourers, most of whom are men, migrate to various parts of the state and adjoining areas (Rogaly et.al. 2001). Within Murshidabad, the study was more specifically in the Bagri region,[11] which has been identified as a high population density area, with high susceptibility to floods,[12] and unequal wealth distribution (Rogaly and Rafique 2003). These factors have together made Bagri one of the leading areas for the origin of migrants to other economically sound parts of the district or elsewhere in West Bengal, and sometimes even beyond state boundaries to other parts of India.

In rural eastern India, seasonal migration for wage work is the key means of livelihood for poor households. It is difficult to make an assessment of the numbers as there are 'no accurate data on the number of seasonal migrants' (Rogaly et. al. 2001). In Barddhaman alone, identified as one the key destinations for agricultural wage-work, it is estimated that more than 500,000 seasonal migrants come from various parts of West Bengal and surrounding states to work for one paddy harvesting season from October to November.[13] These numbers reflect the temporary peaks of demand for labour that this work generates. In addition, seasonal migrants are often employed without any written contract, with informal work arrangements, and different wage rates.

Jalpara, the study village, which falls in Bagri region has a long history of migration from where male migrants have been travelling to intensive paddy cultivation areas in Barddhaman, West Bengal as found in the earlier studies done in the same locality.[14] Since this was a revisit to the same locality, some similarities along with new findings were revealed in migration patterns. These have been reported in detail in another paper by Rafique, Massey, and Rogaly 2006.[15] According to the previous study, all migrants were men, but the research conducted in 2005 found that some women had also started migrating for various types of temporary work. In 1999, men were migrating mainly for paddy cultivation and brick kiln work, however in 2005, it was found that both men and women were migrating for potato and jute harvesting and also travelling to distant places for begging.

Jalpara stretches for one kilometre along a mud road. Less than one per cent of the houses are brick built. Most of them are made of mud and bamboo. The total population (Census June 2005) was 1,303 people living in 328 households. Muslims occupied 288 (88 per cent) of these households while the rest belonged to low-caste Hindus. The household structure was a mix of both nuclear and joint families. Nuclear families consisted of a couple and their children with their own cooking facilities. Joint household had more than one couple sharing a single kitchen. There were 277 (84 per cent) nuclear households and 51 joint households.

Infrastructure facilities in Jalpara were poor. There was no authorized electricity supply, so after sunset the houses were either dimly lit by a lamp or remained dark. Electricity wire supplied by the government passes over cultivable fields. People living near a pole carrying these wires often took electricity from the system illegally. Water facilities were inadequate. Hand-pumps over manually dug wells are along the main road. Most of the villagers live in houses grouped together some distance from the main road and so they have to either walk to the pumps or spend Rs 2,000–3,000[16] to have one installed for their own use. The nearest health centre is five kilometres from the centre of Jalpara and a sub-divisional hospital is fifteen kilometres away. There is one primary school in the village in which four classes are taught in three rooms. Around 15–20 infants and children below five years attend an Integrated Child Development Service Centre each day. For higher secondary schooling, the children have to travel atleast six kilometres.

Transport within Jalpara and its access from and to anywhere outside is difficult. The locality is bisected in the middle by an unpaved mud road. This road was completely water-logged for one week in October during the fieldwork (2005). It became impossible to walk on this road and for several days residents stayed indoors without going out for work, eating whatever was stored in the house. A common means of transport within Jalpara and to all locations was the bicycle. Whether it is going to the hospital six kilometres away, or to the station three kilometres away or to the nearest shopping area three kilometres away, men always travelled on their bicycles, often carrying their wives or children on the back seat. If anyone is ill, or a group of women and children have to travel together, then rickshaw-vans, a flat board, manually pulled, was arranged to take them to the required destination.

METHODS

One of the key methods for primary data collection was life history interviews of thirteen women conducted at different stages of the husbands' migration. Each interview involved several sittings. The different stages covered were: the husband was still at home, husband preparing to migrate, in the husband's absence, and after his return home. This gave a picture of the experiences of women under these different situations. The second and more crucial aim of conducting these life history interviews was to draw on women's past experiences of staying behind too. Past experiences were examined on a temporal scale and under different stages of their life cycle, taking into account their different roles as a daughter, wife, mother, or as a widow. To keep the interaction intact and to facilitate participant observation, the sample households were visited frequently. These repeated visits and engagement in informal chats helped in obtaining detailed information on women's lives. These methods collectively formed an essential database for this research.

MAIN FINDINGS: SEEKING INFORMAL SOCIAL PROTECTION
WHILE STAYING BEHIND

The survey in June 2005 showed that circular migration was a crucial livelihood strategy for 221 households (67 per cent). In the study, circular migration included migration for both agricultural and non-agricultural activities, to both rural and urban areas, within West Bengal and to other parts of India. The maximum period of each migration trip was found to be three months at a stretch, while the minimum was one week.

Migrants were making trips for diverse activities, at different times of the year and for different durations. Paddy work includes transplanting and harvesting. For transplanting, migrants may stay at their work destination for four weeks or less, while harvesting is between two to five weeks. Migration to brick kilns lasts longer, up to six months. It starts in November and can continue until April with fortnightly or monthly returns of the migrant to his home. It was found that migration for road building, construction work, and cable laying was growing. People migrate to Kolkata, which is the nearest city in West Bengal, but they also migrate to other towns and cities in neighbouring states, and to distant cities such as Delhi and Mumbai.

A migrant often makes multiple trips either to the same location at different times of the year or he may choose various combinations of migration. For example, Faizul Sheikh made three trips to various destinations and for different time intervals in 2005: he went to Kolkata in February as a mason for one month, in July the same year he migrated to Barddhaman for paddy transplanting for eight days, and then in November he went to Barddhaman again for paddy harvesting and was away for a fortnight. These frequent absences adversely affect the family members staying behind, who in this study were women and children.

The interviews conducted with women left behind in 2005 and 2006 showed that food was the key necessity to be attended to once the migrant had departed. Women were often left with limited food stocks, which became exhausted if the migrant's return was delayed for any reason. At the same time, it was not possible to keep sufficient stocks of rice and other grains and ingredients for the members staying behind in poor landless households. Take the case of Maruba, a 23 year old Muslim woman who lived in a one-room mud house and did not own cultivable land or livestock. Her husband migrated for three weeks for brick kiln work. He could only manage to leave 8–10 kilograms of rice for his wife and children, which lasted for a week. Similarly Sabrina, a 21 year old Muslim woman, a mother of two daughters, whose husband went to Orissa for urban construction work for two months in November 2005, was left with nothing to eat by mid-December.

The second hardship that women encounter while staying behind is the lack of cash. Only in a few cases were men able to leave some cash for their wives to spend in their absence. For example, Sabrina did not own any land or livestock and had Rs 200 with her to meet any unforeseen expenses as she stayed behind with her two daughters in the absence of her husband for two months. Her husband had migrated to Orissa to work as a mason at a building construction site. He returned home in January 2006. Amrina, another, 45 years old woman who had four children, was left with Rs 100 to meet regular medical expenses for a chronic skin infection. They did not own land; all they had was one goat. In most cases women were left with food stocks, but no cash in hand. As one male migrant, Badsa Ali, aged 34 said, 'I try my best to keep at least Rs 100 or Rs 150 with my wife before I migrate, but fail to do so, so I leave my family almost penniless at home. It is hard to save even that amount of money'.

In a few households, it was found that women were setting out in search of some paid work to fulfil financial shortfalls. This was often in disagreement with their husbands or kept a secret. Lavina Bibi, twenty years old, who frequently remained unwell, often picked green chilli. She sought employment in villages outside Jalpara, and would set for work at 4 am and return by 10 p.m. This enabled her to feed herself and her three children everyday while her husband was away. They had no land or livestock and lived in a dilapidated mud house.

In such conditions, any eventuality requiring cash becomes a serious problem for the household and can push it further into poverty and debt. Health emergencies are the most common crisis. Maruba's two-year-old son fell ill with jaundice and a high fever five days after her husband left for brick kiln work. Similarly, in the case of Manwari, who was twenty-six years old, leased in one *bigha* land every year, had one cow and two goats; on one occasion she had all three of her children suffering from a severe bout of flu. This occurred soon after her husband migrated for paddy transplanting in July 2005, and she felt helpless and confused. Ill health can also be an ongoing situation in migrant households needing constant medication. For example, Sabrina had to spend Rs 20–30 on medicines each fortnight for her treatment of a cyst on her hand and this expense was difficult to bear in her husband's absence.

Food and cash limitations along with ill health can become hardships difficult to overcome or reduce. Women left behind tend to draw on two main kinds of social relations, natal and in-laws, and patron-client relations.

The first preference of most of the women interviewees was to go to their mothers when they needed help. But, whether to approach the mother or mother-in-law to seek help was determined by distance. Luckily for the majority of women, their natal home was either in Jalpara itself or two adjoining villages, Alopara and Parbatinagar, one mile away. This accessibility enabled women to make frequent trips to their natal home almost weekly or fortnightly. Significantly, this proximity encouraged women to seek support from their mother at first and then their mother-in-law. For example, when Maruba noticed that her two year old son had jaundice and a high fever, she rushed to her mother's home in Parbatinagar and asked her mother to accompany her to the doctor. She stayed there for five days, ensuring that her son was given care and attention and regular medicines. After finding that her son's fever had gone, she returned her home in Jalpara. Her husband had been away at a brick kiln all through this time. She did not opt to approach her mother-in-law in this situation inspite of residing in the house next door.

In another case, Tajmira, a twenty eight year old woman, who was regularly left behind with two of her own children and two from her husband's first wife had her natal as well as in-laws house in Jalpara. Her mother resided at the northern end of the locality while Tajmira and her mother-in-law's house was in the centre of the same locality. On asking whom she relied the most for cash or food borrowings, Tajmira's prompt reply was 'my mother', and without pausing she instantly started talking about her relationship with her mother-in-law. She said, '*Sasuri durey- durey* [mother-in-law far-far]. She [mother-in-law] does not love me. In fact she hates me. She is cruel. She only loves male members, the two boys from my surrogate sister [referring to Tajmira's husband's first wife]. She does not love my children, nor gives them anything to eat. If there is no food in my house, she never comes to me or offers me food. She sits in her house with a gloomy face. She takes, but does not give anything. I never go to her house to ask for anything. My mother lives close by; I go to her for all my needs. A mother-in-law always remains a mother-in-law.'

The last remark that Tajmira made about mothers-in-law may not be true in all cases, especially when women have a cross-cousin marriage. This type of marriage where a girl is married to her own paternal or maternal aunt's son was common in the entire Bagri region of which Jalpara was also a part (Rogaly and Rafique 2003). An aunt becoming a mother-in-law may redefine the social protection that a daughter-in-law or in other words a woman staying behind may receive while left alone in the absence of her husband. An example of this comes from Sabrina who was married to her father's sister's son. Sabrina's natal home was in Alopara, the adjoining village and after her marriage she resided in Jalpara with her husband and other in-laws. Describing about her relationship with her mother-in-law she said, 'She loves me a lot. Even after marriage I address her as *phupu* [father's sister]. She hides things from others [daughters-in-law] and gives me raw fish, rice, or vegetables to cook. Whenever my husband is away and I am in need of oil, rice, salt, or cash to buy vegetables or medicines, I first approach my mother-in-law.' Continuing to talk more about the relationship, she said, 'When I was going to give birth to my second daughter, my mother-in-law was with me throughout the pregnancy period. She did so much for me, washed my clothes, cooked my meals, and brought me medicine from the local village doctor.'

In this case marriage to a cousin brought more support for the woman. However, this is not always the case. Razia, a twenty five year old woman with two children under five years of age, was staying behind in her husband's absence. She also shared a similar kin relationship with her mother-in-law. Yet she received neither the same treatment nor the same support. Referring to her mother-in-law she said? 'She has never been a good aunt, so how can she be a good mother-in-law? She never loved me nor did she ever bring any sweets for me in my childhood. Now when I am her daughter-in-law she scolds me and misuses her authority over me.'

Razia's case indicates unfavourable ties that may develop between the daughter-in-law and mother-in-law inspite of having a cross-cousin marriage. Vera–Sanso (1999) warned against making the mistake of presuming that these 'genealogically-related' marriages and ties may always be favourable. In her study among women in rural south India, she found that these forms of marriages make the ties more tense. Referring specifically to Chennai, she said, 'Women in matrillateral marriages often hide unhappy domestic relations from their natal families in order to protect their mothers from emotional distress and, where their fathers had proposed a patri-lateral marriage, from recriminations or beatings. Thus even close-kin endogamous marriage does not ensure good mother-in-law/daughter-in-law relations nor effective natal support for brides.'[17]

Other close relatives, especially brothers may also be of little help as the case of Liki, a thirty year old woman illustrates. Liki was married to Mobin who had earned his living as a migrant since he was a teenager. He did not earn enough to improve the living standards of his family beyond survival. She and her children would survive on just one meal of rice a day when her husband was away. Liki struggled to make ends meet and had also been suffering from a stomach ailment and had been advised to have surgery. Her brothers who resided in houses adjacent to hers in Jalpara, each owning 5 *bighas* of land, refused to help her with her medical expenses. She said 'my brothers are rich for themselves; they don't even look at me or visit my poor mud house. Their children are studying in town. They have money for their own children but not for mine. They see me lying on the floor in pain but don't come or offer any help.'

Similarly, Noorjahan's brother also let her down. Noorjahan, is a fifty year old woman whose son migrates for brick kiln work. In

December 2005 she needed some money to buy food and did not know when her son would return. So she decided to ask her elder brother for some money. Her brother is 'rich', owning ten *bighas* of land and a fertilizer shop, and lives in a brick built house. After approaching him for a loan, Noorjahan said, 'my brother refused to give me any money. Instead he offered me work in his chilli fields for one week so that I could earn some money. I did not expect this from him. I did not know that money could change your own brother's behaviour. It would not have hurt him to put Rs 50 or 100 in my hand.'

Women also draw on patron-client relationships during times of difficulty. Habiba, a 35 year old woman lived in Jalpara with her ailing father. She neither owned land nor livestock. Her husband had abandoned her in the year 2000. Her younger brother migrated for paddy work regularly and in his absence she often approached the rich land owning households in the locality for support. She said, 'Rich people call me for work. There is Sohba Haji, who owns more than 35 bighas of land, I go there. He employed me to harvest paddy in the fields last year. Even Nabib Sheikh tells me to plough his fields. They pay me daily wages of Rs 30. This money is useful for my father and myself. We are able to eat two meals in a day and I also buy medicines for my father from that money.'

Similarly, Amina Bibi, a twenty year old woman was left behind with a four-month old infant in October 2005 when her husband migrated to Kolkata for construction work. In his absence her child became seriously ill and became unconscious. In a panic, she approached Nijban Sheikh's wife for help. Nijban Sheikh and his family live in a three-room brick house and own 12 *bigha* land. Nijban's wife gave Rs 100 to Amina for the child's medical treatment. She also asked Amina to go to the hospital and take Nijban's name to get immediate attention of the doctors. In another case, a fifty two year old widow, Sajima Bibi, whose son was away for jute washing work, approached the gram panchayat member in Jalpara requesting him to issue a ration card for her so that she could receive wheat at a subsidized rate from the local shop. She did not want to rely on her son for food and other living expenses.

But such relationships can also become exploitative. Purvez's study of patron-client relationships in Bangladesh (2005) referred to such associations between rich and poor as a 'vertical relationship' which often turns exploitative and in the interest of patrons as they provide support to the poor by assisting in work or financially.

CONCLUDING REMARKS

Migration of male household members in rural West Bengal does bring in cash, and may ensure food for a part of the year. But it also leaves women and children with a variety of practical difficulties and insecurities to deal with. The kinds of difficulties faced are linked to the generally poor conditions of living for these rural migrant households in West Bengal. The chapter has demonstrated that even if the duration of the separation faced by women is as short as a week, they can face cash and food shortages. In such situations, the support provided by various social relations is critical.

The chapter has discussed the kinds of informal social protection that women who are left behind seek from their relatives. The support that women may get is often determined by residential proximity. Women whose natal homes were either in Jalpara or in adjoining localities, preferred to approach their mother first for any borrowings or other kinds of support. In such cases, the mother-in-law was approached only in circumstances when the mother was unable to provide support. However, the prevalence of cross-cousin marriages in the locality weakened this differentiation between the mother and mother-in-law and a woman staying behind gave equal preference to her mother and mother-in-law (also an aunt) in seeking help. These social relations in Jalpara were crucial for women to seek support in the absence of their husbands.

The other relationship offering a measure of social protection was that between the rich and the poor relatives. Women in general did not have a positive opinion about their rich kin when it came to providing financial or other support. This situation was found in cases where a woman who stayed behind was married into a poor migrant household, and had rich natal kin. She complained of either not being given any help or the help that she was expecting was different from what she was receiving.

This study clearly demonstrates the significance of informal social protection not only for the migrant who departs, but also for members staying behind in the source area. Informal support, be it from a mother or a mother-in-law, rich or poor kin, does matter for women and enable them to overcome and reduce their insecurities and hardships.

## NOTES

1. The author would like to express her thanks to Ben Rogaly and Janet Seeley, co-Principal Investigators of the project, for their intellectual inputs to the work on which this paper is based. She would also like to thank Abdur Rafique who was the co-Lead Researcher along with her, in the project for his constant help in various stages of writing. His work focused on male migrants. The name of the study village as well as names of all respondents have been changed.

2. In other publications, the term 'informal support' has been used rather than informal social protection. (See for example, Rogaly, Rafique, and Massey 2007 ( forthcoming); Massey 2007 ( forthcoming).

   Here I have used 'informal social protection' so as to engage directly with the concept guiding this collection.

3. R. Sabates–Wheeler and M. Waite, 'Migration and Social Protection: A Concept Paper', Working Paper T2, Development Research Centre on Migration, Globalisation, and Poverty, Brighton: Sussex University, 2003, p. 17.

4. J. Breman, *Footloose Labour: Working in India's Informal Economy*, Cambridge : Cambridge University Press, 1996, p. 91.

5. R. Murphy, *How Migrant Labour is Changing Rural China*, Cambridge : Cambridge University Press, 2002, p.69.

6. P. Deshingkar and D. Start, 'Seasonal Migration for Livelihoods, Coping, Accumulation and Exclusion', Working Paper no. 220, London, Overseas Development Institute, 2003, p.30.

7. B. Rogaly, 'Who Goes? Who Stays Back? Seasonal Migration and Staying Put among Rural Mannual Workers in Eastern India', *Journal of International Development*, 15, 2003, p. 626.

8. B. Rogaly and A. Rafique, 'Struggling to Save Cash: Seasonal and Vulenerability in West Bengal, India', *Development and Change*, 34(4), 2003, p. 666.

9. S. Jetley, 'Impact of Male Migration on Rural Females', *Economic and Political Weekly*, 31 October 1987, p. WS–51.

10. M.I. Hossain, I. A. Khan, and J. Seeley, 'Surviving Their Feet : The Importance of Migration for the Livelihoods of the Poor', in I. A. Khan and J. Seeley (ed.), *Making a Living : The Livelihoods of the Rural Poor in Bangladesh*, Dhaka: The University Press, 2005, p. 119.

11. Bagri is the region in between the river Bhagirathi and the river Padma as well as Bangladesh border. The former river has bifurcated the district.

12. See Rafique, 2003 for detailed description of flood-induced migration in the region.

13. B. Rogaly *et al.*, 'Seasonal Migration, Social Change and Migrants', Rights: Lessons from West Bengal', *Economic and Political Weekly*, 8 December 2001, p. 4549.
14. Previous research done in 1999-2000 (See Rogaly and Rafique, 2003; Rafique and Rogaly, 2005).
15. Available at http://www.migrationdrc.org/publications/working_papers/ WP-T17.pdf
16. Equivalent to £25–35.
17. P. Veri–Sanso, 'Dominant Daughter-in-Law and Submissive Mother-in-Law? Co-operation and Conflict in South India', *The Journal of Royal Anthropological Institute*, 5(4), 1999, p. 582.

REFERENCES

Afsar, R., 'Internal Migration and the Development Nexus: The Case of Bangladesh', DFID-RMMRU Conference on Migration, Development and Pro-poor Policy Choices in Asia, Dhaka, 22–24 June 2003.

Breman, J., *Footloose Labour: Working in India's Informal Economy,* Cambridge: Cambridge, 1996.

Carney, D., (ed.), 'Sustainable Rural Livelihoods: What Contributions Can we Make?', DFID, London, 1998.

Deshingkar, P., and D. Start, 'Seasonal Migration for Livelihoods, Coping, Accumulation and Exclusion', Working Paper no 220, London: Overseas Development Institute, 2003.

Devereux, S., 'Making Less Last Longer — Informal Safety Nets in Malawi', IDS Discussion Paper, 373, Brighton: IDS, 1999.

Ellis, F., *Rural Livelihoods and Diversity in Developing Countries,* New York: Oxford, 2000.

Gardner, K., and Z. Ahmed, 'Place, Social Protection and Migration in Bangladesh: A Londoni Village in Biswanath, Working Paper T18', Development Research Centre on Migration, Globalisation and Poverty, Sussex Centre for Migration Research, Brighton: Sussex University, 2006.

Hossain, M.I., I.A. Khan, and J. Seeley, 'Surviving Their Feet: The Importance of Migration for the Livelihoods of the Poor', in I.A. Khan, and J. Seeley, (ed.) *Making a Living: the Livelihoods of the Rural Poor in Bangladesh,* Dhaka: The University Press, 2005.

Jetley, Surinder, 'Impact of Male Migration on Rural Females', *Economic and Political Weekly*, 31 October, 1987, pp. WS47–WS53.

Knodel, J. and C. Saengtienchai, 'Rural Parents with Urban Children: Social and Economic Implications of Migration for the Rural Elderly in Thailand', *Population, Space and Place,* 13 (3), 2007, pp. 193–210.

Koc, I., and I. Onan, 'International Migrants' Remittance and Welfare Status of the Left Behind Families in Turkey', *International Migration Review,* 38(1), 2004, pp. 78–112.

Kothari, U., 'Migration and Chronic Poverty', Institute for Development Policy and Management, Manchester, Working Paper no. 16, 2002.

———, 'Staying Put and Staying Poor?', *Journal of International Development*, 15, 2003, pp. 645–57.

Massey,D., 'Staying Behind and Undergoing Ill Health: Seeking Informal Support in West Bengal, India', 2007, in J. Seeley, and C.R. Abrar, *Social Protection and Livelihoods: The Marginalised Migrants of South Asia*, Dhaka: University Press Limited, forthcoming.

Murphy, R., *How Migrant Labour is Changing Rural China*, Cambridge: Cambridge University Press, 2002.

Narayan, *Voice of the Poor: Poverty and Social Capital in Tanzania*, World Bank, Washington DC, USA, 1997.

Purvez, S.A., 'Building Support for a Living: The Impact of Social Networks for the Livelihoods of the Poor', in I.A. Khan, and J. Seeley, *Making a Living: The Livelihoods of the Rural Poor in Bangladesh,* Dhaka: The University Press, 2005.

Rafique, A. 'Floods, Poverty and Seasonal Migration', *Economic and Political Weekly,* 8 March 2003, pp. 943–5.

Rafique, A., and B. Rogaly, 'Internal Seasonal Migration, Livelihoods and Vulnerability in India: A Case Study', in Tasneem Siddiqui (ed.), *Migration and Development: Pro-Poor Policy Choices,* Dhaka: University Press Limited, 2005.

Rafique, A., D. Massey, and B. Rogaly, 'Migration for Hard Work: A Reluctant Livelihood Strategy for Poor Households in West Bengal, India', Working Paper T17, Development Research Centre on Migration, Globalisation and Poverty, Sussex Centre for Migration Research, Brighton: University of Sussex, 2006, available at http://www.migrationdrc.org/publications/working_papers/WP-T17.pdf

Rogaly, B., 'Who Goes? Who Stays Back? Seasonal Migration and Staying Put among Rural Manual Workers in Eastern India', *Journal of International Development,* 15, 2003, pp. 623–32.

———, J. Biswas, D. Coppard, A. Rafique, K. Rana, and A. Sengupta, 'Seasonal Migration, Social Change and Migrants' Rights: Lessons from West Bengal', *Economic and Political Weekly,* 8 December 2001, pp. 4547–58.

Rogaly, B., and A. Rafique, 'Struggling to Save Cash: Seasonal and Vulnerability in West Bengal, India', *Development and Change*, 34(4), 2003, pp. 659–81.

———, and D. Massey, 'Straw in the Elephant's Mouth? Social Protection for Temporary Work Migrants in West Bengal', 2007, in J. Seeley, and C.R. Abrar, *Social Protection and Livelihoods: The Marginalised Migrants of South Asia,* Dhaka: University Press Limited, forthcoming.

Sabates–Wheeler, R., and M. Waite, 'Migration and Social Protection: A Concept Paper, Working Paper T2', Development Research Centre on Migration, Globalisation and Poverty, Sussex Centre for Migration Research, Brighton: Sussex University, 2003.

Vera-Sanso, P., 'Dominant Daughter-in-Law and Submissive Mother-in-Law? Cooperation and Conflict in South India', *The Journal of the Royal Anthropological Institute*, 5(4), 1999, pp. 577–93.

Winkels, A. and W.N. Adger, 'Sustainable Livelihoods and Migration in Vietnam: The Importance of Social Capital as Access to Resources', Paper presented at International Symposium on 'Sustaining Food Security and Managing Natural Resources in Southeast Asia: Challenges for the 21st Century', Chiang Mai, Thailand, 8–11 January 2002.

# 12

# Social Protection and Migrant Support

*Priya Deshingkar and John Farrington*

## What Does the Evidence Show?

Instruments such as the National Sample Survey or the Census are not designed adequately to capture circular migration, and official estimates showing some 10 million (1 per cent of the population) seasonal migrants are widely regarded as serious under-estimates. At the other extreme, estimates as high as 150 million are almost certainly over-estimates. The true figure probably lies at around 100 million, as adding up the numbers in major sectors and occupations employing migrant workers shows: the textile and garment industry employs 35 million of whom many are migrants, construction (30 million), brick kilns (10 million), street vending (10 million), rickshaw pulling (8 million), truck drivers and helpers (5 million), quarries and mines (500,000), salt pans (150,000), and prawn processing (at least 100,000).[1] In addition, at least half of the estimated 20 million domestic workers in India, waiters in small restaurants, and room boys in small hotels are probably migrants.

Policy initiatives in respect of circular migration are currently inadequate partly because of these under-estimates, and partly also because powerful urban electorates are ill-at-ease with the prospect of increased in-migration. There is perhaps therefore little political incentive to make official estimates of migration more accurate.

The contribution made by migrants to the national economy is, for these reasons, substantial but largely unquantified. Despite this contribution, most remain on the margins of society, contributing cheap labour but unable to influence their pay or working and living conditions. Migrants are rarely full citizens in their place of work. In the formal context, they lose voting rights, as well as ability to access healthcare and government schemes such as the public distribution system (PDS). It becomes less easy for them to access free education for their children.[2] Less formally, they are often regarded as illegal residents and may be subject to police harassment. Journeys to and from work can be hazardous, with cheating over tickets on public transport and the constant threat of theft. They also face discrimination more generally because they often belong to historically disadvantaged groups such as the scheduled castes or scheduled tribes.[3] Women and girls from these social groups rarely receive 'equal pay for equal work' and so are even more heavily discriminated against in the labour market.

Although there are a few instances of migrants having influenced policy making directly, grass roots level organizations have lobbied on their behalf for better living and working conditions. A few organizations have found ways of helping migrants to reduce the costs and risks of migration, and one of the largest migrant support programmes in the country has been reviewed in this volume (Chapters 5 and 10).

Thus, migration has many costs and risks associated with it that are difficult for poor and vulnerable people to cope with. A lack of proper housing and sanitation and lack of access to subsidized food through the PDS are among the most acute problems that migrants face. The poorest are stuck in the least remunerative options because they do not have the skills or networks to move up the job ladder. They cannot negotiate with employers and are often subjected to discrimination at the destination, especially if they are from the disadvantaged groups.

India is currently going through a transition from an economy consisting of very large numbers of small and marginal farms to one where the structures of agriculture and industry are changing rapidly in response to globalizing forces, environmental stresses, and population pressure. But change of this kind underpins the conundrum at the core of this book: policy and the media—as well as much of the Indian citizenry—recognize and broadly welcome this economic transformation; by contrast, they largely fail to recognize the role of migrants in helping to achieve the transformation. Most damagingly for migrants, policies are still premised on bimodal patterns of 'rural' or 'urban' livelihoods, with almost complete neglect of the new reality, which is that for many households and individuals, livelihoods have become multilocational.

Land fragmentation, drought, increasingly severe groundwater scarcity, and the consequent inability of agriculture in many areas to provide more than a single season's employment, as well as the increasingly uncertain financial environment facing farming, all help to 'push' labourers into other occupations. Rapid urban growth and with it the demand for labourers in construction, brick-making, and small-scale services, all help to 'pull' workers into new areas and occupations, despite the risks and isolation from family that migration poses. Opportunities for learning new skills also beckon. At a more anecdotal level, labourers, especially from the SCs and STs, see enhanced prospects of breaking out of restrictive caste norms in the more socially fluid environment of urban areas (as is evident in the Chandpur case in Chapter 8, as well as in Chapters 6 and 9). The uptake of migration opportunities is in some measure a response to market signals, but is by no means purely a market transaction in the neoclassical economics sense. Information is imperfect and transactions costs are high. Good personal contacts are almost everywhere a prerequisite for securing migratory work quickly and at minimum risk. This is particularly evident in the Bihar case (Chapter 6).

This is not to say that efforts to increase agricultural productivity and growth no longer have a role in poverty reduction—indeed, they remain necessary, but are no longer sufficient. Given the fragmentation of holdings, limited soil and water resources, and the pressures of the global economy, agriculture alone will be insufficient to achieve widespread poverty reduction. Not only are small farmers exposed to many new risks due to price volatility, but also many marginal areas are unlikely to provide significant opportunities for expansion of agricultural production and employment creation. This points to the need to recognize that:

a) Other sectors such as urban areas and manufacturing may be equally if not more important in some contexts. For instance, from the panel data in AP and MP, it is clear that a combination of commuting and circular migration to take advantage of such opportunities is of growing importance: more than half of the sample households now have at least one member either migrating or commuting, and among the poorest categories (SCs and STs) migration and commuting combined contribute more than half of net household income (Chapters 3 and 4). Even where income from migration and commuting is insufficient for productive investment, it can help to repay debts and to smooth consumption.

b) Despite the widespread discrimination against SCs and STs, migration and commuting are among the very few ways that poor people have of enhancing their skills and so progressing to better opportunities, given the limited scope for local off-farm employment, especially in the more remote villages, and the limited availability and often poor quality of government training schemes. STs are in a weaker position to commute, in terms of the remoteness of their villages and lack of skills, and this is represented in the figures, with much of the growth in circular migration attributable to STs, especially in MP, Rajasthan, and Jharkhand (Chapters 4, 5, 6, and7).

c) Efforts to create sustainable livelihoods within difficult and marginal areas may yield poor results. Indeed there is some evidence that, precisely because of their greater mobility, landless labourers are better off than marginal farmers in locations where agriculture remains, or has become, highly risky and urban labour markets have expanded.

d) In addition, migration and commuting allow the rural poor to make a substantive contribution to overall economic growth, especially via their contribution to the construction industry, and recognition of this is pivotal to the development of new policy towards migrants.

Huge amounts of money are currently invested in improving productivity in marginal areas – for example, in excess of $1000 million has been invested in watershed development projects in India. Given the fiscal, environmental, institutional, infrastructural, and governance constraints faced by these initiatives, marginal areas have shown little improvement over the years and are unlikely to change dramatically in the next 10–20 years. The goal of making people in rural areas better off through these initiatives and so keeping them there seems illusory. On the other hand, well-supported rural-urban links can reduce regional inequalities by transferring some of the benefits of construction and urbanization to poorer regions. The benefits of intensive agriculture can be redistributed in the same way via rural-rural migration. There is evidence that remittances and migration earnings are stimulating agriculture and improving living standards in sending areas.

It is very likely that circular migration will continue to increase in India as an increasing population of young adults bridges the gap between rapid economic growth in some locations and stagnation in many rural areas. Forecasts on labour mobility and migration trends in Asia, prepared by the Economist Intelligence Unit, indicate that all major Asian countries, especially the Philippines, Malaysia, and India, but with the exception of Japan, will experience increases in their working age populations. A positive outlook for economic growth for the region as a whole will drive demand for labour to 2015.[4] In absolute terms, China and India will have the largest increases in working age populations by 2015 (88 million and 148 million respectively).

Although the demand for skilled labour will probably increase in some sectors, the demand for unskilled labour will continue to increase for informal employment in road maintenance, construction, cable networks, and coastal activities where mechanization continues to be limited despite growth.

While earlier projections expected temporary migration to go down, current trends indicate that a growing number of people are choosing to keep one foot in the village because of social ties, lower costs, other safety net aspects, and a long-term intention to pursue a better life in the village. Commuting has emerged as an important form of mobility for many working poor. Women and children who migrate independently or accompany men need special attention as they are more vulnerable, often carry a heavier work load and are systematically underpaid. A combination of political will and bureaucratic commitment is needed to enforce existing regulations that have been designed to protect migrant workers.

As far as national evidence on migration is concerned, there is an urgent need for more disaggregated data on occupations that capture part-time and seasonal activities. Census and National Sample Surveys need to be supplemented with additional modules. In addition, valuable information on seasonal migration can be gleaned from the many existing and ongoing village-level research projects on rural livelihoods implemented by regional research centres and universities.

Unlike other countries in East and Southeast Asia, where demographic features and development policies may reduce the flow of temporary migrants, circular migration and commuting in India are likely to grow and the government urgently needs to take steps to make these more remunerative and less painful for the poor.

## CURRENT TYPES OF POLICY RESPONSE IN SUPPORT OF CIRCULAR MIGRANTS

The lack of clarity in official positions on migration—often, if anything, veering towards a denial of the contribution that migration makes to the economy and prompting efforts to 'relieve distress' in order to keep migrants in rural areas—all mean that official support for migrants is almost non-existent. Such (still very limited) support as there is has been devised and implemented by NGOs. Their migrant support programmes fall into four broad categories, most of which have operated on a very limited scale to date:

### The Social Protection Model

This model provides subsidized services related to job information, rights awareness creation, and other support. Social protection aims to reduce poverty and vulnerability by promoting efficient labour markets, diminishing exposure to risks, enhancing their capacity to protect themselves against hazards, and interruption/loss of income.

The Migrant Labour Support Programme (MLSP) of the Gramin Vikas Trust is an example of this. The MLSP emerged from the DFID-funded Western India Rainfed Farming Project (WIRFP) a participatory rural development project in the tribal areas of Gujarat, Rajasthan, and Madhya Pradesh. MLSP was established in 2003 in the districts of Ratlam, Jhabua, Dhar (MP); Banswara and Dungarpur (Rajasthan); and Dahod and Panchmahals (Gujarat). The project has set up a number of resource centres known as Palayan Seva Kendras (PSK) in sending and receiving areas, offering services to migrant workers to help them to reduce the costs and increase the returns to migration (Box 12.1). By 2006 it had issued more than 17,000 ID cards to migrant workers which considerably reduced the difficulties that they faced while travelling and during their temporary stays at the destination (CMS 2006).

BOX 12.1: SERVICES PROVIDED UNDER THE MIGRANT SUPPORT
PROGRAMME OF THE GRAMIN VIKAS TRUST

Protection
- Identity cards
- Insurance facilitation
- Protection of assets and family members

Communication
- Telephone booth and mobile phones
- Messaging services

Information to migrants
- Information—on government schemes,
- on techniques and technologies relevant to their occupations,
- on contractors,
- on places where labour is in demand

Information to contractors
- on the availability of labour.

The MLSP is also helping to create awareness of rights among workers

The rationale of the social protection model is that poor migrants cannot fend for themselves in a job market that is dominated by labour market intermediaries and employers who are better informed and connected than they are. They are in need of support to reduce their vulnerability but are unlikely to be in a position to pay for, or be willing to pay for services on a full cost recovery basis immediately. The services provided will enable them to access better jobs and reduce the level of uncertainty and harassment that they face in the job market.

Like any subsidy approach, this kind of approach has attracted criticism for being expensive and economically unsustainable. However, critics under-estimate the time that it takes to attract poor, risk-averse and uneducated workers into contributory schemes. While industrial worker costs may be borne by industry (see market based approach below), other poorer workers who migrate on a free lance basis and switch jobs rapidly may require more support. Some social protection is available via the mutual, informal support that women offer to each other when husbands take on migrant work (Chapter 11). However, it is clear that this is limited in scope, and if it is to expand, this will have to be via more formal mechanisms.

## The Market Based Approach

This model works with existing labour market patterns and offers services on a cost recovery basis. An example of such an approach is the initiative called Mazdoor.org proposed by Samarthan (a leading NGO in Madhya Pradesh working on rural employment and human rights issues), and the World Bank funded District Poverty Initiatives Project (DPIP) in Madhya Pradesh. This will provide skills enhancement and certification programmes, advice and information on jobs, and help workers to link up with government schemes on insurance and workers funds. They intend to work within the existing structure of industry and the labour market, that is, recognize that capital and labour are highly mobile and that capital/industry locates itself where cheap labour can be accessed. They also recognize that a majority of industrial workers are not named on the employment registers of industries and are recruited by intermediaries who are not accountable to anyone under the law. Mazdoor.org will take on responsibility for the welfare of the workers even though it is the responsibility of the industry and employers under law. For this they plan to make industry pay service charges. A further example is provided by LabourNet, an NGO based in Bangalore which has developed a database of 4,500 migrant construction workers, with the intention of improving job *information* for them (*Outlook Business* 2008).

## The Labour Union Model

This is a rights-based approach and works for better implementation of labour laws and regulation of labour flows. Some NGOs like Prayas in Rajasthan (Katiyar 2005) and DISHA in Gujarat (DISHA 2004–5) believe that unionizing migrant workers will go a long way towards realizing their rights, improving their bargaining power in the market, and prevent exploitation. Prayas has set up a union of migrant workers who work in cotton fields. One of the main objectives of the Union is to regulate the supply of labour because they feel that an excess supply situation lowers the bargaining power of the migrant. They have enrolled over 1,500 recruiting agents or 'mates' and the Union has put out a charter of demands. It has set up around 16 manned check points at all the border crossings between Gujarat and Rajasthan. As a result, employers have offered a partial hike in wage rates and negotiations are continuing. A similar approach has been adopted by the Bandhkam Majoor Sangathan (BMS) established by DISHA in Ahmedabad. Both Prayas and DISHA are also engaged in policy advocacy for the amendment of the Inter-State Migrant Workmen Act which they argue is unimplementable in its current form.

## The Rehabilitation Model

The best example of this is the work done by ActionAid with brick kiln workers in Orissa and Andhra Pradesh. ActionAid conducts raids on brick kilns together with the police to release bonded migrant workers and rehabilitate them. They believe that migration of this kind is akin to trafficking, where workers are lured on false promises, often borrow money from recruitment agents which they repay through punishing work schedules, their movement is restricted at the work site, and wages are well below the legal minimum. In addition, women and children are also exploited in various ways and living conditions are appalling.

Although these models offer much promise, they are by themselves incomplete. For many types of challenges faced by migrants, a combination will be needed of these kinds of support, together with changes in (or better enforcement of) government legislation, and in some cases more information will need to be collected on migrants' needs. We now examine a number of challenges faced by migrants, and the potential role of statutory provisions, advocacy, and support programmes in response to each.

## WHAT ISSUES DOES POLICY NEED TO RESPOND TO, AND HOW?

### Wage Discrimination

Although migrant workers earn more as construction workers or trench diggers (Rs 100–20 for men and Rs 70–90 for women) than they would as casual labourers in rain-fed agriculture (Rs 35–50 for men and Rs 25–30 for women), they rarely have written contracts and are at risk of being cheated or being paid late. Migrants need access to information (on jobs, wages, and rights) and also need help with bargaining for better wages and help with approaching the police, and other relevant authorities.

### Health And Safety

Migrant workers' health and safety are often at risk, especially in brick kilns, quarries, construction sites, and small industrial units. Regulations governing health and safety exist but are rarely enforced. Their improved enforcement will require a combination of advocacy and awareness creation among migrants of their rights in order to put pressure both on employers and on the relevant authorities. Efforts to unionize construction labour, or to forge links with existing unions, as well as pressing government to conduct necessary inspections, may pay off here.

### Child-Related Issues (Child Labour, Education)

One of the most serious costs of migration is the interruption and discontinuation of schooling among the children of migrants.[4] In Orissa and Andhra Pradesh (Chapter 3), a number of NGOs are working with the government to facilitate the education of migrant workers' children through the District Primary Education Programme (DPEP). In Maharashtra, sugar mills now have to run a school for the children of migrants working in the factory. This is an area where existing government schemes such as the Sarva Shiksha Abhiyan can be made to work better for migrants.

NGOs, researchers, donors, and policy makers need to work closely together to develop ways of helping the poor to earn enough without sacrificing the future of their children. Providing incentives for education, changing school timings, and other win-win measures need to be given serious consideration. Mere bans on child labour have not brought results.

### Access to Benefits at Destinations, Such as Public Distribution System

Providing migrants access to the public distribution system (PDS) at their destinations constitutes a more complex problem, though one which computerized databases may be able to tackle. State governments are aware of the need to address the problem and discussions have been held between the Food and Civil Supplies Departments of different state governments to introduce 'roaming'

PDS cards. Mobile ration cards and temporary ration cards for migrants have been piloted in Maharashtra and Andhra Pradesh but at a very small scale and usually through a G.O. (government order) issued by a Collector. The government of Rajasthan has been working with GVT to develop a system of providing subsidized grain to rural-urban migrants within the state. Very little information is available on how these pilot projects have fared. Important lessons can be learned from these experiments.

There is a need for policy change at the highest level that recognizes the need to match the administration of existing subsidies for the poor—that is, principally on foodgrains—to the needs of a mobile population.

### Establishing Personal Identity

Migrants tend to attract the attention of police and other authorities, especially at public places such as railway stations, in part because they are notably different from local populations and provide easy scapegoats. Where they are able to establish their identity through some semi-official means, this threat recedes. Ideally, to make improvements here requires action from both NGOs and the government. Thus, for example, learning from the work of Aajeevika Bureau, the Government of Rajasthan has allowed its name to be used on the identity cards of migrants from southern Rajasthan who cross the state border into Gujarat for seasonal work there. Substantial reductions in harassment are reported as a result (Chapters 5 and 10).

### Access to Housing

There is no housing provision for circular migrants. To address this basic need would reduce the hardship faced by migrants considerably. As of now, the needs of circular migrants do not appear to be reflected in the Jawaharlal Nehru National Urban Renewal Mission (JNNURM) plans. Additionally, there are a number of initiatives for improving slums across India and these need to take into account the specific needs of temporary residents.

### Providing Migrant-friendly Financial Services

Migrants still continue to hand-carry money at great risk or remit their savings through expensive, inefficient, or unsafe means. Some private banks have now started to recognize the need for financial services for migrants. For example, both ICICI Bank and the Indian Bank have recently launched remittance services for Tamil migrants from Thirunelveli who stay in the slums of Dharavi in Mumbai. Some NGOs have also entered this area. Adhikar, an NGO in Orissa has been helping migrants in Gandhidham in Gujarat in remitting money to Orissa. They started this service after the 2001 earthquake, when they found more than 10,000 migrants from Khurda district working in and around Gandhidham—at the Kandla port, free-trade zone, Indian Farmers Fertilizer Cooperative Limited (IFFCO), and for the Railways. Adhikar was supported by the research and innovation fund of CARE India's CASHE (Credit and Savings for Household Enterprises) project.

Providing migrants with pre-migration loans could help reduce their dependency on agents and contractors. This is being done by the Aajeevika Bureau through its newly established financial company the Rajasthan Shram Sarathi Association (*Outlook Business* 2008). It offers a 'break away loan' to prospective migrants to allow them to migrate without the help of an intermediary thus reducing the likelihood of underpayment, exploitation, and ultimately bondage. The initiative has been supported by the ICICI Bank. Labour Net, a Bangalore based group running a portal on labour issues has also set up micro-insurance initiatives linking construction workers with HDFC Chubb and Healing Fields, an NGO. This scheme provides health insurance of up to Rs 28,000 for a premium of just Rs 450.

## Improving Skills

A majority of poor migrants are unskilled or semi-skilled at best. An improvement in skills increases their prospects of finding more remunerative employment. A nationwide initiative is being planned by the Ministry of Textiles to provide training in skills for rural people from BPL families to enable them to find work in the textile industry during the XI Plan. The industry which is second in importance after agriculture in providing jobs in the country, currently employs between 35 and 55 million people (estimates vary) in the value chain (spinning, weaving, processing, knitting, and apparel-making). It is projected to generate an additional 6.5 million jobs (skilled and unskilled) by 2012 (*The Hindu Business Line*, 26 Sept 2007). Under the scheme, training will be provided through 400 Textile and Apparel Training Centres across the country.

Some industries that depend on migrant workers and where the demand for skilled workers is rising, have been quick to design training programmes for upgrading the skills for prospective workers. For example, the Lanco group, a leading infrastructure company based in Hyderabad has set up a number of training institues for youth in rural and urban areas in Andhra Pradesh under its Lanco Institute of General Humanitarian Trust (LIGHT). Lanco has projects in power, infrastructure, construction, and property development with a market value of around Rs 160,000 million.

On a smaller scale, NGOs such as Aajeevika Bureau in Rajasthan (Chapters 5 and 10) have also started training programmes to help migrants to find better jobs. The Bureau is working with the government of Rajasthan to train over 200,000 SC/ST youth who have been educated up to the VIII standard through a scheme called 'Eklavya'. Similarly the DFID-supported Madhya Pradesh Rural Livelihoods Project is linking up with the government of Madhya Pradesh initiative of employment oriented training for rural youth to include migrant workers.

## Improving Transport Services and Communications

There are certain peak seasons for migratory movement when migrants, especially women with babies and infants, have to travel in distressing conditions. Although private transport operators fulfil part of this requirement, the situation can be vastly improved if the need for additional transport is recognized at the policy level. With the rise of commuting, transport networks are even more important and any regulatory effort on informal transport providers should recognize the importance to poor people's livelihoods.

In sum, there is an urgent need for recognition at the policy level of the importance of migration and the rapidly growing importance of commuting for rural livelihoods. This will have implications for planning in a number of sectors including urban development, rural development, urban infrastructure, housing, transport, and the flexibility of pro-poor services and programmes.

NOTES

1. Estimates of textile workers from Ministry of Textiles http://texmin.nic. in/msy_20010621.htm; construction workers from Chen (2007); brick kiln workers from ILO (2005); numbers of street vendors from GOI (2004); estimates of rickshaw pullers from the Centre for Rural Development which runs rickshaw banks in several states; truck drivers from an HIV/ AIDS control programme reported in *Business World* (2008); mine and quarry workers from Ghosh and Roy (2007); estimates of salt pan workers from BOBP–IGO (2006).

2. They have legal rights to send their children to school but often do not for a number of reasons, for example, because it is difficult to do so in the middle of a term or because they lack the necessary networks. Language may also be a problem.

3. These groups accounted for more than 250 million people in 2001 (167 million SCs, 86 million STs and other minorities). Official statistics show that SCs and STs are more deprived than other social groups. At the all India level, poverty among STs was about two times higher than non-SC/STs, the poverty gap ratio being 2.10 and 1.7 times higher among SCs compared to non SC/ST groups. But there were variations across states. The disparity between SCs and non-SC/ST groups was particularly high in Punjab, Haryana, and Rajasthan with poverty disparity ratios of 5.31, 3.98, and 3.72 respectively. Thus, poverty among the SCs was about five times higher in Punjab, about four times higher in Haryana, and about two and half times higher in Rajasthan than the rest of the non-SC/ST population (Thorat and Mahamallik 2005).

4. The current recession will slow down economic activity in a number of Labour absorb sectors but the long-term trend is still likely to be an increase.

5. The America India Foundation estimates that at least 6 million children miss school in India every year because they migrate with their parents.

REFERENCES

BOBP–IGO, 'The Saga of India's Salt Workers', *Bay of Bengal News*, Bay of Bengal Programme Inter-Governmental Organization, Chennai, India, March 2006, pp. 37–40.

CMS, 'Impact Assessment Of The Migrant Labour Support Programme', Catalyst Management Services, Bangalore, 2006.

*DISHA Annual Report*, 2004-5, Ahmedabad, India.

Ghosh, M. and S. Roy, 'Contribution Of Small-Scale Mining To Employment, Development and Sustainability—An Indian Scenario', *Environment, Development and Sustainability*, 9, 2007, pp. 283–303

Government of India, *National Policy for Urban Street Vendors/Hawkers*, Ministry of Urban Employment and Poverty Alleviation, 2004.

Katiyar, S., 'Short term Migration in South Rajasthan—Incidence and Impact', Sudrak, Udaipur, Rajasthan, 2005.

*Outlook Business*, 'Workers without Borders', in *Outlook Business*, 20 April – 3 May 2008, pp. 72–6.

Thorat, S. and M. Mahamallik, 'Persistent Poverty—Why Do Scheduled Castes And Scheduled Tribes Stay Chronically Poor', Paper Presented at CPRC-IIPA Seminar on 'Chronic Poverty: Emerging Policy Options and Issues', 29 and 30 September 2005, Indian Institute of Public Administration, New Delhi.

# Glossary

| | |
|---|---|
| *Rabi* | Winter Crop Growing Season |
| *Kharif* | Monsoon Crop Growing Season |
| *Bhagiya* | Share Cropper |
| *Mestri* | Labour Contractor |
| *Mistri* | Mason |
| *Mukkaddam* | Labour Recruiting Agent |
| *Haveli* | Large Palatial House |
| *Zari* | Embroidery Using Metal Thread |
| *Halwai* | Sweet Maker |
| *Dhana* | Locality |
| *Kutcha* | Made with Mud and Thatch |
| *Pucca* | Made with Bricks and Mortar |
| *Bigha* | Local Measure of Land Area varying from a third of an acre to an acre |
| *Kattha* | 1/20 of a Bigha |
| *Naukar* | Attached Servant |
| *Adivasi* | Tribal |
| *Dalit* | Those who were traditionally regarded as untouchables |
| *Mandal* | Administrative Unit of 4–5 Villages in Andhra Pradesh |
| *Panchayat/Gram Panchayat* | Village Level Council |
| *Namkeen* | Savoury Snacks |
| *Jowar* | Sorghum |
| *Toowar/Tur* | Pigeon Pea |

# Contributors

SHAHEEN AKTER, Research Associate, Overseas Development Institute, London.

REENA BADIANI, PhD Candidate, Economic Growth Center, Yale University, Research Scholar at ICRISAT in 2006.

PRIYA DESHINGKAR, Research Fellow, Overseas Development Institute, London.

JOHN FARRINGTON, Senior Research Fellow, Overseas Development Institute, London.

WHITNEY GANTT, Program Officer, The Grameen Foundation Technology Center, Seattle, WA.

ELON GILBERT, Research Associate, Overseas Development Institute, London.

BHARATI JOSHI, Programmes Coordinator, Aravali (Association for Rural Advancement through Voluntary Action & Local Involvement), Jaipur.

RAJIV KHANDELWAL, Director, Aajeevika Bureau.

HARENDRA KUMAR CHOUBEY and DHANANJAY KUMAR, Research Associates, A.N. Sinha Institute of Social Studies, Patna.

SUSHIL KUMAR, Research Associate, Overseas Development Institute, India.

SOPHIE LLEWELLYN, PhD Candidate, Department of Anthropology, McGill University, Canada.

DEEPTIMA MASSEY, PhD Candidate, Development Research Centre (DRC) on Migration, Globalisation, and Poverty, University of Sussex.

LAXMAN RAO, Research Associate, Overseas Development Institute, India.

ABLA SAFIR, PhD Candidate, CREST (Centre de Recherches en Economie et Statistique), Paris.

ALPA SHAH, Lecturer, Department of Anthropology, Goldsmiths, University of London.

PRAMOD SHARMA, Research Associate, Overseas Development Institute, India.

# Index